SHELTON STATE COMMUNITY
COLLEGE
JUNIOR COLLEGE
LIBRARY

D0857127

KF
380
.B34

Ball, Milner S.

The promise of
American law

DATE DUE

Aug 8 '80			
APR 2 6 1989			
OCT 0 ' 1993			
DEC 2 2 1998			

The Promise of
American Law

Milner S. Ball

The Promise of American Law

A Theological, Humanistic View of Legal Process

Discarded
SSCC

The University of Georgia Press  Athens

Copyright © 1981 by
the University of Georgia Press
Athens, Georgia 30602

All rights reserved

Set in Palatino

Design by Richard Hendel

Printed in the United States of America

Library of Congress Cataloging in Publication Data

Ball, Milner S.
   The promise of American law.
   Includes bibliographical references and index.
      1. Law—United States.   2. Judicial process—
United States.   3. Law and ethics.   I. Title.
KF380.B34   349.73   81-4325
ISBN 0-8203-0572-3   347.3   AACR2

TO JUNE

who has taught me the amazement of

daily beginning again.

"[T]he great problem in politics, which I compare to the problem of squaring the circle in geometry . . . [is]: How to find a form of government which places the law above man. . . . [T]he conflict between men and laws, which places in the state a continual internecine war, is the worst of all political conditions."

—Jean-Jacques Rousseau,
"Letter to the Marquis de Mirabeau"

"The story by which revolutions are saved is the story in the reality and power of which revolutions are freed from their fate and freed for the pursuit of their appointed end: the making room for freedom and a new beginning and a new order of human affairs."

—Paul L. Lehmann,
The Transfiguration of Politics

"[T]he privilege against self-incrimination—the essential mainstay of our adversary system—is founded on a complex of values. . . . All these policies point to one overriding thought: the constitutional foundation underlying the privilege is the respect a government— state or federal—must accord to the dignity and integrity of its citizens."

—Earl Warren,
Miranda v. Arizona

Contents

🙢 PREFACE   xi

🙢 INTRODUCTION   1

🙢 CHAPTER ONE
BEGINNING AND AUTHORITY   7
Possible Sources of Authority 8 / The
Founding Act as Authority 9 / The
Beginning as Authority: An
Alternative 11 / Communal Beginning
and Political Possibilities 12

🙢 CHAPTER TWO
STORY IN LAW   16
Preserving the Past and Legitimacy 18 /
Story, Participation, and Law 18 / Present
Understanding and Judgment 22

🙢 CHAPTER THREE
LAW IN PLACE   29
An Original Association of Law with
Space 29 / Public Place 30 / Private
Place 32 / Interdependence of Public and
Private 33 / Property 34 / Courts 40

🙢 CHAPTER FOUR
JUDICIAL THEATER   42
The Theatrical Elements of Courtroom
Action 43 / Courtroom Action as a Distinct
Type of Theater 54 / The Functions of
Judicial Theater 57

Contents

CHAPTER FIVE
THE IMAGE OF COURT AS
THEATER OF BEGINNING:
JUDGMENT AND PROCESS   64
Judicial Process and Judicial Decisions 66 /
The Clarity of the Process 72

CHAPTER SIX
PERSONAE   82
The Masks of Court and Society 82 /
Personae as Property 85 / The Being and
Action of Court 93

CHAPTER SEVEN
JUDICIAL PROTECTION OF THE POWERLESS   95
Why the Powerless? 96 / The Cost: *DeFunis*,
Bakke, *Weber*, and *Fullilove* 101

CHAPTER EIGHT
CAROLENE PRODUCTS   106
The Footnote Four Theory 106 / The
Decisional Shape of the Theory 110 /
Conclusion 124

CHAPTER NINE
LAW, LANGUAGE, DEATH, AND LIFE:
LAW SCHOOL   126
Diagnoses 127 / *The Legal
Imagination* 128 / Teaching Law and Teaching
Its Meaning 130 / Law as Metaphor 136

NOTES   139

INDEX   205

 Preface

Anyone who writes about law is indebted to the work of many others. In addition to the prominent jurisprudents and constitutional authorities, from whom I have obviously learned much, I have depended upon the less well-known but no less formidable scholars like my former colleagues at Rutgers-Camden Law School, Ed Chase, Roger Clark, and Hunter Taylor.

I have also been well instructed by my valued colleagues at Georgia, whom I forbear to name save for Dean Rusk, who has been to me, since his elevation to the rank of law teacher, uncommonly generous of his time, his learning, and his support. There are other lawyers and judges who have been too kind to be forgotten but are too numerous to list. The notes will indicate the many others outside of law, like Karl Barth, Dietrich Bonhoeffer, and Hannah Arendt, to whom I have turned. Notable among these others is Paul Lehmann, whose astonishing life and work continue daily to inspire and instruct. I do not summon this cloud of saints to endorse or to share responsibility and blame for this book. They are innocent. I only wish to thank, not implicate them.

Dean Russell Fairbanks of the Rutgers-Camden Law School and Dean Ralph Beaird of the Georgia Law School made research and writing time available to me. I am grateful for their encouragement and their daring.

The manuscript could not have been prepared without the skill of Meredith Ellard, for whose indispensable, uncomplaining help I am grateful.

Studies for first one part and then another of this book were originally published as law review articles. It had not been my plan simply to stitch these pieces together, a possibility which would have proved impossible of fulfillment anyway. In fact, I have had to discard what I had originally thought would be a centerpiece. All of the original studies have been reworked, in some instances beyond substantial and formal recognition. I am indebted to several law reviews for first publishing and then allowing me to recycle them to a new use even though the originals may not be detectable: to the *Rutgers-Camden Law Journal* for material which has been utilized, for the most part, in Chapter One—originally published as "Authority and American Courts," 8 *Rutgers-Camden L.J.* 563 (1977); to the *Stanford Law Review* for material which has been incorporated in Chapter Four—originally published as "The Play's the Thing: An Unscientific Reflection on Courts Under the Rubric of Theater," 28 *Stan. L. Rev.* 81 (1975); to the *Iowa Law Review* for materal which surfaces largely in Chapter Seven—originally published as "Judicial Protection of Powerless Minorities," 59 *Iowa L. Rev.* 1059 (1974); and to the *University of Chicago Law Review* for the piece which served as the basis for Chapter Eight—originally published as "Review: *The Legal Imagination,*" 44 *U. Chi. L. Rev.* 681 (1977).

The Promise of
American Law

⚜ Introduction

This is a book about American Law, especially American law courts. It belongs in that category of thinking about law which has a popular constituency in the United States. Such thought is not the province alone of jurisprudential schools or of academic lawyers like me. Law bears upon the lives of us all and is an expression of the sovereignty of the people. Critical thinking about law is thus a popular preoccupation as well as a general civic right and responsibility.

American law is a human enterprise. It is illuminated by and illuminating of other human undertakings such as politics, story, and theater. Moreover, lawyers are asked to take on a seemingly limitless range of problems in our society. Law cannot be done and should not be analyzed as though it were discrete. Inexplicably, however, we do not often intentionally bring to our understanding of law much from the wide range of nonlegal endeavors and materials which are its matrix.

A federal judge, a good one, once told some of my students who were about to graduate that they should not read Thucydides, Aeschylus, and the like but that they should read instead the great trials, and the famous lawyers, and the celebrated closing arguments like those of Clarence Darrow. However, that same judge has rendered decisions in conflicts that raise questions about life and death whose answers are better informed by poets, historians, and prophets than by barristers.

One cannot deny that law is and must be reductionist. When they are brought to law, disputes and grievances have to be worked into judicially cognizable and manageable form. A certain amount of professional single-mindedness is therefore necessary, even enviable. Nevertheless, the apparatus of judgment includes dynamics, commitments, biases, predilections, senses, and thought which arise from sources anterior to juridical learning and which are not always acknowledged. Law is reductionist, but it has a context.

My aim is to participate with others in making contextual thinking about law self-conscious. To this end I have ventured, a wild ruminant, into fields outside the law, other disciplines in which I cannot claim, much less establish, competence. This is a confession. I make it frankly and early for, although it will not excuse lapses in scholarship, it will allow me to get on with the seductive delight of the business at hand. Otherwise, I should be impressed into inaction by the knowledge that moves are available to check every effort to advance beyond the limits of my expertise.

Some of the concepts I employ are familiar in discussion about law. One example is the proposition that judicial review is appropriate when it is invoked in protection of powerless minorities. I think that an alliance between the judiciary and minorities makes for a sensible, fit theory of judicial review. Others disagree. I shall get to all of that in due course. The point here is that the idea is familiar, its dispute a sign of the familiarity.

There are other ideas which are undisputed and unfamiliar; they have been raised infrequently or not at all in recent jurisprudential discussion. I have in mind, for example, the identification of the judicial process as theater, or the narrative and spatial connotations of law hereinafter examined.

What I aim for in conjuring other disciplines is discovery of questions properly engaged in discourse about law. We are still in a time of experimentation and so of essays rather than of systems. This book proceeds largely in the letter of the declarative, but it is really carried forward by the spirit of the interrogative. It is no more than an essay, a form which is, as Justice Felix Frankfurter observed, "tentative, reflective, suggestive, contradictory, and incomplete."[1]

This is not to say that I proceed at random. I am guided by the reality of the beginning. To speak about the beginning in the way which I do is not novel or idiosyncratic, although it may be unfamiliar and does warrant brief, introductory comment. The notion of beginning is to be found in Plato, Virgil, and, recently, Hannah Arendt. My own emphasis upon and understanding of beginning, however, comes from the biblical tradition rather than from any of these other sources.

I write in the wager that the biblical tradition is the most fruitful medium for understanding, judging, and celebrating the secular world, including law. My wager is that a theological standpoint will provide a view of law in context and in relation to other human enterprises. If it pays off, I shall have exposed to you connections which will aid clarification, assessment, and affirmation of what is really going on in what is happening in law. It should not be necessary to this payoff that you share my theological premises, only that you grant them to me.

There is in the Church's past and present a noble attempt to serve ethical decision making by portraying God's will as a prescribed text that is a blend of the Bible, natural law, and tradition. This celestial text is thought to be accessible to human reason but is not wholly written or fully known. This text of higher law provides a standard against which one can measure mundane legal texts composed of statutes and court decisions.

This attempt is respectable and useful and has engaged the minds of many good people who have sought to render the Christian faith intelligible and practical. But I think it is wrong. On the one hand, it tries to make into timeless, universal ordinance, and rational structure suitable for text, the will of God, which is always particular, personal, and living. On the other hand, it treats human law, best understood as act and event, as though it, too, were prescription and rule also suitable for text.

There is another strand in the tradition of systematic theology which has sought ethical guidance in historical realities and relationships rather than in prescriptive texts. Dietrich Bonhoeffer, for one, found God's commands to be given the historical forms of mandates: work, marriage, governmental authority, and Church. Karl Barth detected in Bonhoeffer's proposal lingering elements of rational structure and arbitrariness (why these four mandates and not others?). So Barth set about to state for ethics the God-man relationship in a way that was not so much different from Bonhoeffer's as better, *i.e.*, less arbitrary and more directly drawn from the self-revelation of the God of the Bible. He therefore described God's command as an ethical event, an encounter between God and man, between God, self-characterized as Creator, Reconciler, and Redeemer—Father, Son, and Spirit—and man as the one created, reconciled, and redeemed. The will of God thus understood is not given in orders or mandates—still less in texts or natural law—but in spheres and relationships, one of which is that of the Creator and created.

I do not intend any substantial departure from this latter tradition when I adopt the formulation "beginning." I only wish to bring this tradition to bear upon American law. On the theological side, the selection of "beginning" is not arbitrary. There is both ancient and recent precedent for focusing upon "God's self-identifying self-communication in Jesus of Nazareth as a *new beginning*."[2] "Beginning" is a relational term of creation, reconciliation, and redemption.

On the jurisprudential side, lawyers have long since grown accustomed to discussion of the prominence and legitimating role attributed to principle in the law. The root word of principle is the Latin *principium*, and *principium* meant both principle and beginning. I choose the latter word in preference to the former because it educes the historical sense of *principium*, aids exploration of law as event and history, and connotes the fertile typological ground relating the biblical tradition and law, systematic theology and jurisprudence.

The New Testament community was given life in the death and resurrection of Jesus, the new exodus prefigured by the first exodus from which the Old Testament community took its life. The archetypical biblical beginning has a corresponding type in the beginning of the American people. I do not mean that there is an exact equivalence. I do not mean that Americans are the chosen people of God. I do mean that the biblical history is what informs our decision about the good and evil, about what is to be affirmed and what disaffirmed in American history as well as in history generally.

In the exodus, God created for himself a people. By this creation the people became a community with God. There was to be a common history. This commitment of God to his creation was fulfilled in the death and resurrection of Jesus, the Word given to humans as covenantal partners with whom God declares common cause. The vertical community between people and God creates also at the same time a horizontal community of the people with one another.

The communal characteristic of the biblical beginning is answered by the covenantal mutuality of the American beginning. The founding was a joint venture, participation in which yielded equal dignity. This experience of engagement in a common enterprise was not extended to all, notably not to blacks. For that exclusion and oppression, the founders stand under judgment, as Thomas Jefferson proclaimed on at least one occasion. It was a great, grievous offense. There were others. Nevertheless, in a simultaneity of opposites, we can at the same time discern in the beginning made by the founders—not altogether in spite of themselves—an exchange of promises and binding together into a body politic which is a reflection of the biblical mode. This is to assert no more than that there is continuity in history, that the biblical faith claims to have identified its real source, and that pressure exerted by this source may be found vented in the men and events that brought America into being. What this may tell us about our law is the subject I pursue in the following pages.

For a start, I shall examine the source of authority, that which gives legitimacy to American law, in terms of beginning. This is the subject of Chapter One. Because the beginning gives rise to story as its medium of communication, Chapter Two is devoted to the relationship between law and narrative. Then, because space is the necessary complement of story, Chapter Three explores the spatial referents of law, exemplified by the legal construct we label property. Chapter Four is a discussion of the judicial process as a form of theater, the intersection of story and space in court. The courts, I suggest, are a kind of political theater. They are theater of the American beginning which reenacts and enlarges the mutual dignity of the beginning. Chapter Five then raises one consequence of the judicial process so understood: courtroom action offers a normative guiding image to judgment within court and to the political community without. Chapter Six discusses the legal mask, the legal *persona*, as a form of property which equips citizens for participation in the joint enterprise set in motion by the beginning. Chapter Seven argues that, in their substantive judgments, the courts are to be especially solicitous of those who are powerless, the most likely to have been excluded from the common venture. Chapter Eight spells out in technical terms a conceptual legal theory for invocation of the judicial protection of powerless minorities. The whole is concluded in Chapter Nine by a brief word on law as a metaphor of life or of death and on the challenge to the teaching and practice of law so understood.

The teaching of law appropriately seeks positive correlation with the nature of law. In order to conform to the beginning and so have legitimacy, the judicial process exhibits mutuality, which it does by providing in court and implementing in the society the fact as well as sense of participation in a common undertaking. Good teaching of law appropriately finds ways to create the same kind of experiment by drawing students into a joint, exploratory venture. The case method of teaching law can be wooden and can stultify students so that it really teaches the oppression of the powerless and denies the legitimating essential of law. It need not be that way. A course on

6

Introduction

property law can, like property itself, equip people to participate in a joint enterprise by embarking on one in the classroom. The last chapter thus examines teaching as journey, a methodology which corresponds more fully with the essence of law and of life.

The critic and essayist Nicola Chiaromonte observed that "all great theater is concerned with the life of the community by way of individual cases."[3] I allow the same of all great law. The *basso continuo* that supports the howsoever diverse themes of the various chapters which follow is the attempt to discern in law the life of the community. I understand the authentic life of the community to be the biblical new beginning, the basis for the most adequate analysis of as well as aspiration for the secular doing of law.

Chapter 1

❧ Beginning and Authority

Law requires authority for permanence. If law is backed by force and not authority, then it is unstable; it is vulnerable to erosion by arbitrariness and inconsequence and to overthrow by rebellion and superior force. Questions about authority are always in the wings ready to make an entrance, which they have done with some frequency in the last two decades in politics and theology as well as in jurisprudence.

Questions about authority, the absolute that validates American law, originally appeared in the exceptional circumstance of the Revolution: If the king be overthrown, who or what supplies legitimacy to government? The civil rights movement, the crises associated with Vietnam, Watergate, oil supply, the economy, and the sense that we have lost control of the government of affairs have more recently brought authority to stage center. The problem of authority has continued all along, albeit usually in less acute form, in the more common circumstance of judicial decision making.

When courts review the acts of legislators and administrators or determine private controversies, they have the authoritative last word. This arrangement may not be axiomatic, but it is settled.[1] By what right is it so? By what right does a judge strike down a statute, or require busing of school children, or rule on disputed facts? These are questions about authority, the same kinds of questions that have been with us since the Revolution.

In public law, the Constitution is the accepted basis for decision. The Constitution must be construed, however, especially when the applicable provision is open-textured like the equal protection or due-process clauses. What, besides text, guides and anchors judgment?

In private law, precedent and the pull of deciding like cases alike, the rule of *stare decisis*, is the agreed basis for decision. *Stare decisis,* however, is really a theory of possibilities[2] rather than a binding restriction. This being so, what determines the choice between available precedents or constructions of fact that may determine the outcome of a case? What does a judge turn to, and what in turn legitimates the judicial decision? These, too, are questions about authority.

🎎 Possible Sources of Authority

Certainly the Constitution is the material source of authority in the United States. But this is to designate the start rather than the end of the inquiry, for the Constitution's authoritativeness rests upon its ordination by the people.[3] We might then try saying that "the people" is the source of authority and we would be nearer the truth but for the fact that, while the consent of the people does explain the power of the government, "the people" is an insufficient explanation for authority. If it is correct that "in America the law is King,"[4] then the authority of law cannot be predicated upon the people. If this is a "government of laws, and not of men,"[5] then men cannot be the origin of legitimacy. Unless we are to have it both ways, law requires a source other than the people for its legality. (As the quotation in this book's epigraph indicates, Rousseau thought resolution of this problem to be critical.)

One early American attempt at resolution was to ascribe authority to the Constitution but to do so because the Constitution was the embodiment of certain immutable principles. These principles of natural law, antecedent to the people and only acknowledged by them, could then be viewed as legitimating their issue.[6] There was and is a commanding, also highly diversified, tradition of natural law, and it is understandable that natural law was invoked in the second sentence of the Declaration of Independence.[7] The reference in the Declaration is not only to "the Laws of Nature"; there is added, "and of Nature's God." The grammatical conjunction arose from a theoretical union. The eighteenth-century mind did not always or necessarily distinguish God and natural law.[8]

In our own time, Hannah Arendt attempted a somewhat different answer to the question about authority. It was her suggestive thesis that, rather than the Constitution, natural law, or nature's God, the constituting act itself is the enduring source of authority.[9] The greatest success of the founders, she observed, was the provision of a stable foundation for freedom—a separate, vastly more difficult achievement than that of liberation. To be sure, the Constitution was the crown of their success. Arendt's point, however, is that the constituting act, more than the Constitution, is the source of authority. It is an intriguing notion that invites further, considered attention.

❦ The Founding Act as Authority

Arendt was not the first to cause us to believe that there might be a source from which even the Constitution's authority is to be derived and that this source is somehow to be located in the beginning of the republic. Abraham Lincoln leads us to the same conclusion. For example, of the two principal documents of the beginning, the Declaration and the Constitution, it was to the former which Lincoln customarily appealed. He held that the nation had been born with the sentiments expressed in the Declaration and that the Declaration revealed the American *politeia*,[10] our fundamental political fact.[11] For Lincoln, the pivotal statement in the Declaration was that about equality, and he referred to it in the Gettysburg Address as the "proposition" to which the nation is dedicated.[12]

If we allow ourselves to be instructed by Arendt and Lincoln, then we can see that the verbal reality of the Declaration took shape in deed in the congress assembled where each member had the distinction of participating "in the government of affairs,"[13] persuading and being persuaded—the singular activity of equals.[14] The caucuses, town assemblies, and conventions actualized the *politeia* verbally embodied in the Declaration of Independence. The proposition that "[w]e hold these truths to be self-evident, that all men are created equal" is one face; the mutual exchange of pledges and deliberation was another face of the positive reality of América that appeared at its founding. Now we bundle the people, the words, and the events together and celebrate them as the Fourth of July.

This fundamental reality had been prefigured by the first colonizers. The *Mayflower* and its passengers landed outside the jurisdiction of the Virginia Company and so outside the jurisdictional authority of their patent.[15] The colonists needed law for which they needed authority. They solved the problem by the exchange of prom-

ises. On board the *Mayflower* in 1620, Saints and Strangers cove-
nanted and combined themselves into a political body with an act and
a document that provided a legitimating foundation to their law: "We
. . . solemnly and mutually in the presence of God, and of one another, covenant and combine ourselves together into a civil body politic; . . . by virtue hereof to enact, constitute, and frame . . . just and
equal laws, ordinances, acts, constitutions and offices." [16] The cove-
nanting and combining provided authority for law.

The Mayflower Compact was the earliest of a multitude of com-
pacts and combinations. And it was this covenantal tradition that lay
behind the Declaration of Independence and the founding act of the
republic. In the covenantal tradition, the legitimacy of government is
a derivative of the constituting act of binding together into a civil
body politic. The people thus formed may then choose and frame a
government.

In developing her proposition about the constituting act as the
source of authority, Hannah Arendt proposed that what rescues the
beginning from a vicious circle is the act of beginning itself. She
makes note of the fact that, in the Greek (*arché*) and the Latin (*principium*) languages, the same word connotes both "principle" and
"beginning." [17] She argues that the act of beginning is saved from
arbitrariness because beginning and principle are coeval. As she
paraphrases Plato, "For the beginning, because it contains its own
principle, is also a god who, as long as he dwells among men, as long
as he inspires their deeds, saves everything." [18] In the American republic, she says, the beginning was identical with the singular appearance of mutual promise and common deliberation.

> The principle which came to light during those fateful years
> when the foundations were laid—not by the strength of one
> architect but by the combined power of the many—was the
> interconnected principle of mutual promise and common delib-
> eration; and the event itself decided, indeed, as Hamilton had
> insisted, that men "are really capable . . . of establishing good
> government from reflection and choice," that they are not "for-
> ever destined to depend for their political constitutions on
> accident and force." [19]

Arendt's is an attractive resolution of the problem of authority in
the republic. An American "god" of mutual promise and common de-

liberation is a better, more comprehensive explanation than others which have been offered: the force of an unlimited sovereign, for example, or a postulated basic norm, or a rule of recognition read out of social facts. For all its power, however, Arendt's solution does not go far enough. The American beginning, like the men who precipitated it, was not autogenetic. Morever, if this beginning was a god, it was a badly flawed one. Arendt is correct to seek authority in the beginning. She was wrong not to find that the beginning of America is affirmed and disaffirmed by another, transcendent beginning.

🌿 The Beginning as Authority: An Alternative

Arendt traces beginning, via Virgil, back to natality and suggests "that men are equipped for the logically paradoxical task of making a new beginning because . . . the very capacity for beginning is rooted in natality, in the fact that human beings appear in the world by virtue of birth."[20] The problem with this explanation is that no capacity inheres in natality, which is itself a consequence. She does not get us all the way back to the root of things.

There is a more penetrating alternative. Arendt furnishes a clue to it by referring us to Augustine. In the course of portraying the connection between natality and new political beginnings, she cites, as a complement to Virgil, Augustine's statement, *"Initium ergo ut esset, creatus est homo*—'That there be a beginning, man was created.'"[21] Augustine's point however was quite different from that of Virgil and of Arendt.

Augustine was prepared to agree with the Platonists that man is cleansed only by a *principium* which determines what comes after.[22] But the principle-beginning must be accurately discerned. Augustine specifically attributed the shortcomings of Rome and the Platonists— and I would add Arendt—to their acceptance of a defective *principium*.[23] Not just any beginning will do. According to Augustine, beginnings can be understood and undertaken only in the context of the biblical beginning.[24] In his view, the purification necessary for a new and lasting political beginning comes not by natality and flesh, "but by virtue of the Word by which [flesh] was assumed, when 'the Word became flesh and dwelt among us.' . . . The *Principium*, therefore, having assumed a human soul and flesh, cleanses the soul and flesh of believers. Therefore, when the Jews asked Him who He was, He answered that he was the *Principium*." [25] The Roman and Platonist error lay in the refusal "to recognize that Christ is the *Principium* by whose incarnation we are purified." [26] This *principium* is "the supreme reality, . . . the one fundamental principle for individual regeneration and for social reformation, the point of departure for a fresh experiment in human relationships, on the acceptance of which rests the only real hope of fulfilling the promise of secular life." [27]

What frees men and women from being destined to depend for their political constitutions on accident and force is the biblical beginning. This beginning is the source of new political beginnings. It displaces the love of power with the power of love so that people are not hostage to cyclical, capricious fortune and, freed from the destructive attachment to interests, may exchange and keep civil promises, thereby beginning a *novus ordo seclorum*. [28] Hannah Arendt's statement "that the very capacity for beginning is rooted in natality, in the fact that human beings appear in the world by virtue of birth," must thus be restated: The very capacity for political beginning is rooted in the Nativity, in the fact that the Word appeared in the world by virtue of His birth.

🦎 Communal Beginning and Political Possibilities

Arendt specifically rejects the biblical convenants as the matrix of convenanting into a political body. She maintains that the Puritans believed in a compact between God and Israel that implies government by consent but that does not imply a political body in which rulers and ruled would be equal, *i.e.*, where rulership no longer applies. [29] She thinks that "the belief that God retains his sovereignty and refuses to delegate it to any earthly power 'setteth up Theocracy . . . as the best form of government.' " [30]

Such an assessment, however, misses the horizontal effect of intersection with the vertical. The community of people with God creates the community of people among themselves. The communion of saints, as Augustine understood, is not theocratic but democratic. Love empowers self-giving without fear or illusion and so allows people to be most fully human and to participate in a fully human politics.

In the Augustinian vision, there is a city of God. It recruits its citizens from all races and cultures, imposes upon all the same obligations and duties, and rejects the claims of any superman-savior because of the assumption that all are sinners. The leadership of the community differs "both in purpose and technique from any of the various types of leadership current in the secular world. This is the episcopate, a name as [Augustine] says, 'not of distinction but of work.'"[31] The members of the association "pledge themselves in a new oath or sacrament . . . conceived not as an act of self-surrender analogous to that whereby a citizen of this world resigns his will into the keeping of a temporal sovereign, but rather as a covenant of emancipation from temporality."[32]

Subsequently, Luther and Calvin were also led to affirm the communal effect horizontally of vertical communion with God. They insisted upon the centrality of communion as sacrament and social act. In their minds, the priesthood of believers stood for the proposition that each believer, rather than utilizing his own independent line of communication to God, was to "be a Christ" to his fellow—each his neighbor's priest.[33] Moreover, conciliarism, not theocracy, was to the Reformers "the constitutional principle which gives at once order and freedom to the exercise of the spirit of communion and the priesthood of the people."[34] By propounding conciliarism, they intended recognition of the old conciliarist tradition. Whereas theocracy conceived of divine influence entering human affairs through a governing head, conciliarism affirmed that "authority flowed from the divine Spirit diffused throughout the body of the Christian people, and accordingly that the fundamental organ of authority was a council of the Christian people or their delegated representatives."[35]

Arendt is not the only one to have misread the covenant tradition as supportive of theocracy or of individualism. This misreading is partially responsible for the failure to perceive the bearing of the biblical tradition of beginning upon the beginning of America. There is another cause: in interpreting American origins, theorists have displaced the covenant tradition with the tradition of the social contract. The latter, too, derived government and law from a compact. The fictional compact of this tradition, however, was really more a pretext than a context for law.

In the tradition of the social contract, the natural human condition in which individuals were cast was conceived as one of war and death[36] or of confusion and disorder.[37] Accordingly, individuals formed civil society for the protection of life[38] or property.[39] To this end and by contract, individuals yielded up power, authority, and right to a leviathan;[40] they subjected themselves to a monarch or legislative body[41] or to the community and majority rule.[42] While the power to vary their contract with the government might have been retained by the people,[43] the retained power did not negate or qualify the theoretical and practical consent of the individual to be subject to that government.[44] This alienation or transfer of power and authority was then said to be ratified tacitly by succeeding generations of individuals. The social compact was merely a justification for law rather than its ground and content.

In contrast to the social contract, the covenant tradition does not rest on a surrender of a preexisting individual power to another entity. The people and their power are created by the covenant. To consent is to accept the proposition that the people become a people in the election of God. The covenant is a matter of receiving, not preserving, the self or its property. The attendant duty involves no submission, save that of becoming the people that they are. Obedience is not submission to a higher power or greater authority but is a response to the present reality that has called the people into being. The content of the law is the covenant that creates the people. The people are not alienated from their law. It follows that succeeding generations are not made party to a mythic compact by implied consent. They affirm a contemporaneous covenant by participation in, and acceptance of, the identity of the people whom the covenant creates. The covenant thus constitutes the people, and it constitutes them governors.

The founding fathers did employ some of the language and thought-forms of the social contract tradition. Nevertheless, convenantal realities were prominent in their acts, and covenantal ideas were prominent in their minds.

Thomas Jefferson is an example. (Because he was so many, I must be careful to specify the Jefferson of the Declaration and not any of the postrevolutionary Jeffersons.) As Jefferson wrote it, the Declaration was a covenantally oriented tract. Gary Wills has demonstrated that this Jefferson was instructed by the moral sense school of Scottish divines.[45] According to this theory, we begin in society, not isolation, bound by the ties of affection which then form the basis for government.[46] The political world is viewed in communal, covenantal terms. As Jefferson came to believe, the "political bands are those of benevolence, formalized by compact to continue an existing affection."[47] What had bound the American to the British people was "fraternal love."[48] So the Declaration was an action for breach of covenant, "a renunciation of unfeeling brethren."[49] His talk of "affection," "unfeeling brethren," and "former love" can only seem oddly out of place to "those who think of Jefferson and his time as hard bargainers into the individualistic contract of John Locke."[50] They will appear as perfectly natural to those prepared to see in Jefferson's approach a type of the Augustinian, covenantal insight that love is the prior question of politics.

The Mayflower Compact, the Declaration of Independence, and the founding act of the republic are the issue of the City of God. This is not to say that America is or was the new Jerusalem—a foolhardy assertion barred by, besides much else, black labor and black misery, the "primordial crime" of the society.[51] It is to say that the fundamental fact of America is the legacy of the biblical beginning. From that quarter come judgment on the American republic and its law and a continuing challenge for their reformation.

In sum, authority saves revolution from self-destruction. It stabilizes by legitimating law. The search for the source of authority leads from the Constitution to the constitution of the society, from the beginning of the republic to the biblical beginning. The immediate, material repository for authority is the Constitution. The Constitution draws authority from the constituting act. The constituting act evidences community. The community is enabled and instructed by love, love comprehended in the affirmation, "In the beginning was the Word . . . . And the Word became flesh and dwelt among us." The reality thus affirmed characteristically issues in civic mutuality, *i.e.*, equality made actual by covenant, by exchanging pledges and common deliberation. It is this reality that is the source of authority. Law has permanence as it serves and conforms to this reality, the reality of the biblical beginning to be discerned in and transcending the beginning of America.

Chapter 2

🜁 Story in Law

I have proposed that the beginning is the source of authority for law. Now I must attempt to say how the source of authority so understood affects and clarifies law.

I think that the beginning emerges in the courtroom. It is the subject that is continuously playing in the courts as a kind of theater. On the way to exploring this proposal about courts as theater of the beginning, I am going to pause at two intermediate points: the evidence of first story and then place in law. These are not detours.

Both story and place are brought to our attention by the prism of beginning. Also, they are basic components of theater. Consideration of them will prepare for the later dramaturgical discussion and also, I hope, illuminate some aspects of law along the way.

Story is characteristic of the biblical account of the beginning. Theology is done in the Bible by telling stories. There are no abstractions. In the Old Testament, the story of the exodus, the event that constituted the people of Israel, plays a pivotal role and is frequently repeated. The Old Testament scholar Gerhard von Rad established that the central Hebraic confessions of faith were recitals of the mighty acts of God, that these brief credos could be isolated in numerous biblical passages, and that they constituted the core biblical theme.[1] Deuteronomy 6:20–25 (RSV) is one of the key passages in which the theme is sounded.

> When your son asks you in time to come, "What is the meaning of the testimonies and the statutes and the ordinances which the Lord our God has commanded you?" then you shall say to your son, "We were Pharaoh's slaves in Egypt and the Lord brought us out of Egypt with a mighty hand; and the Lord showed signs and wonders, great and grievous, against Egypt and against Pharaoh and all his household, before your eyes; and he brought us out from there, that he might bring us

in and give us the land which he swore to give to our fathers. And the Lord commanded us to do all these statutes, to fear the Lord our God, for our good always, that he might preserve us alive, as at this day. And it will be righteousness for us, if we are careful to do all this commandment before the Lord our God, as he has commanded us."

Much of the Old Testament can be understood as the repetition and elaboration of the exodus story, carried backward to the creation and forward to Israel's present. The story is then taken up and taken over in the New Testament story of Jesus, who descends into Egypt, is brought out, and is then tempted in the wilderness for forty days, corresponding to Israel's forty years. In a new exodus, Jesus descends into death and is brought again to life. The Bible is composed of these stories and others related to them.

Like the biblical account, American law proceeds through narrative. The relationship between the one and the other is as complex as that between the biblical and American beginnings. The connections may be traced back to the first European settlers of this country, who viewed the transatlantic voyage as their crossing of the Red Sea. Instead of trying to decipher all these connections, I want to direct attention to the fact of their method—narrative. We do law the same way that the Israelites did theology: in the telling of stories. The connections lie in the linking of the stories.

We sometimes try to dress American law in blackletter rules and give it the appearance of abstraction, but the singular fact about American law and American thinking about law is court. The Supreme Court was a unique contribution of the founders to the art of government, and courts have played a special role in the United States ever since. The courts are not all there is to law, and the other branches of government require discussion. But the courts are predominant. American concentration on courts is a contribution to jurisprudence, just as the Supreme Court was a contribution to government. It has permitted us to see that the judicial process is not adjectival and that it is itself of substantive significance in understanding law. Any attentive observer of courtroom action will quickly become aware of how important story is to the process.

The importance of story to law is worthy of being explained rather than being explained away. The explanation appears to me to be the same as that for the importance of narrative in the Bible: beginning takes story for the most adequate communication. The present chapter will examine those elements of story distinguished by service in communicating the beginning in law.

✳ Preserving the Past and Legitimacy

In subsequently taking the form of a story, the exodus event is preserved. Story has this conservative effect. It quickens memory and prevents people and events from subsiding into oblivion. The capacity of story to rescue is one of the chief purposes Herodotus had in mind in writing his history[2] and helps to explain its presence in law.

As I said in Chapter One, authority lies in the American beginning placed in the context of the biblical beginning. The founding, like the exodus, is preserved in memory by talking about it over and over again.[3] Thus, at moments of high drama or great need in the affairs of state, political leaders seek to evoke authority by telling the story which allows recurrence to the foundation of the political community;[4] the examples of Presidents Lincoln in the context of the Civil War[5] and Johnson in presenting to Congress the Civil Rights Act of 1964[6] come immediately to mind.

These occasional performances in the other branches of government are the daily office of the judiciary. The courts are the institution in our government given to continual talk about the past.[7] History is not peripheral to their task. It is not a decoration for opinions. The courts are the principal conservators of the story of beginning. By preserving the story of origins, they preserve their authority in significant part.

✳ Story, Participation, and Law

The courts are not simply conservators of the past. The beginning is brought to life for us when we participate in it, which we can do through story. The courts give us this opportunity by their continuation of the story of beginning.

The participatory character of any story is evidenced on an elemental level, for story, like laughter, is inherently communal, something shared among equals, a joint enterprise of speaker and hearer. For this reason many stories have no further point than their telling. The exchange itself is what is sought and is sufficient. Perhaps this is the simplest meaning of having one's day in court, the occasion for a story. At least in early America, it may have been that "it was a secondary matter with the client whether he won or lost his case, so the 'pleading' was loud and long."[8]

At another level, story provides an inclusive, humanizing perspective. Thus, Herodotus wrote to preserve the achievements not only of the Greeks but also "of the Asiatic peoples."[9] Similarly, Aeschylus in *The Persians*[10] portrays those people, foes of the Greeks, with sympathy and praise. *The Persians* was performed only eight years after the battle at Salamis in a war in which both the playwright and his audience had fought. Story permits even the recent enemy a place of equal dignity. So also does the drama of the courtroom elevate perspective when and if it works; judges and juries are led beyond prejudice, and the larger audience, the society as a whole, is enabled to look with equal eye upon offenders and offended, the feared and the abused, the powerful and the weak.

At a still more complex level, story also allows for a kind of participation in the events reproduced in the telling. Story opens a breach in the barrier of time. It opens the past to the present and the present to the past. In the Deuteronomic passage cited earlier, the exodus story breaks down the distinction between narrator and audience, and also the distinction between both narrator and audience, on the one hand, and the participants in the events recounted on the other. It is "we" who were slaves in Egypt, were brought out, given the promised land, and preserved alive "as at this day."[11] Form is thereby matched to content.

In the biblical beginning, God summoned a people to participate with him in his creation. The point is drawn out by the account of the Sabbath. On the seventh day God rested, not from weariness or the exhaustion of ideas for further things to create, but in order to allow humans to join with him in creation. It is a gloss upon the exodus in which God elects the Israelites, whose election makes them covenant partners with God.

In the American beginning, citizens exchanged promises and decided together how they should govern themselves. They entered a covenant and a common venture. To be at the beginning was to be a participant in a joint enterprise. To tell and to hear the story of it is also to participate in a joint enterprise. The story does what it is about. It is "the verbal form of freedom." [12]

Earlier, I noted that the courts are the governmental institution given to continual talk about the founding events.[13] And I observed that this talk is conservative; it preserves the beginning. But it is also, I must now add, liberating because of the participation it induces in the events recounted.

This participation in the narrated events has consequences both for the present and for the past. Its chief effect upon the present is to align contemporary attitudes and approaches along the axis of the founding. "We" take and share part in the beginning. The repeated story of the founding draws succeeding generations into the continuation of what was there begun.

In turn, the past is given extension in time, quantity and quality. The beginning is extended into the present to contemporary participants, succeeding generations and successively broader circles of citizens, those who would otherwise have been excluded by time or by other barriers like racial prejudice. The foundation is, in Madison's phrase, "improve[d] and perpetuate[d]." [14]

The story of beginning conserves. It ties back to the foundation. The story also liberates. It provides for innovation. As the institutional bearers of the story of beginning, the courts are thus "a kind of constitutional assembly in continuous session." [15] By returning to the story, they participate in and allow contemporary generations to participate in the beginning.

Accordingly, in giving play to the story and in keeping with it, the courts are to assure broad participation in the processes of government. For example, where a majority of the citizenry was "stymied" [16] because of the allotment of representation, the courts removed the restriction through reapportionment.[17] "One person, one vote" [18] allows for full participation in the electoral process. Where a powerless minority rather than the majority is frustrated, the courts are to be especially solicitous. When black Congressman Adam Clayton Powell was refused his seat by the House of Representatives, the Supreme Court made positive response to his suit for redress.[19] The Court's opinion did not discuss it but could well be explained on the ground that it was "very important to show Negroes that the political process is for them as well as for whites."[20]

The same provision for participation is brought to bear upon all governmental processes, not just voting and representation. It applies also in administrative proceedings.[21] And it bears upon private relationships and transactions. For example, where a consumer or tenant has not been a true participant in a bargaining process, an "agreement" may be struck down or amended by the courts on this ground, among others, as an adhesion or unconscionable contract.[22]

Assuring participation in these howsoever various processes assures citizens of the opportunity to exert influence. In order to be genuine, this participation must carry with it the potential for real influence. But if this is so for involvement in governmental and other processes, then it must also be so for what I have referred to as participation in the beginning, the involvement of narrator and hearers in the events of the story. That is to say, if an audience takes part, then it must exert some influence upon the story. The participation of succeeding generations in the founding events must be effective or potentially effective in some way. And in fact this proves to be the case.

In an elegy for John F. Kennedy, W. H. Auden wrote:

> What he was, he was:
> What he is fated to become
> Depends on us.
>
> Remembering his death,
> How we choose to live
> Will decide its meaning.[23]

The future of the past depends on us. A parallel observation has been made about the constitutional convention. We have a picture of what happened there which comes to us from various hands and which is generally consistent. What is not available "is any external check upon either the accuracy or the completeness of that picture. The conceptions of what occurred at Philadelphia remain . . . 'ours.'"[24]

The beginning of America was. It is also fated to become. Its meaning remains to be decided by present choices made in remembering it. The story is still being written. It is ours.

By deciding and providing for all citizens to decide the meaning of our past, the courts render the past vulnerable to corruption. There is no guarantee that the influence that participants exert will be beneficent. The past can be revised to suit present need by the courts or by others.

Although it is vulnerable, the American past has proved relatively resistant to propagandizing for two reasons. The first is the resiliency of the past itself. Many ordinary Americans at the time of the separation from England had their own, different agendas and need for other revolutions. Nevertheless, "the wonder is that so many . . . Americans of humble circumstance saw their own aspirations bound up with independence." [25] The beginning was inclusive and unified in a way that has been difficult to revise.

The other explanation for the relative resistance of the past to corruption is the relative success of the very present participation which is the source of vulnerability. The participation of powerless minorities is preventive. Nondominant minorities have histories that run "on different tracks and with different timetables." [26] A society which includes and nurtures these minorities will include also their tracks and timetables in its memory of the past. By taking their frames of reference into account, the majority will forever make fresh discoveries about its origins.

Insofar as the courts and the society which is their audience decide in favor of contemporary diversity, therefore, they keep faith with the past and decide that it will be ever richer and not closed or deceptively, officially made to seem what it never was. A recruitment of nondominant minorities may thus be found to arise from and to enhance the story of the beginning with its dialogue between past and present.

Law is allowed to conform to the authorizing, living reality of the beginning through participation generated by story. Story in law not only saves the events for memory but also augments the vitality and mutuality of the beginning.

✥ Present Understanding and Judgment

In addition to the preserving and augmenting service which it renders the beginning, story is also employed to deliver the beginning to the living. In the Bible, meaning and purpose are gathered from reflection upon what has happened. Story informs every generation's understanding of itself and of life.[27] It did so then, and it does so now. It sustains the sense of appropriateness,[28] the sense of who we are, where we have come from, and where we are going. The ordering capacity of story is the other purpose Herodotus had in mind for his history besides that, mentioned earlier, of keeping brave men and deeds fresh in memory. It was an attempt to discover why the Greeks and barbarians fought one another, a search for the *logos* according to which all things are governed.[29] His conclusion was wrong; he chose the wrong *logos*. But there was nothing wrong with his method, *i.e.*, story.[30]

Because it provides entry to meaning, tradition and its transmission were passions of the American founding fathers. For all their talk about natural law and reason, it was to history, recent and ancient, that they turned for help in the task of making the nation. Experience was their "least fallible guide."[31] Moreover, because "influence over government must be shared among all the people," history, in Jefferson's assessment, was to be also the chief subject of public education.[32] "History, by apprizing [the people] of the past, will enable them to judge of the future," he believed.[33]

History's enablement of judgment is particularly evident in law, for it is through the telling and connecting of stories that law is made. Indeed, if narrative were alien to legal thought, law would be a hopeless enterprise. The archetype of legal discourse is the courtroom performance. A story is told. The story is connected to other stories and ultimately to the story of origins. Legal judgment—a recognition scene[34]—emerges from this recurrence to and association of events.

A lawyer forms the story of his client, first for himself and then for judges and juries, by discerning and emphasizing or deemphasizing given elements under the influence of earlier courtroom stories. Story is the way a lawyer understands, makes sense of, and presents a case. Courts arrive at a decision about a case by replaying it in their minds in search of the fit of its parts and the fit of the whole with prior stories.[35] Story is the way courts come to and explain judgments.

In this process, the story of origins may be more or less near the surface but is always controlling, a possibility that can be explored by understanding that the juridical telling and connecting of stories is a kind of typology. The typological enterprise requires the story of beginning for its point of departure and for a continuing basis of interpretive selection.

Properly speaking, typology originated in the Christian under-standing of events in the Old Testament as prefigurations of events recounted in the New.[36] It is an approach to texts and events that ex-poses continuity in history. Because it was predicated upon the con-tinuous revelation of God's presence in acts in time, it extended beyond scriptural exegesis to become later a form of political dis-course: Cromwell and Charles II as Davidic types, for example.[37] The American settlers then discerned in their own crossing of the wa-ter and entry into a promised land contemporary types of biblical events.[38]

It has been argued that typology "lost its religion"[39] and came down to nineteenth-century America as a structure of thought that was not necessarily or explicitly theological.[40] And one Old Testament scholar proposes that typological thinking is an elementary function of all thought and interpretation.[41] In the context of the present discussion, it is unnecessary to determine whether the typological thinking of lawyers and judges is an instance of a more generalized mode of a biblical typology which has or has not lost its religion. The point is that to think like a lawyer is to think typologically; one story is placed in understanding as a type of another or of others.

In the typology of the common law, a case—the event compre-hended by a judicial decision—is framed for subsequent use by the opinion that supplies the justification for the outcome.[42] The future of the case is both restricted and freed by the words of the opinion. There are limits because the case may not be said to stand for what the opinion denies. But the words are rarely, if ever, cast in rigid ca-nonical formulae. Rather, the good opinions tend more to the memo-rably epigrammatic: "Danger invites rescue."[43] The epigrams serve as guideposts. They are mnemonic references to stories or are stories themselves. To state the issue of a case is to express the interpretive possibilities of a story.[44]

As compared to case law, the process of statutory interpretation is more circumscribed by the form of the language that the word-event assumes.[45] A statute is, no less than a case, an event. It is a legislative act. The legislative event, however, is given canonical terms that only permit a court "to say that the legislature pushed some policy to the limits of the language it used, without also supposing that it pushed the policy to some indeterminate further point."[46] The limits do not mean that statutory construction is a departure from typology but only that its field of play is more certainly delineated. Legislative acts are amenable to narrative. One event is still connected to and understood in terms of another; a court's judgment intermediately completes a sequence of events initiated by the legislature's action.

The founding events underlie both common and statutory law.[47] They are more immediate to and more easily discussed in the context of constitutional law. Constitutional law is not confined to exegesis of discrete textual passages.[48] Although the separate parts of the Constitution do provide distinctive insights, the whole also makes continuous sense. And although the separate parts do have diverse historical backgrounds, the Constitution as a whole refers to the story of the founding. This story is the focal point for interpretation; it provides coherence, scope, and unity to the various passages and to the separate events which underlie them.[49] Thus, for example, Chief Justice Warren's opinion for the Court in *Miranda v. Arizona*[50] surveys the particular history of the self-incrimination clause and its association with John Lilburn but then places that history in the context of the founding and the *principium* of the mutual dignity of citizens.[51]

The Constitution is an opening to a legitimating history. In interpreting the Constitution, the courts are concerned with the story of the beginning to which the Constitution is a reference. The bearing of those events upon present ones is an expression of the afterlife of the founding, which supplies both inspiration and guidance.

Inspiration is necessary because the typology of common, statutory, and constitutional law does not establish exact correspondences. One story does not replicate an earlier one, just as the American beginning did not replicate the biblical beginning. One event is only a shadow, only a type of another. Cromwell is not David. The Pilgrims and Puritans are not tribes of Israel. The Supreme Court is not the constitutional convention. Ernesto Miranda is not John Lilburn. The United States of today is not that of 1776 or of the 1860s. The exposure of connections, therefore, is an apperceptive enterprise. It is not determinate.[52] There is room for argument and critical need for imagination.

Typology effects advances in law by associating unlike stories which, once related and in retrospect, appear to have belonged together. It is the more powerful the greater the distance between the events whose association is yet apt.[53] *Macpherson v. Buick Motor Co.*[54] upheld a decision that Buick Motor Company was liable for injury to a man who was the driver of one of its cars but who had not been an immediate purchaser. Cardozo's celebrated[55] opinion in the case is exemplary in its linking of a wide variety of events including the sale of a falsely labeled poison,[56] an exploding boiler,[57] a falling scaffold,[58] and the collapsing Buick. In property law, disparate acts or omissions—from the introduction of "divers lewd women"[59] into the premises of a boarding house to green fluid leaking from an air conditioner onto the terrace of an apartment[60]—have been typologically linked to the expulsion of a tenant by the landlord and so are "constructive" evictions discharging the obligation to pay rent. If such connections are not made the law cannot progress. That is why inspiration is necessary to the enterprise.

This dependence upon inspiration exposes law to error—misconnections and disconnections. That is why guidance is necessary. One form which error takes is the fantastic, in which all things become types. The appeal of this form lies in consistency and disinterestedness. For instance, George Wythe's judgments were renowned for their detachment; they "were all as between A and B, for he knew nobody, but went into court as Astrea was supposed to come down from Heaven, exempt from all human bias."[61] But to see only and always abstract types is myopic. It causes the corrective capacity for important human perceptions to atrophy. Thus, knowing nobody and seeing only *A* and *B*, Wythe could judge that slaves were types of chattels; he was blind to persons.[62] Benjamin Cardozo and the Restatement of Torts also resorted to alphabetical types; Helen Palsgraf as *A* and the Long Island Railroad as *X* and *Y*.[63] The discernment of people as types, all *P*s and *D*s, *A*s and *B*s, *X*s and *Y*s, produces cases which lose their concretion and slip their moorings in reality. The real effects of what they are doing is hidden from the judges and their potential critics.

Another, similar form of error is the proposal of fabulous associations. In *Illinois v. Allen*,[64] the Supreme Court determined that a disruptive defendant might be found in contempt of court or bound and gagged or excluded. Such a determination was necessary, according to Justice Black, to show that "our courts, palladiums of liberty as they are, cannot be treated disrespectfully" and to insure that they "remain . . . citadels of justice."[65] The association of binding, gagging, and excluding defendants with exoneration of palladiums of liberty is unfit.[66]

The cure for typology run amok is to keep the enterprise fixed to realities. In contemporary law as in the theological hermeneutics of a former day, "there is a medium between those that cry down all types, and those that are for turning all into nothing but allegory."[67] That medium lies in being "true to history."[68]

To fasten the judicial approach to real people and events does orient it and protect it against deficiency and excess. However, to speak of truth to history as the solution raises the prior question about selection: Which are the historical realities to fix on; how discriminate between the fundamental and the contingent?[69]

In order to select, one must have a standpoint. Generally, the story of the beginning of the republic will serve as the ground for judgment, the basis for selection. But much that happened at the beginning is to be disaffirmed, denied extension into the present.[70] Slavery is an example. Wythe's connection between slaves and chattels was a typological connection, and it was invidious but could not be judged so if the only ground for judgment were the American beginning.

The story of the founding is penultimate. There must be some better vantage point. Such an Archimedean point need not be taken up outside of or apart from history. It does not have to be ahistorical— "celestial secret books"[71] or an ideal world of which this one is no more than an illustration. Nor need a transcendent perspective take other than narrative expression, *e.g.*, prescriptive command, fundamental value, basic norm, neutral principle, or rule of recognition. It would be a mistake to assume that there is a form of words more adequate to reality than story. "Who says what is . . . always tells a story."[72]

The question is not whether but which story is decisive. The present era is a promising one in which to put the question, for it has made available a variety of stories of origins.[73] The diversity is welcome. One neither rejects nor presumes upon this pluralism in concluding that it is the biblical story which impresses itself upon us as the accurate and compelling account of existence, "the true *logos* or account of being and movement in the universe."[74]

I hold that the biblical story is background to the story of America's beginning and that it is in the light of the former that the latter is itself finally to be construed. Who says what is always tells the biblical story and receives from it the answer to contemporary questions, like the one in Deuteronomy, about "the meaning of the testimonies and the statutes and the ordinances."

I do not mean that judges and jurors must all be Jews and Christians or that those who are should respond to litigants with scriptural quotations. Judges and jurors hold many faiths or no faith at all. This diversity is in keeping with the beginning and should be encouraged. The citation of biblical proof texts is alien to the beginning and should be repudiated. My point is that the biblical story impresses itself upon us as saturating history with comprehensibility and that this power to make intelligible is as available in law as anywhere else.

Chapter 3

❧ Law in Place

If the beginning occurred in time, it also occurred in place. This is the other half of the concretion and historicity of God's revelation of himself in the biblical narrative. God's will for his people is not to be sentimentalized. That is why Barth says that God and man, as historically articulated figures, meet in *Bereiche*, *i.e.*, spheres, ranges, or provinces. Human beings and the commands of God do not exist out of place anymore than out of time. They have locality.

Deuteronomy is again instructive.[1] According to that book, "all the commandments and statutes and the ordinances" were proclaimed to the Israelites "that they may do them in the land which I give them to possess."[2] The giving of the Mosaic law was coincident with the conquest of the land of Canaan. And the continued occupation of that land was conditioned on the doing of the law. In this tradition, legal bounds have their material counterpart and field of operation in the boundaries of a promised land.[3]

Like the command of God, American law is no brooding omnipresence. It, too, takes place. Our fathers brought forth a nation "on this continent."[4] And the continent is certainly the turf of the American story and the Constitution. But the law courts are their particular places. Law has many places: law offices, law schools, police stationhouses, etc. The courts, however, remain the prototypical place of American law. The subject here is the sense in which the courts have provided place for the story of beginning as the source of authority. In the next chapter, I shall then take up the issue of how the story and place of the judicial process are a kind of theater.

❧ An Original Association of Law with Space

A story, we say, takes place. And it does. So does law. The spatial connotations of law are not unique to the Hebraic tradition.

The Greek word *nomos*, which we now translate "law," had early de-
noted "both 'pasturage' or 'feeding-place' and secondarily 'dwelling-
place,' quarters," so that the adjective *ennomos*, "which later means
'keeping within the law,' 'law-abiding,' has the older sense of 'quar-
tered' or 'dwelling' in a country, which is, as it were, the legitimate
range of its inhabitants."[5] Thus, compared to the scientific notion of
law, *nomos*, as F. M. Cornford observed, signified "a range or province within which defined powers may be legitimately exercised."[6]

For the settlers too and the founders, law was related to place. As I
noted in Chapter One, because the Pilgrims anchored in Province-
town harbor, they were outside the bounds, outside the jurisdiction,
of the Virginia Company and so beyond the law. One explanation for
the Mayflower Compact is that, according to the later account of
William Bradford, some of the Strangers on board "let fall . . . that
when they came ashore they would use their own liberty, for none
had power to command them, the patent they had being for Virginia."[7] Landing outside the geographical limits of the Virginia Company required setting new legal limits.

Later, Madison was to be uniquely fascinated with the size of the
land governable within and because of the constitutional framework,
the singular American contribution to the world of "the experiment of
an extended republic."[8] The Constitution fit the land. We still feel this
old coincidence of law and land. The places where we grow up in this
country help to define our American identity, realigning our instincts,
it has been observed, "like a shadow Constitution."[9]

✹ Public Place

Territorial boundaries, institutional arrangements, and other structural issues are not separable in constitutional history from
human, personal concerns.[10] The two are intertwined because the end
of the founding was a space in which people might exercise freedom
and equality in fulfillment of their humanity.[11] We need a place where
we may come together, see and be seen, pursue public happiness,[12]
and give expression to our citizenship. Law sets the scene.

The constitutional separation of powers fixes boundaries for the exercise of power, spheres of legitimate functioning. Montesquieu
taught that "[p]olitical liberty is to be found . . . only when there is no

abuse of power. . . . To prevent this abuse, it is necessary from the very nature of things that power should be a check to power."[13] Law does not oppose power but allows the powers to oppose each other. "[A]s it relates to the constitution,"[14] law separates the powers and demarcates the ranges within which each is to be contained and act as a check to the others. The aftermath of the Watergate crimes gave the Supreme Court occasion to reaffirm the point. Chief Justice Burger declared that it is up to the Court to "delineate claims"[15] to power advanced by other branches of government. None may overstep its limits, which are kept under the watchful, referee's eye of the Court. Thus, the judicial power

> can no more be shared with the Executive Branch than the Chief Executive, for example, can share with the Judiciary the veto power, or the Congress share with the Judiciary the power to override a Presidential veto. Any other conclusion would be contrary to the basic concept of separation of powers and the checks and balances that flow from the scheme of a tripartite government. We therefore reaffirm that it is the province and duty of this Court 'to say what the law is.'[16]

In addition to this separation of powers among the branches of government, there is also the national-state division of federalism.[17] Although the general trend since the 1930s has been toward enlargement of the sphere of federal power,[18] there have been exceptions,[19] and the states have remained the dominant unit of government in the daily affairs of law.[20] There has been disagreement about whether the boundaries between state and federal government are to be maintained through the political and not through the judicial process. Notwithstanding how it is supervised, federalism, like the separation of branches, defines and contains governmental power.[21]

A further containment of power through subdivision is one of the by-products Madison hoped for from the size of territory and larger number of people governable in the American system.[22] "In a free government," he observed, "the security for civil rights must be the same as for religious rights. It consists in the one case in the multiplicity of interests, and in the other, in the multiplicity of sects."[23] Diversity would be preserved and made fruitful for decision making through representative government. Public views were to be passed through the medium of an elective body so as to refine them.[24] Or, as one court has put it, representative government is a way to guard against "rashness, precipitancy and misguided zeal; and to protect the minority against the injustice of the majority."[25]

Separating the branches of government, federalism and voter diversity balance power against power. The division and subdivision arrests the tendency of power to overreach and destroy itself. Were it otherwise, power would become tyrannous and eliminate the range of freedom. In Montesquieu's words, "[t]here would be an end of everything."[26] As it is, the republican dispensation of constitutional law preserves the political sphere, the public space of the story of the beginning.

🗝 Private Place

Determination of the boundaries of the *res publica* requires consideration of a variety of factors, among them one of critical relevance to this discussion: privacy. The boundaries of the political are established by reference to the compass of the private sphere over against it, the private place which the American story takes.

In a country where government is said to be of, by, and for the people, some explanation is due the necessity of separating a private over against a public sphere.[27] Because rulers and ruled are said to be identical, there should be no disjunction between the people and their government and a corresponding absence of any need to protect citizens from government. There are two reasons for establishing a private realm.

One is the inherent worth of privacy. Political associations are not the only ones there are. The ties of family and religion are also basically human. Thus, for example, religious life is "exempt from the authority of the Society at large," Madison wrote. "The duty of every man to render [homage] to the creator . . . is precedent both in order of time and degree of obligation, to the claims of civil society."[28]

The other reason is the necessity of definition. Granting the worth of both public and private life, they must be distinguished. The private no less than the public requires limitation. Even "virtue itself has need of limits."[29] Accordingly, the Bill of Rights draws bounded ranges for both "private rights and public happiness."[30]

Within the public sphere, there is a separation and division of powers. Within the private sphere, there is a correspondent differentiation. Modernly, for example, antitrust law is "designed to control the exercise of private economic power. Competition is relied upon as the primary mechanism of control."[31]

There is a further set of limits within the private sphere that has less to do with circumscribing power than with safeguarding secrecy. Secrecy is inappropriate in the political realm. The system of checks and balances is designed in part to insure exposure. But secrecy does have a place in the private sphere. Dietrich Bonhoeffer observed that "God himself made clothes for men; and that means that in *statu corruptionis* many things in human life ought to remain covered. Exposure is cynical."[32] Privacy is protected by actions for trespass to property, for example, and specifically by the so-called right to privacy,[33] which is primarily concerned with freedom from publicity by mass communication.[34]

✣ Interdependence of Public and Private

Law designates public and private spheres for politics and persons. In doing so, it separates or differentiates. Montesquieu, however, observed that law was not divisive. "Laws, in their most general signification, are the necessary relations arising from the nature of things."[35] The partition effected by law is a means to something else. Law distinguishes in order to relate.

In the public sphere, the system of checks and balances is a regime for the relationship and growth of the powers. Because "there is a necessity for movement in the course of human affairs," Montesquieu wrote, the three powers "are forced to move, but still in concert."[36] Each part is preserved and multiplied in strength precisely because each is kept to its appointed place by the others in a kind of isometric muscle-building exercise for the body politic.[37]

The same thing is true in the private sphere. Law establishes limits in order to protect spaces within and across which individuals may be related. As Thoreau noted, individuals need sufficient distance from each other when they begin "to utter the big thoughts in big words. You want room for your thoughts to get into sailing trim and run a course or two before they make their port . . . . also, our sentences [want] room to unfold and form their columns in the interval. Indi-

viduals, like nations, must have suitable broad and natural boundaries, even a considerable neutral ground, between them."[38] Distance
is necessary to the development and genuine exchange of feelings
and thoughts.[39]

The economy of dividing legitimately to relate is descriptive also of
the division into public and private spheres. Each contributes to the
other exactly because of their counterpoised integrity of distinction.
The issue has been explored by Richard Sennett.[40] His conclusions
about the mutual benefits which accrue to the public and private from
their independence had to be drawn largely by negative inference
from the dissolution of their separation in the modern period. When
the personal and the political are confused, the quality of both deteri-
orates. In the public domain, Sennett notes, impersonal issues fail to
arouse passion and only arouse passion when they are falsely treated
"as though they were matters of personality."[41] This development in
the public sector then creates a concomitant problem for private life.
"The world of intimate feelings loses any boundaries; it is no longer
restrained by a public world in which people make alternative and
countervailing investment of themselves. The erosion of a strong
public life therefore deforms the intimate relations which seize people's wholehearted interest."[42] As Sennett discovered, a dissolution
of boundaries between public and private robs both of their particular characteristics and so destroys the ground for their mutual enrichment.[43] Without independence there can scarcely be
interdependence.

❦ Property

Property is a principal means by which law establishes
spheres for the legitimate exercise of power and for the legitimate expression of relations.

Property may arise from basic instinct. Defense of one's house and
the land around it can be viewed as a personal code; "you step on my
land, you step on me, goes an old mountain saying."[44] Or as Oliver
Wendell Holmes put it, property "is in the nature of man's mind. A
thing which you have enjoyed and used as your own for a long time,
whether property or an opinion, takes root in your being and cannot

be torn away without your resenting the act and trying to defend yourself."[45]

Whether or not property is a consequence of instinct, an animal territorial imperative,[46] it is also and primarily a legal artifact. Thus Blackstone, who thought the origins of property "probably founded in nature," concluded that for all present intents and purposes it is "entirely derived from society."[47] And as Bentham, who also believed property arose from "sources anterior to law," came to affirm, "property and law are born together, and die together. Before laws were made, there was no property; take away laws, and property ceases."[48]

As a creation of the law, property shares with the Bill of Rights the function of marking a boundary between the public and private spheres. To protect property is to protect the private realm against encroachment by the public. A man's house is guarded as though it were his castle in the interest of protecting the integrity of the private space. According to the saying ascribed to William Pitt, "The poorest man may in his cottage bid defiance to all the force of the crown. It may be frail; the roof may shake; the wind may blow through it; the storms may enter; the rain may enter—but the King of England cannot enter; all his forces dare not cross the threshold of the ruined tenement."[49] Unlike the Bill of Rights, property also sets boundaries within the private sphere. It is a protection against encroachment by private as well as public parties.

The separating and distancing which law effects through the device of property is a particular instance of the general proposition that law sets limits in order to express relations. It binds power in order to give expression to the bonds of association. Thus property is ultimately a way by which law expresses the relation of individuals and of public and private spheres. Property and politics are interdependent.

POSSESSION

There is another conception of property that runs counter to the one I am presenting here. This other conception is basically antipolitical. Its basic premise is that property is an object to be possessed, an extension of personality rather than a place for persons. In this conception, property may be a piece of the American dream, but it cannot be the place of the American story.

This conception is neither barren of attractive aspects nor without notable exponents. Cicero, for one, believed that possessions sustained individual independence, "inactivity without loss of standing and activity exempt from risk."[50] And Walter Lippmann gave modern, more pungent expression to the same sentiment. Lippmann thought that liberty had been maintained where and insofar as the mass of people had enough wealth to sustain themselves if they lost their jobs for expressing their opinions. "There is no surer way to give men the courage to be free than to insure them a competence upon which they can rely," he wrote. "That is why . . . the American's conviction that he must be able to look any man in the eye and tell him to go to hell [is] the very essence of the free man's way of life."[51]

The problem with this approach lies in the core idea of possession, which is destructive of politics for three reasons. First, when "the free man's way of life" is predicated upon property as possession, then inevitably the public and private spheres are no longer held in counterpoise. Cicero and Locke argued that government exists for the purpose of making private property secure. That is, the public realm is thought of as existing for the sake of the private, which has priority.[52] And peace and prosperity rather than freedom and justice can then be thought of as the objects of the national desire.

For politics to be the affair of free people, it is certainly true that public service must be left to choice. It cannot be compelled. But to say that governmental service may not be required is far different from saying that the state exists in order to "make the world safe for property."[53] The public realm is not established to protect the private realm for those who choose always to remain within it. Politics exists also for itself. And, in some respects, the private domain exists for the sake of the public.

Second, the belief that property is something to be acquired means that the state itself, *res publica*, like *res privata*, can be possessed. The republic then belongs to the people not in the fit sense in which a stage may be said to belong to the actor but as a thing that can be owned.[54] Either things public become an extension of private power, or things private are subsumed under things public.[55]

Third, and most insidious, the desire to possess does not admit of mutuality and common participation, the characteristics of American politics at the beginning. Ownership is by nature monopolistic and is naturally inimical to politics. As Blackstone declared in a famous, eu-

phoric passage on the possession of property, "it is that sole and despotic dominion which one man claims and exercises over the external
things of the world, in total exclusion of the right of any other individual in the universe."[56] Possession is competitive and can only be
satisfied at the expense of others. When the public sphere becomes
an arena for the contention of competing interests, the government as
arbitrator can at best arrange a temporary armistice of contending
factions.[57]

In his shrewd anatomy of the Roman Empire, Augustine observed
about acquisitiveness that inevitably "what is longed for either suffices for none, or not for all."[58] In consequence, the earthly city "is
often divided against itself by litigations, wars, quarrels, and such vic-
tories as are either life-destroying or shortlived."[59] Thus, he remarks,
Cain "the founder of the earthly city was a fratricide."[60] This "archetype of crime" found "a corresponding crime at the foundation of"
Rome.[61] Romulus slew Remus, "for he who wished to have the glory
of ruling would certainly rule less if his power were shared by a living
consort. In order, therefore, that the whole glory might be enjoyed by
one, his consort was removed; and by this crime the empire was
made larger indeed, but inferior, while otherwise it would have been
less, but better."[62] The drive to possess the glories of property can
scarcely be a stimulus to politics. It brooks no living consorts. As
Blackstone said, it is sole, despotic, and exclusionary.

Suburban America is an iconography of Blackstone's notion of
property ownership. The suburbs are "a haphazard, disjointed picture, a landscape that, close up, has many pleasant little corners but
as a whole is nonsensical, contradictory, in some ways downright
crazy."[63] There is lacking the organizing center formerly and para-
bolically supplied by a church, town hall, common, or courthouse,
some coherent center of community life. Instead, there are frag-
mented private realms with no points of contact and interchange.
There are "centers," shopping centers, for example, but they are exactly not centers.[64]

As one observer explains, land-use patterns in suburbs have not
followed those of the Jeffersonian yeoman farmer or the country gen-
tleman, both of whom viewed land as something to be worked.
Rather, the ideal chosen has been that of the leisured rich living in the
midst of estates surrounded by luxury.[65] Subdivisions are mini-estates
with class segregation and antisocial absorption. Each house stands

on a separate plot of ground backed by a fenced-in private recreation system. Backyards are pleasure instead of vegetable gardens. The pursuit of happiness in politics is transposed into the pursuit of private interest and private leisure.[66]

Instead of serving as the base from which citizens become engaged in public affairs, a plot of land is made a retreat into which individuals withdraw, a bedroom away from work. Suburbs are subdivisions, but, unlike the divisions effected by the separation of powers, they do not preserve and generate political power. They subordinate politics to possession so that politics becomes the pursuit in public of private interests. Law is stood on its head.

The inversion has been endorsed by Chief Justice Burger. In *Eastlake v. Forest City Enterprises, Inc.*,[67] the Court upheld a city's practice of requiring popular referenda for zoning variances. In that case, the necessary 55 percent majority approval had not been given to a recommended zoning change that would have allowed the respondent to construct a multifamily apartment in Eastlake, Ohio, a suburb of Cleveland. The Chief Justice, writing for the Court, likened such referenda to town meetings and asserted that the referendum "is a means for direct political participation, allowing the people the final decision, amounting to a veto power, over enactments of representative bodies. The practice is designed to 'give citizens a voice on questions of public policy.'"[68] The Chief Justice's confusion of mind is arresting. In effect, he mistakes the French for the American Revolution, the plebiscite for political participation. He also mistakes the private writ large for the public sphere. And then he accepts property as the end rather than as the base for public action.

It has been correctly observed that *Eastlake* is one of the products of a view according to which the local zoning process is a "joint exercise of the prerogatives of private ownership [, and] the municipality is a club, which enjoys the mandatory and exclusive membership of its residents and landowners. And majority will—however insular, unjust, or irrational—prevails."[69] On the *Eastlake* model one may cultivate, undisturbed by the courts, the appetite for ownership of property, its value artificially inflated by the absence of other classes and races, if one captures the polls as a device of exclusionary dominion. But on this model, property is a denial of the beginning.

POLITICAL GROUNDS

According to the other notion of property, the one which I have pursued here—*i.e.*, that it provides place for people and is not an object to be possessed—the legal referents of property are predominantly spatial rather than possessory, and the chief end of property is politics. As I understand it, private property and public affairs are linked neither by polar opposition[70] nor by the common denominator of possessability but by the fact that both are places for being human in. Private property is the place of the person; the public forum the place of citizens. As such, they are together places for the story of beginning.

Possession of property, to the degree that it is material and relevant, is, like the possession of goodness in Augustine's reckoning, "increased in proportion to the concord and charity of each of those who share it . . . and he who is most willing to admit others to a share of it will have the greatest abundance to himself."[71]

Property is fulfilled in exchange. It is therefore political rather than antipolitical, inclusively relational rather than monopolistic. So conceived, it becomes a medium for the expression of our communal nature as we know and receive ourselves from the beginning.

Jefferson understood property in this fashion as the commerce of equal citizens. It was for him a medium of exchange of those who had exchanged promises of fidelity and was thus productive of solidarity.[72]

Madison was affected by the same view. The first illustration Madison offers of what he refers to as "the larger and juster meaning of property" is "opinions and the free communication of them."[73] And he adds that "the praise of affording a just security to property should be sparingly bestowed on a government which, however scrupulously guarding the possession of individuals, does not protect them in the enjoyment and communication of their opinions, in which they have an equal, and, in the estimation of some, a more valuable property."[74]

By nature, such property requires others and is valueless if its possession is sole and despotic. To have a property in the enjoyment and communication of opinion is to have secured spaces for them, first for private independence of perspective and then for public appearance, sharing, and enrichment.

In his later years, Jefferson repeatedly urged that counties be divided into the even smaller unit of wards. These wards would constitute the division of the republic "from the great national one down through all its subordinations, until it ends in the administration of every man's farm by himself."[75] What he envisioned was not withdrawal into the civic apostasy of mini-estates in the suburbs but "elementary republics," enclaves within which people would be independent and from which they would be competent to participate in the "government of affairs."[76] In his vision, there would be a "gradation of authorities, standing each on the basis of law, holding every one its delegated share of powers, and constituting truly a system of fundamental balances and checks for the government."[77]

The fruition of property as a ground of liberty is ultimately political. It is neither a bedroom nor a pleasure garden nor a fortress which allows one "to look any man in the eye and tell him to go to hell."[78] Rather, it is a place—a foothold or platform—whereon to gather independence of thought to be shared and so invested in politics. On the Jeffersonian model, opinion begins on the farm, is exchanged in the ward, and is refined through the media of graded, representative bodies. In this way, property enriches both public and private spheres and expresses the covenantal commitment we have to each other from the beginning.

🐌 Courts

The spatial connotations of law, expressed in property, take specific physical shape in the courtroom. The rooms themselves are singular and have even been described in hyperbolic religious terms.[79] Thus far I have treated story and place separately for analytical purposes. In the event, in the judicial process, they are inseparable, different aspects or dimensions of the same reality.

Their inseparability emerges graphically in the recent volume *Court House*, a collection of photographic studies of courthouses as the center of community life.[80] One of the book's supplementary essays observes how it is that "[c]ountless dramas have been played out within and around these landmark buildings. It is they that have brought our heritage of law most directly to the people. In a very real sense, they are our history."[81] The argument of the book is that the study of courthouses is a "way of reconstructing the American people's story."[82] These places and that story are of a piece.

The coherence of story and place in court suggests that court is an instance of theater, political theater of the beginning. This is the subject of the next two chapters. In Chapter Six, I shall return to the spatial notion of property and its specific connection to judicial theater.

Chapter 4
❦ Judicial Theater

The beginning of America, comprehended in the context of the biblical beginning that is the ultimate source of authority, generates story and takes place. The courts are a particular and particularly important place where the American story unfolds. They are human, humanizing spaces within which the story of our beginning comes contemporaneously alive. As such, they are theaters.

The identification of judicial proceedings as theater has been glossed over, as though theatrics were an expendable, intrusive embarrassment to the scientific and businesslike austerities of the courts.[1] I choose to acquiesce in rather than to deny the court's theatricality.[2]

A theater is a place for live performance. Therefore, as has been observed, the production of plays, unlike the production of goods, cannot be streamlined.[3] A performance of *King Lear* requires about as much time and labor now as it did in Elizabethan England. Output per working hour could be significantly increased in the theater only by radically transforming its quality, dynamics, and nature, as for example, by abandoning the intimate medium of live performance for the quite different mass media of television or film. Productivity gains are simply precluded in theater because what the performer does—live performance—is an end in itself and not the means to production of some other good. Inasmuch as it is invulnerable to greater technological efficiency through mass production or speedier processes, theater cannot reduce its costs.

The same is true of the public functions of courts. Some aspects of judicial administration are undoubtedly subject to modifications that would increase its productivity, but there is little that can be done to cut the time and labor of trials and oral arguments. Their costs can only multiply. A question, which gathers urgency as court work loads and docket congestion increase, is whether current modes of trial and oral argument based on live presentation ought to be discarded altogether.[4] If courts are viewed as producers of judgments, then conceivably other means—videotape, recordings, more exclusive use of writings—could be employed to make the same product more efficiently. But economy of this sort would really be diseconomic, a radical transformation of the judicial system, because courts are not primarily in the business of making decisions. The live presentation of cases in the courtroom, although a means to the end of judgment, is also an end in itself.[5] Trials and oral arguments are to the judicial system what performance is to drama. The play's the thing.

Certainly, judicial proceedings have long been recognized as a source of drama, as is attested by the works of playwrights from Aeschylus[6] to Shakespeare[7] to Daniel Berrigan.[8] And not infrequently, the courtroom hs been a setting for dramatic moments and dramatic confrontations as trial lawyers, judges, and jurors well know. This service of judicial proceedings as source and setting for drama suggests, but is not to be equated with, the allied notion that judicial proceedings are themselves a type of theater. It is this last idea—courts as theaters—that is the subject of the present chapter. In subsequent chapters I shall then explore the senses in which we may say that courts, as theaters, are spaces for the unfolding story of the beginning—courts as theater of beginning.

The Theatrical Elements of Courtroom Action

THE ELEMENTS OF FORM

Clarity may be served, if at the risk of belaboring simplicities, by beginning with some preliminary comments on the theatrical elements of courtroom action: its physical characteristics, audiences, and format.

Physical Characteristics

The courtroom is, or should be, a theatrical space, one that evokes expectations of the uncommon.[9] Unlike the interior of the familiar Broadway theater, the court lacks a stage, curtain, and footlights, and its house lights are not darkened in signal of an imminent theatrical event. Nevertheless, the design and appointment of the court-room, enhanced by costuming[10] and ceremony,[11] do create a dramatic aura.[12]

Theatrical effects are such dominant factors in the physical identification of a courtroom that their absence may raise doubts about whether a court that lacks a properly theatrical aspect is really a court at all. For example, the absence of courtlike features from the place in which a prisoner was convicted for contempt of court was instrumental in overturning that conviction in *Thompson v. Stahl.*[13] Thompson had been arrested for public drunkenness and then taken to a booking room, where his allegedly boisterous behavior drew the contempt sentence. The booking room, located beneath a jail, contained three magistrates' desks behind a steel screen at one end and, at the other, a holding cell where the prisoner was placed. The court observed that "a locked cell . . . in the United States (the 'dock' at the old Bailey notwithstanding) connotes a *jail* rather than a court."[14] Words of warning by one of the magistrates to the prisoner Thompson to be quiet "did not convert the holding cell nor the booking room into a court, nor did they set the stage for any valid exercise of contempt power."[15] Too much should not be made of a phrase, perhaps inadvertent, yet the possibility is raised that a court must appear to be a court architecturally, and that this appearance may be instructively described as the setting of a certain kind of stage.

The *type* of stage to be set, of course, must be accordant with the particular nature and demands of courtroom theater. For example, *Roberts v. State*[16] demonstrated that the staging appropriate to legitimate theater may be inappropriate to the theater of law. In that case:

> The court removed the trial from the courtroom to the theater, and stated as a reason therefor: "By reason of the insufficiency of the courtroom to seat and accommodate the people applying for admission . . . it is by the court ordered that the further trial of this cause be had at the Keith Theater," and thereupon the court was adjourned to Keith Theater, where trial proceeded.
>
> The stage was occupied by court, counsel, jury, witnesses, and officers connected with the trial. The theater proper was crowded with curious spectators. Before the trial was completed it was returned to the courtroom and concluded there.

At the adjournment of court on one occasion the bailiff announced from the stage: "The regular show will be tomorrow;
matinee in the afternoon and another performance at 8:30.
Court is now adjourned until 7:30." [17]

A town playhouse is an inappropriate setting for court because it
may lend itself to actions that belong to vaudeville or legitimate theater but not to courtroom theater. This difference between court and
playhouse is one of species rather than genera, although Chief Justice
Warren, concurring in *Estes v. Texas*,[18] apparently did not perceive it
as such. In that case the Court reversed the conviction of Billy Sol
Estes on the ground that televising his trial had infringed the fundamental right to a fair trial. Among other things, the layout of the
courtroom had been changed to permit installation of a television
booth. Chief Justice Warren believed that this change ignored the importance of the courtroom. The courtroom "in Anglo-American jurisprudence," he wrote, "is more than a location with seats for a judge,
jury, witnesses, defendant, prosecutor, defense counsel and public
observers; the setting . . . is itself an important element in the constitutional conception of trial, contributing a dignity essential to 'the integrity of the trial process.'" [19] He found that the physical alteration of
the trial process could divert it from the fair and reliable determination of guilt to entertainment, commercialization, or political education.[20] He referred to the lower courts' error of allowing television
cameras and coverage as returning "the theater to the courtroom," [21]
and he cited the *Roberts* case to make concrete his fear of the kind of
"staging of criminal proceedings" to which televising trials might
lead.[22]

There is no disagreement between the position taken herein and
Chief Justice Warren's assessment that the courtroom is more than a
nakedly functional location, that this something more is essential to
the trial process, and that the integrity of the process is to be preserved against accommodation to ulterior purposes. Disagreement
arises over characterization. Televising trials should not be characterized as a return of the theater to the courtroom for two reasons.
First, television is to be distinguished from live performance; they are
different media. The introduction of television to trials, as to plays, is
the introduction of a mass, electronic medium into an intimate, live
one. Television no more returns theater to the courtroom than it does

to the playhouse; rather, it represents the transformation of a medium. Second, theater cannot be returned to the courtroom since theater has never left it. What can happen is that one type of theater can be inappropriately imported into another. The correct objection to show trials, produced for commercial or political reasons, is an objection not to theater per se but to the misappropriation of one type of theater with its own purpose—trials—for some other type with different, sometimes dishonorable, purposes. Thus, if courtrooms are something more than functional locations, this something more is their theatricality—their appropriateness to the singular theatrical action of judicial proceedings. In a word, a courtroom is, following Bentham, a "judicial theatre" or "theatre of justice." [23]

Audience

While they must provide something more, courtrooms, like theaters, have seats for an audience. Plays can be written and read as literature or rehearsed to empty houses. But a play is only completed, only really a play, in live performance before an audience. [24] An audience is no less important to courtroom action. In court, there are potentially three audiences: spectators, jury, and judge. While these participants are more specifically the subject of constitutional protection than is courtroom design, it need scarcely be said that this protection has not (although it should have) been tied to their character as audience whose presence is necessary to consummate a theatrical event.

The presence of spectators is subject to limitation, but a criminal trial may not ban the public altogether. [25] Constitutionally, open proceedings are viewed as a safeguard to fair trials for defendants. [26] Something of the sense in which the public may be *theatrically* necessary may underlie the observation of one court that the judicial process "does not unfold legally and normally" when it "takes place behind closed doors"; [27] "participants in secret proceedings quickly tend to lose their perspective, and the quality of the proceedings suffers as a consequence." [28] The public not only monitors what happens in the courtroom but may also help the active participants keep their perspective, thereby prompting them to perform their proper roles.

Gerhard Mueller detected a broader theatrical reason for public presence. After noting that criminal trials were "the theater and *spec-*

taculum of old rural America,"[29] he pointed out that entertainment was not the sole explanation for the popularity of trials.

> It was felt to be the business of everyone in the county to be present when in their name justice was dispensed . . . . It still is the people's trial, although they no longer may officially acclaim the judgment as did the *Umstand* of our Germanic past or the spectators of frontier days. Popular justice is public justice—it is play with popular emotions while doing or restoring right.[30]

The presence of the public is desirable, but there is no guarantee that onlookers will exercise the right to attend. However, their absence does not mean there is no audience, for there is another, the jury. Like spectators, the jury is a subject of constitutional protection[31] and is viewed, at least in part, as a public witness that can check potential governmental oppression.[32] Unlike the right to public trial, the right to jury trial may be waived,[33] and in both criminal and civil cases there are instances in which the right to a jury trial has been held inapplicable.[34] However, when a jury is employed, it is, more decisively than a group of onlookers, a part of the trial event; as the finder of fact, it is the immediate audience for whose response the case is produced in the courtroom.[35]

In the instance of nonjury proceedings, should public spectators not attend, the judge will be the only audience. The judge then performs in several capacities, including that of spectator.[36] A one-person house is minimal, but it is enough. "Can the theater exist without an audience?" Jerzy Grotowski asked, and answered, "At least one spectator is needed to make it a performance. So we are left with the actor and the spectator. We can thus define the theatre as what takes place between spectator and actor."[37] A judge or panel of judges, the irreducible minimum, is sufficient to support a performance of judicial theater.

Format

Besides the physical appearance and audience for theater, judicial proceedings provide the format of drama. Protagonists confront one another,[38] present conflicting versions of the past, and establish a problem to be solved. As one commentator has observed,

[t]he opening statement is the exposition which, by not di-
vulging all, creates suspense. The artful order in which witnesses are called sets up crisis and climax. Conflict, the gist of
any lawsuit, is developed during cross-examination and im-
peachment. Timing is always important; to maintain jury
interest the climax should not come too soon, although, deflat-
ing as it may be for counsel's ego, it rarely seems to occur
during the closing argument. Attention is given to costuming:
"Be sure to wear a dark dress."

If this all smacks of manipulation, it is. Like a play, a trial
must be produced.[39]

At trial, the principal actors are the witnesses and the parties litigant.
Overall direction of the action is the responsibility of the judge, who
controls what happens.[40] Yet to a certain extent, the judge, like the
jury, also performs as an actor. Similarly, attorneys perform both as
directors (in producing the presentation of their clients' cases) and as
actors. The dual role of judges, juries, and attorneys at trial is a product of the fact that trials actually encompass two distinct plays: the
small play, the advocate's production of his client's case (played primarily to the jury or the judge); and the larger play, the trial as a
whole (played before the public audience at large).[41] On appeal, attorneys are the principal actors. They take the part of their clients and
theatrically as well as legally *represent* them.[42]

THE ELEMENT OF METAPHOR

The case which an attorney presents for judgment in court
is an admixture of fact and law. The facts are called facts because they
are not, we hope, fiction. The interaction of the facts and the law
is guided by a logic that may be described, following John Dewey, as
an "experimental and flexible logic,"[43] or a logic "relative to consequences rather than to antecedents."[44]

The selection of facts and law is guided by their interaction with
one another and with a third element, their potential for presentation
in court. The elements of presentation—the rules of evidence, the
case of the opposing side, the dynamics of the proceeding (including
surprise and improvisation), the quality of evidence and witnesses,
and the compellingness of the law—are considered just as carefully

by an attorney as are the facts and the law. The dominant element in the presentation with which he will be concerned is the need to persuade the appropriate decision-makers, first to a judgment that the claim is judicially cognizable, and then to a judgment favorable to the party represented.

The consequential logic, which to a degree governs the selection of facts and law, coupled with the attorney's need for a persuasive presentation, distinguishes the legal case from a scientific investigation. Dewey, for example, hastened to add to his description of the workings of experimental logic the demurrer that "I do not for a moment set up this procedure as a model of scientific investigation; it is too precommitted to the establishment of a particular and partisan conclusion to serve as such a model." [45] What distinguishes the case from scientific investigation helps to establish it as a form of dramaturgy. The case persuades histrionically. This point is neglected when the courtroom is thought of as a laboratory or a research library, with the mistaken consequence that the methods employed in the courtroom are urged to approximate "the methods of historians or physicians or geologists." [46] The methods are better understood as those of playwrights, actors, and directors, and may be described as the making of metaphor.

What is meant by metaphor? In reference to the play *The Cherry Orchard*, Francis Fergusson explained that "the larger elements of the composition—the scenes or episodes, the setting and the developing story—are composed in such a way as to make a poetry of the theater: but the 'text' as we read it literally, is not." [47] The poetry, the metaphor, is not necessarily to be found in the words of the text. Rather, it is to be found in the histrionic elements which "can only be seen in performance or by imagining a performance." [48]

About a production of the play *Akropolis*, which he characterizes as "a poetic paraphrase of an extermination camp," [49] Grotowski describes how, as the play begins,

> [i]n the middle of the room stands a huge box. Metallic junk is heaped on top of it: stovepipes of various lengths and widths, a wheelbarrow, a bathtub, nails, hammers. Everything is old, rusty, and looks as if it had been picked up from a junkyard. The reality of the props is rust and metal. From them, as the action progresses, the actors will build an absurd civilization; a

civilization of gas chambers, advertised by stovepipes which will decorate the whole room as the actors hang them from strings or nail them to the floor. Thus one passes from fact to metaphor.[50]

The passage from fact to metaphor is what the advocate seeks. It is the passage from the materials of fact and law (the text) by means of courtroom presentation (the performance) to a persuasive statement of what is to be done in a given situation (the metaphor).

The advocate's presentation of a case, the creation of courtroom metaphor, is marked by the coincidence of the opposites of fact and illusion. Illusion here is not falsehood but facts selected and established through artful, sometimes fortuitous, sequence. This convergence is the paradox of theater. In an essay on Nicola Chiaromonte, Mary McCarthy commented that "[t]he sphere of ultimate, irreducible reality which is the stage is also the licensed sphere of illusion."[51] In the course of years of reflection upon the paradox of theater, Chiaromonte had pursued the original, remarkably simple, and fruitful insight that theater is "a sequence of actions performed by actors"[52] which constitutes the "repetition, re-enactment of an already accomplished fact (rather than simulation of a set of facts still in the course of happening)."[53] In the playhouse, as in the courtroom, an event already completed is reenacted in a sequence which allows its meaning to be searched out. Chiaromonte concluded:

> In the theatre, the main thing is the drama, the conflict of individual situations, of ideas and passions—the clash of characters who are left, so to speak, on their own. If this is so, then the fictional element—fabulation—loses all importance. What matter are reflection and judgment. As for the plot, it plays exactly the same part as played by the corpus delicti in a law court. It has already happened and is now being re-examined, mounted on the stage for inspection—not the exterior episodes, as in a film, but the relevant and material acts, those we would turn over in our minds, in the course of reflection.[54]

At its best, the presentation of a case is a coincidence of reality and illusion, not in the sense of perjury, but in the sense of theatrical metaphor—the reenactment of relevant and material elements for reflection and judgment. Although elusive, this paradoxical interplay of reality and illusion does seem to correspond with the deeper truth of the way we experience life,[55] which is to say that it is a strength, and not a weakness or fault, in both the playhouse and the courtroom.[56]

DEFENDING THE ANALOGY

Is Courtroom Action Really Metaphor?
Several objections may legitimately be raised to viewing the courtroom as a theater. One is that it asks too much and the wrong things of the word "metaphor." A brief defense of its use here may prove useful.

"Metaphor," Lon Fuller has observed, "is the traditional device of persuasion. Eliminate metaphor from the law and you have reduced its power to convince and convert."[57] Certainly the law does employ metaphors. Fuller illustrated his point with a consideration of the metaphor "constructive notice."[58] An additional point is attempted here: attorneys not only use linguistic metaphors but also produce histrionic metaphors. Constructive notice is a metaphor. A presentation which makes out a case of constructive notice is also a metaphor. Like the performance of a play, the presentation of the advocate's case seeks to persuade, and it does so openly. It is a metaphor and not a lie. Insofar as there is duplicity through selection and formulation of facts, the duplicity is open and generally accepted. Judge, jury, and public expect the attorney to offer the construction of facts and law most favorable to the client; his purpose and point of view are apparent.

Like metaphor, the attorney's presentation is a mode of persuasion. Also like metaphor, the attorney's presentation proceeds by substitution. According to one popular authority, "a metaphor is a tacit comparison made by the substitution of the compared notion for the one to be illustrated."[59] The court case is a tacit comparison in which presentation of selected fact and law is substituted for the events themselves and the prior law.

There are several reasons for the substitution. The plainest is that the past cannot be reproduced exactly, so that in the nature of things some substitution cannot be avoided.[60] Another is constitutional policy, which may require deliberate exclusion of certain evidence in criminal cases.[61] A third reason arises from the task of judgment, which requires interpretation rather than a formless flow of information.[62] Finally, and most basically, the very theory of our justice system, as Justice Holmes put it, "is that the conclusions to be reached in a case will be induced only by evidence and argument in open court, and not by any outside influence."[63] This process is to be preserved even against *truthful* outside influences.

> A publication likely to reach the eyes of a jury, declaring a witness in a pending cause a perjurer, would be none the less a contempt that it was true. It would tend to obstruct the administration of justice, because even a correct conclusion is not to be reached or helped in that way, if our system of trials is to be maintained.[64]

This may or may not place truth and justice in conflict,[65] but, in any event, it does suggest that our system of trials seeks to do justice in a particular and artful manner[66]—in a metaphorical manner, it seems proper to say.

Trials Persuade. Does Theater?

Besides maintaining that it overloads "metaphor," another possible objection to the position adumbrated here is that, if, as has been maintained, it is the precommitment of a case to a partisan conclusion that distinguishes it from scientific investigation, then this same precommitment distinguishes it as well from theater. In other words, judicial proceedings are not theater because theater is its own end (art for art's sake) or has some end other than that of persuading to a judgment (entertainment or cathartic excitation to pity or fear, for example).[67]

Yet, art in general and theater in particular do persuade to some conclusion. If the objective is parochial or political, then the artist's product may be, perhaps corruptly, propagandistic. If the objective is broad (for instance, a view or experience of human life), then it is contemplative. Either way, there is an objective of persuasion. For example, Chekhov proposed that

> the writers whom we call eternal or simply good and who intoxicate us have one very important characteristic in common: they move in a certain direction and they summon you there too, and you feel, not with your mind alone, but with your whole being, that they have a goal, like the ghost of Hamlet's

father who does not come and trouble the imagination for nothing. Some, depending on their caliber, have immediate objects: abolition of serfdom, liberation of their country, politics, beauty, or, like Denis Davydov . . . , simply vodka; others have remote objectives: God, immortality, the happiness of mankind, and so forth. The best of them are realistic, and paint life as it is, but because every line is permeated, as with sap, by the consciousness of a purpose, you are aware not only of life as it is, but life as it ought to be, and that captivates you.[68]

Of course, a play does not guide its audience, as a case guides the jury, to either an immediate decision or to a decision with immediate consequences for the life, freedom, or property of another.[69] Judgments made in response to a play, other than critical ones about the play's quality, are longer range and have to do more with perceptions of life and one's own identity.[70] The question is whether this difference destroys the proposition that the case is theater or only distinguishes the theater of the courtroom from that of the playhouse. The latter alternative has been chosen here.[71]

How Far Does the Analysis Carry?

Added to the objections that the present analysis abuses both "metaphor" and the notion of theater is the further objection that the analysis is inapplicable to the methods by which some important judicial decisions are reached.

Trials, in which the greatest range of theatrics is exhibited, are a method for resolving only certain types of factual disputes. Kenneth Culp Davis drew a useful distinction in this regard between adjudicative and legislative facts. Disputes about adjudicative facts ("facts about the parties and their activities, businesses, and properties, usually answering the questions of who did what, where, when, how, and why, with what motive or intent") are those appropriate to resolution by trial.[72] Legislative facts ("general facts which help the tribunal decide questions of law, policy, and discretion") are appropriate for oral argument and briefs, the typical procedure of appellate courts.[73]

Cases before appellate courts are governed by emphases, subject matter, and methodology different from those of trials. Appellate emphasis is upon legislative fact, although adjudicative facts are neither unimportant nor without effect.[74] The subject matter is superficially the action of a lower court. The methodology places greater reliance upon argumentation and briefing and allows for extra-court development of legislative facts by the decision-maker.[75]

The essentials of theater, however, are as clearly discernible, if less protean, in appellate as they are in trial courts. Facts and law are shaped into material which informs both a text and a histrionic presentation in a theatrical space before an audience. On appeal, the attorney's role as actor dominates that as director. Indeed, appellate attorneys are more authentically actors and more purely representative of their clients than their trial counterparts.[76] And their performance, their oral contest, is or may be critical to the outcome.[77]

To say that courtroom presentations are as essentially theatrical when they are appeals as when they are trials does not, however, address those instances in which judicial decisions are made without either trial or oral argument. The Supreme Court, for example, makes many decisions about whether or not to grant certiorari, decisions that are based upon documents. This choice of cases is of considerable importance to the Court's judicial responsibility, as the debate about a national court of appeals has reminded us.[78] The selection of cases and the subtle policy decisions it involves are judicial but not the product of histrionic proceedings. They do bear upon theater for they control which cases, which plays, will be produced. But judicial decisions which are the end product of exclusively documental occasions are not themselves theater. This limitation need not scuttle the analysis undertaken here if it be agreed that histrionic proceedings are the typical, though not exclusive, mode for reaching judicial decisions.

✣ Courtroom Action as a Distinct Type of Theater

Their physical context, audiences, format, and use of metaphor invite examination of courtroom proceedings as a type of theater. Before exploring the import of the theatricality of courtroom action, we will find it useful to fix more clearly, if still preliminarily, the identity of judicial theater as a distinct type.

THEATER OF THE ABSURD

One of the characteristics of judicial theater is its ordered sequences and exchanges. Disruption of the order may make it something else or may expose the fact that it has already been made into something else—perhaps theater of the absurd, a categorization suggested for the Chicago conspiracy trial.[79] The attorney's part in the specified flow of initiative and response, according to Geoffrey Hazard, is "not soliloquy but—the pun is irresistible—a trialogue, a series of ordered exchanges with the judge and opposing counsel," interference with which means that "the lawyer's appearances and cues are lost or disordered and at some point his role and reason for being there simply collapse."[80] The same may be said of defendants.[81]

Superficially, courtroom disruption converts judicial theater into another and incompatible type. However, it may be that attorneys and defendants abandon their preassigned roles because they believe that the courts have already abandoned their own proper roles. About the Chicago trial, for example, the possibility was ventured that, had the judge "consistently avoided playing it like a minstrel show, then defendants might not have played it like a circus."[82] More broadly speaking, if the courts are perceived as instruments of oppression rather than of justice—if they are perceived to be not really courts—then notwithstanding the decorous behavior of judges, disorderly conduct may occur as an anguished protest against injustice and an appeal for justice.[83] My point is simply that whether disruption be instigated by the parties, their counsel, or the judge, it does make of the proceedings something other than the forensics of judicial theater.

THE MORALITY PLAY

In addition to theater of the absurd, another type of theater from which judicial theater may be distinguished is the morality play. Especially criminal but also civil trials have been likened to morality plays.[84] The analogy fails for two reasons. First, the *dramatis personae* of morality plays were symbols or personified abstractions like Everyman, Goods, Fellowship, and Beauty.[85] Although episodes and character groupings might vary from one morality play to another, the endings were always the same.[86] In contrast, courts deal with individuals, the outcomes of whose cases have at least the potential for being neither preprogrammed, predictable, nor uniform. Insofar as trials are prepackaged and routine rather than unique, it would seem that they are not really trials and might qualify as *immorality* plays.[87]

Second, morality plays featured symbols and a uniform conclusion because they were unapologetically and unrelievedly didactic— glosses on medieval Christian dogma. A trial is not the dramatization of a sermon. Insofar as it is made a platform for moralizing or a forum for educating, a trial is not a trial. Trials may indeed have an educative effect, but they have this effect when, instead of deliberately undertaking to teach, they treat the parties as individuals. In his concurring opinion in *Estes v. Texas*,[88] Chief Justice Warren noted that the Soviet Union's trial of U-2 pilot Francis Gary Powers sought both to determine the guilt of the individual and to provide the public with an object lesson. This divided purpose "undercut confidence in the guilt-determining aspect of the procedure and by so doing rendered the educational aspect self-defeating."[89]

THE SATURNALIA AND PLAY

Quite the opposite of the morality play but equally distinct from courtroom theater is the saturnalia, an extravagant entertainment or orgy which gives vent to passion and in which all are participants.[90] The failure to distinguish between actors and audience may render saturnalia inimical to all types of theater.[91] In any event, saturnalia are incompatible with judicial proceedings. First, active participation by spectators imperils the forensic sequences no less than does disruption by attorneys and defendants. More important, mob scenes and the gathering and release of passion overrun reasoned deliberation and reduce the potential for protecting defendants' rights.[92]

To distinguish judicial theater from saturnalia is not to distinguish it from play, which may be understood, following Johann Huizinga, as "a free activity standing quite consciously outside 'ordinary' life as being 'not serious,' but at the same time absorbing the player intensely and utterly. . . . It proceeds within its own proper boundaries of time and space according to fixed rules and in an orderly manner."[93] Orgies abandon limits and thus abandon play; court proceedings spring from play. In the course of an examination of the ancient relation between play and law, Huizinga found that the lawsuit had originally been, in the strict sense of the word, an *agon*, a match or struggle, which (notwithstanding and even because of its seriousness, tension, and emphasis on winning) was a form of play.[94] He discovered that an agonistic element, chiefly in the form of verbal battle, was still to be discerned in the lawsuit.[95] The engagement of adversaries in a serious legal contest is agonistic but not orgiastic and is thus an expression of play.

THEATER OF FACT

The type of theater most obviously parallel to judicial theater is theater of fact. Theater of fact is documentary in appearance. Its scripts may consist of edited transcripts of hearings or trials. Father Berrigan, for example, simply lifted out portions of the transcript of his trial in order to make the text for a play.[96] Theater of fact is politically oriented, and its effect is generally accusatory. Hochhuth's *The Deputy*[97] does not differ greatly from a prosecutor's case, played in a theater to an audience sitting as a jury. What finally distinguishes judicial theater from theater of fact, and from other types to which it may bear similarity,[98] are the immediate judgment rendered in the courtroom and the consequences that attend it. An audience is not a jury. This distinction is only typological, however, for judicial proceedings remain theatrical in essence.[99]

✻ The Functions of Judicial Theater

As a distinct type of theater, courtroom action is highlighted by ordered exchanges, nonprogrammatic individuality of outcome, and contest or play. The construction and analysis necessary to deliver an object to judgment could be provided without these histrionics. A court system can be hypothesized, for example, in which cases would be handled entirely by mail. Therefore, I want to turn now to some of the contributions made by live judicial theater. It is the theatrical character of courts that makes them spaces of freedom, human places where the story of beginning is augmented as it comes alive.

COMMUNICATING NONVERBAL INFORMATION

It may be that live performance communicates nonverbally some of the information that the decision-maker must take into account.[100] Demeanor evidence is an example. While it is undeniable that documents lack the capacity to convey nonverbal information, it has been contended that videotape may do so as well as live presentation.[101] Opinion on the issue will likely continue to be divided, since the communication of nonverbal information is not easily tested or analyzed.[102] It would seem, however, that what is true of plays is true as well of cases: "The little ritual of performance, given just a modicum of competence, can lend to the events represented another dimension, a more urgent reality."[103]

REDIRECTING AGGRESSION

Further, the theatrical character of lawsuits also allows them to redirect aggression. Aggression, the need to fight and have revenge, is acted out[104] and is thereby ritually expressed and controlled.[105] It is in this sense that "[t]he right to sue and defend in the courts is the alternative of force."[106]

The continued capacity of lawsuits to rechannel aggression depends upon several factors, one of which is their gravity, that is, their convictive and absorptive power.[107] This power may arise from the fascination and purgation of the action itself, as was the case with the "good show" in early American courtrooms.[108] Or interest may be engaged and satisfied by the stakes. Money damages, decrees, or imprisonment give to judicial theater a moment missing from that of Broadway. They do not, for all that, make it any the less play; they simply make it more serious.[109]

Besides their gravity, another, more decisive factor that maintains legal proceedings as an alternative to other forms of aggression is their fairness. The procedures and conventions of the courtroom set judicial proceedings apart from the world of common, daily affairs. Acceptance of this play world cannot be commanded. Judges, like referees, can penalize for irregularities—by dismissing suits, handing down contempt citations, ordering the binding and gagging of defendants. But these can be no more than remedial measures. Punishment for infraction after the fact does not generate the necessary, precedent willingness to accept the special world marked off by court rules and conventions. Acceptance of judicial proceedings must be voluntary and is consequently dependent upon the perceived fairness of the courts.[110]

If acceptance of the rules of play ultimately depends upon their fairness, acceptance of the play world they mark off depends upon that world's making good on its express and implied promises. Playgoers bring with them to the theater a "willing suspension of disbelief,"[111] a willingness not to see an actor and a bare stage when presented with Macbeth and Birnam Wood come to Dunsinane. This "negative faith in the existence"[112] of the play world can be violated as a result of any of several causes: a lapse in writers' or actors' skill or a failure of artifice and craft in staging. The really serious offense for which the license granted theater is revoked is its failure to redeem the pledge to entertain or supply catharsis or mirror nature—in a word, to be theater.

Participants in judicial proceedings also bring with them a willing suspension of disbelief. It is manifested in their willingness to observe the rules and forms of the proceedings, their willingness to abide by the outcome of the proceedings, and their willingness not to dismiss the legitimacy of the legal system, characterized though it may be by curious formulae, arcane rites, and untoward results. Like the license granted theater, this willingness will answer for any sustained length of time only to the system's reasonable degree of success in doing what it promises, in this case, justice.[113]

ENCOURAGING IMPARTIALITY

Courts may not always or even frequently do justice, but their theatrical quality does contribute to their potential for doing justice by encouraging disinterestedness in the decision-makers. As actors, the judge and jury are asked to play parts in a government of laws and not of people. Fulfillment of the roles enables judgments that rise above prejudice and that, therefore, will more likely be just. Not the least hoped-for result of the theatrical trappings and conventions of judicial proceedings is to educe such performances.

Judge and jury are audience as well as actors[114] and in this capacity also may be encouraged to make unprejudiced judgments. Actors may be drawn beyond themselves by the roles they play, but they are not thereby totally absorbed in their parts, for they maintain control of the characters they create on stage.[115] An equivalent mix of involvement and detachment is also possible for the audience.[116] A production that works absorbs the audience. The involvement is not total, however, for there remains a separation arising from consciousness that what is being witnessed is a theatrical action. The separation allows the audience to make impartial judgments about what it sees.

Bertolt Brecht observed the phenomenon of audience involvement and separation and exploited it through the "alienation effect." Alienation, in this sense, "is the art of placing an action at a distance so that it can be judged objectively and so that it can be seen in relation to the world—or rather, worlds—around it."[117] Alienation stimulates conscious judgment by keeping the audience from simple identification with the characters of the play. Such alienation is encouraged by the manner in which the performers look at themselves as they perform.[118] Brecht noted of one production,

> The performer's self-observation, an artful and artistic act of self-alienation, stopped the spectator from losing himself in the character completely, i.e. to the point of giving up his own identity, and lent a splendid remoteness to the events. Yet the spectator's empathy was not entirely rejected. The audience identifies itself with the actor as being an observer, and accordingly develops his attitude of observing or looking on.[119]

This same attitude of limited identification with attorneys or parties while observing them and forming judgments about them is the attitude appropriately developed in judge and jury as audience.[120] The courtroom equivalent to alienation may arise from the way attorneys present their cases, from the comments by the judge, from bench conferences, and the like, all of which may remind the judge or jury that a decision about the action must be reached.[121]

In a sense more profound than that of Brecht's "alienation effect" and its courtroom equivalents, the distancing necessary to good judgment lies in the very nature of drama and the dramatic. As Chiaromonte observed in writing about Aeschylus, a "current or recent event . . . had dramatic value to the extent that the poet was truly able to 'give it distance,' to contemplate it by raising himself above the emotions and passions of the moment."[122] Thus, Aeschylus' *The Persians* was "the loftiest example of civic poetry" because of this distancing effect, which "caused his townspeople to contemplate not the grandeur of their deed, but solely and strictly the law of the gods that had led to the ruin of the huge Persian force."[123] It represented "the triumph of the poet's mind over the victory of his country and . . . his own victory."[124] It is a dramatic triumph and, even if possible in other media, is preeminently associated with drama. When courtroom theater is effectively and really that—*i.e.*, when it is theater, when it is dramatic—then decision-makers are put in position to judge not so much with blindfolded as with equal eyes.

INDUCING CREATIVITY IN JUDGMENT

To the suggestions that live presentation may communicate nonverbal information, redirect aggression, and encourage impartiality, there may be added another: it is perhaps an inducement to creativity in judgment.[125] Of the cases that come to court, one estimate placed at 30 to 40 percent of the total those that can be decided but one way because they clearly fall within the ambit of a clearly and authoritatively stated rule.[126] Even in these "clear" cases, live presentation may promote the search for imaginative alternatives if it makes disposition less mechanical by giving force and appeal to the position of the party against whom the rule is to be applied.[127]

Live presentation is more certainly an active element in the unclear cases. In these it may give more urgent reality to the particular facts that establish distance between a given case and a general rule or that expose a given case to competing rules.[128] Performance of cases, by thus contributing to indeterminacy, helps to bring about the conditions for creative resolution. It may also have some influence upon the creativity that is exercised in those conditions. This influence may extend no further than some potential of performance to dispose the decision-maker to respond in kind, that is, creatively rather than routinely or with formulae. Or, live presentation of cases may have a suggestive influence upon the substance and methodology of judgment, a possibility I shall develop in subsequent chapters.

It should not be concluded from the foregoing discussion that live presentation seduces courts into making undisciplined judgments. Judges may yield to bias and prejudice but not in consequence of live presentation. A legal judgment may be creative without being undisciplined. In this regard it is like fine art. Although original, as Kant observed, "there is still no fine art in which something mechanical, capable of being at once comprehended and followed in obedience to rules, and consequently something *academic* does not constitute the essential condition of the art." [129] The formal requirement that judges, unlike artists, state reasons for what they have done offers added assurance that discipline will be exercised. [130]

THE PERFORMANCE AS A WHOLE

If the advocate's presentation of his client's case is a form of theater which is played to the judge or jury and which contributes to judgment, there is also the theater of the courtroom itself—embracing all that goes on within—played to the public at large. It is the function of this drama to provide an image of legitimate society. In this sense, it is importantly an end in itself. As is true of theater generally, so of judicial theater: the performance is the "good" consumed. The courts are not so much in the business of producing decisions— finding facts, fixing liability, convicting the guilty, protecting the innocent, etc.—as they are of giving a performance.

I have said that the authority of the beginning is communicated through story tied to place. The courts are the paradigmatic spaces where the dramatic narrative of our beginning is recurred to and augmented.

If the presentation of a case is a metaphor, the same may be said of the larger courtroom drama of which it is a part. And if metaphor is "saying one thing and meaning another, saying one thing in terms of another," [131] then what is said by the courtroom performance as a whole is what legitimate society is.

In fulfilling what John Marshall saw as its duty to say what the law is, the judicial branch does not merely utter decisions, disembodied words. It is the exemplar of law. In its ceremony, its costuming, its performance, and its treatment of participants, it embodies the legitimate exercise of power within a given sphere. Judicial theater is itself a continuous way of saying, in things and acts within appointed spaces, "what the law is." [132]

In the biblical beginning, a people was brought into being by the covenant which God cut with them. This vertical community between the people and God issued in the horizontal community of the people with each other. They were covenant partners with each other because of their covenant partnership with God. In the priesthood of believers, as Luther said, each is priest to the other. What the observer remarks about the community of faith is this horizontal or political mutuality: the common dignity of those engaged in a joint venture, the equality of participation of those who share a history ("See how these Christians love one another").

I have said that evidence of this same kind of politics may be found in the exchange of promises that constitutes the founding and continuation of the American enterprise. The courts are a kind of constitutional assembly in continuous session insofar as they carry this joint venture forward. When the courts, by their process, give people significant roles to play, parts of real importance and dignity, then we find people being treated as they are in the beginning. Then covenantal mutuality is recreated. Then what the law is is performed. And then the source of its legitimacy—the authority of the beginning—is played before us.

The story of law (Chapter Two) and the place of law (Chapter Three) coincide in the judicial process as theater, the subject of this chapter. It is as theater that the judicial process serves the beginning. How this is so and with what effect are the issues I am now set to explore.

Chapter 5

🐚 The Image of Court as Theater of Beginning

Judgment and Process

In court, the beginning is continually playing. "[T]he purpose of playing," Hamlet instructed his actors, "was and is, to hold, as 'twere, the mirror up to nature."[1] In commenting on this line, Eric Bentley observed that the mirror is held up "not to the picture people have of themselves but to nature, that is to people as they really are—a very different matter."[2] American courts hold a mirror up to our political nature, ourselves as we really are and know ourselves to be from the beginning.[3]

When the courts do mirror who we really are, our better self, they give a normative image. As Bentley went on to say about Hamlet's instruction on holding the mirror up to nature, "Though art imitated life, it did not do so for the record, but in order to improve life."[4]

If who we really are is who we are to become, then who we really are indicates what we are to do. We must learn to seek guidance not from prescriptive texts but from the personal, historical, relational reality of the biblical beginning. This reality discovers to us our nature and destiny and may be discerned in and through the American beginning as well as the ongoing judicial process. Ronald Dworkin has labored mightily to free jurisprudence from dependence upon celestial secret books and to persuade us that there are answers, right answers, which are not drawn from texts.[5] He has sought to convince us that judges are not asked to apply rules so much as to recognize rights, for which litigants contend with arguments of principle. He is to be applauded for having shown us that the burden of judgment is not in applying rules or in formulating policies and that we are ennobled by the robust give-and-take of legal argumentation. But if he has freed us from the ideology of prescriptive texts, he has not set us free enough. The notions of principle and right still partake of static, rational construct and are arbitrary to that extent. I want to move completely beyond prescriptive texts and thus adopt the formulation "beginning" in place of "principle" and "theatrical masks" (or "*personae*") in place of "rights." I agree with Dworkin that there are right answers. I disagree about the form of and means for discovering these answers.

Again I take Deuteronomy as my point of departure. You will remember that the Deuteronomist gave statement of the meaning of the law by reciting the exodus story, the story about the origin of the people. The story said who the covenant people were, and it answered the question about the meaning of law. The theologian Karl Barth once noted about Israel's law,

> There is no abstract cult-regulation, no abstract legal norm, no abstract moral law. Everything that God wills is an exact expression of the fact that those of whom He wills it are His own—an exact counterpart of the "great and terrible things" which God had already done for these men . . . . The Ten Commandments and the various ceremonial, legal and moral enactments, are not independent and cannot be separated from this antecedent. They receive and have from it their specific content. They are merely part of the law of the life of the people led by God out of Egypt and into Palestine. It is because it is this people, because it would not exist without these "great and terrible things" done by God, because it owes its existence to these acts of God, that it is bound and obliged to keep the command of its God. And in content each of the commands reflects and confirms the fact that Israel is this people, the people created and maintained by these acts of God. *Thou* shalt! means, *Israel* shall! and everything that Israel *shall* is only an imperative transcription of what Israel *is*, repeating in some sense only what Israel has become by God, and what it must always be with God.[6]

In America, no less than in ancient Israel, what the people *shall* is only an imperative transcription of what the people *is*. Who we really are is discovered in the beginning and imaged in court. As it is theater of the beginning, the judicial process thus sustains judgment and is a guide to society. The process itself is an image of what is to be done. I focus on the process here to discover first how it bears upon judgment and second what specific measures must be taken to maintain its proper role in judgment.

❧ Judicial Process and Judicial Decisions

I have already noted some of the contributions made by live judicial theater: communication of nonverbal information, redirection of aggression, encouragement of impartiality, inducement of creativity, and the performance of what the law is. As theater of the beginning, the judicial process also figures in making specific judgments.

ENLARGING THE MIND

Live courtroom presentation correlates with the mental processes whereby judgments are formulated. Judge Joseph C. Hutcheson, Jr., explained how, in the cases not easily resolved,

> the judge may, reconciling all the testimony reconcilable, and coming to the crux of the conflict, having a full and complete picture of the scene itself furnished by the actors, re-enact the drama and as the scene unfolds with the actors each in the place assigned by his own testimony, play the piece out, watching for the joints in the armor of proof, the crevices in the structure of the case or its defense. If the first run fails, the piece may be played over and over until finally, when it seems perhaps impossible to work any consistent truth out of it, the hunch comes, the scenes and the players are rearranged in accordance with it, and lo, it works successfully and in order.[7]

The word "hunch" is loaded and, one suspects, was deliberately employed for its provocative effect. For present purposes, however, attention should be focused upon Judge Hutcheson's account of the prelude to the "hunch." The decision-maker plays the performance over; the case is reproduced in the mind. The reproductions rearrange scenes until they work; that is, the case is played over from different points of view until it yields a consistent and satisfactory judgment.

Kant discovered that judgment is enabled by the "enlarged mind."[8] He found an enlarged mind to be indicated by the habit of reflecting upon one's own judgment from a universal standpoint that is established by shifting ground to the standpoint of others. This is not a matter of thinking like or empathizing with or being led by others. It is a matter of thinking for oneself in the position of others. According to Kant,

> we have quite got into the way of calling a man narrow (*narrow*, as opposed to being of *enlarged mind*) whose talents fall short of what is required for employment upon work of any magnitude (especially that involving intensity). But the question here is not one of the faculty of cognition, but of the *mental habit* of making a final use of it. This, however small the range and degree to which a man's natural endowments extend, still indicates a man of *enlarged mind*: if he detaches himself from the subjective personal conditions of his judgment, which cramp the minds of so many others, and reflects upon his own judgment from a *universal standpoint*.[9]

It may not damage Kant's insight too greatly to bring it to bear, as he did not, upon judicial decision making. The courtroom presentation invites the decision-maker to play the case over in his mind from the standpoint of the plaintiff or prosecutor, from the standpoint of the defendant, from the standpoint of judges who have decided similar cases in the past, and from the standpoint of reasonable people in general, on the way to reaching a valid judgment. The courtroom presentation may act in this way as a stimulus to the enlarged as well as the impartial and creative mind. It may encourage the critical faculty to take account of various representations, "in order, as it were," as Kant said in a different context, "to weigh its judgment with the collective reason of mankind, and thereby avoid the illusion arising from subjective and personal conditions which could readily be taken for objective, an illusion that would exert a prejudicial influence upon its judgment."[10]

The end of impartiality and enlargement of mind in the courtroom is, immediately, the act of judgment. I say this in order to add two amendments. First, Augustine had objected to stage plays because "the hearer is not drawn . . . to help the other, but only is he invited to be sorry with him." [11] As Augustine's view has been characterized, plays aid "the forces of demoralization by stimulating the tragic emotions only to drain them away into the barren sands of inactivity," as is also true "of irresponsible amatory adventure, which gives rise merely to a fluctuating heat barren of foresight." [12] This potential prostitution of the dramatic is curtailed in the courtroom play because action in the form of a judgment is always its end, even though the judgment may not always be relieving.

Second, Kant wished to avoid the cramping effects of subjective personal conditions that insert prejudice into judgment. That is why he commended weighing one's judgment with collective reason. However, there is another alternative to subjective personal conditions than that of a universal standpoint. What Kant sought—freedom from prejudice—is better achieved from a particular, historical (if transcendent) standpoint. This is the possibility commended to us by the Hebraic and Christian traditions. I have termed this possibility the biblical beginning that we may discern in and transcending the American beginning. We are invited to reflect upon our judgment from a biblical standpoint. One weighs his judgment with the specific history of the community of faith rather than with the collective reason of mankind.

The judicial process correlates with and excites the process by which the mind is set free from illusion and fear. As theater of beginning, it allows typological connections to be made between the stories that unfold in court and the story of beginning, between the drama of the case at hand and the drama of who we really are, between the human realities of the controversy and the authentic human reality of the beginning.

I shall say more about these connections in the next two chapters. Indeed, Chapter Eight will be given over to an extended discussion of one such example, the protection of powerless minorities. Just now I only want to point out that the theatrical mode of court aids judgment by stimulating connections that enlarge the mind and that it does so insofar as it prompts us to make connection with the beginning. Let me give a specific illustration.

LONGBOAT, JURY BOX, STAGE:
United States v. Holmes

The American ship *William Brown* sailed from Liverpool on March 13, 1841, bound for the United States. She carried a cargo, a crew of seventeen, and sixty-five passengers. The passengers were Scottish and Irish emigrants, mostly women and children. In mid-ocean, the ship struck an iceberg and soon went down with thirty-one of the passengers. The remaining passengers and all the crew escaped. Ten people, including the captain, made away in a small jolly boat. The first mate, eight sailors, and thirty-two passengers crowded into a longboat. The two boats separated.

The longboat was so full that its gunwale cleared the water by only a few inches. It also lost a plug and was in danger of swamping. Chunks of ice floated around the boat. After some hours of calm, a continuous rain began, a wind came up, and the sea grew heavier. Some twenty-four hours after they first entered the longboat, at about 10:00 P.M., the crew, on orders from the first mate, began to jettison passengers. Fourteen male passengers were thrown overboard. The following morning two more were cast out. Shortly thereafter, a passing ship rescued the longboat. It still contained a week's provisions. Five days later the jolly boat, with the captain, was picked up. Those who were rescued eventually made their way to Philadelphia. Most of the crew then disappeared.

The defendant, Holmes, one of the seamen who helped to jettison the passengers, was indicted under a federal statute providing punishment for manslaughter on the high seas and brought to trial.[13] He was charged with casting into the sea one Frank Askin, an Irish youth, whose two sisters apparently leaped into the sea voluntarily to follow their brother in sacrifice. (They were the only women lost from the longboat.) Upon trial, the jury returned a verdict of guilty against Holmes with a recommendation of mercy. The court sentenced the prisoner to a term of six months at hard labor[14] and payment of a fine of twenty dollars. A pardon was sought, but President Tyler refused it since the court had not joined in the petition.

Critical to Holmes's defense was the argument that the case could not be judged. There was no way with square, rule, and compass to measure the circumstances of so dark and terrible a night; the case could only be tried in a longboat, overloaded and sinking in an icy sea, where a state of nature existed impossible of judicial reckoning.

Critical to Holmes's conviction was Judge Baldwin's insistence in his instructions to the jury that the jury had both the capacity and the responsibility for judgment in the courtroom. Holmes's criminal act would have been justified by necessity if there had been immediacy of peril, a fact to be decided by the jury. But it was also for the jury to decide about the relation between the parties. A sailor is under the duty to preserve passengers. Enough sailors must be saved to manage the lifeboat. If there are more sailors than required for navigation, then the sailor is bound to set a greater value on the life of his passenger than on his own, and "imminence of danger cannot absolve from duty."[15] The case therefore came within the "ordinary rules"[16] and could be decided not according to a state of nature but according to the law which "is made to meet but the ordinary exigencies of life."[17]

Generally, conduct must be blameworthy to be criminal. The effect of Holmes's defense was to ask the jurors to determine blameworthiness on the basis of what they would have done in the circumstance. The judge charged the jury, however, to decide blameworthiness on the basis of what the defendant could prove in court. Furthermore, the defendant's own assessment of his conduct in the circumstance was not to be considered as an element tending to make out his case. The sailors had made their decision in the longboat. The citizens in the jury box were to make theirs in court.

This decision would not require that the jurors imagine themselves in a longboat. It would be unnecessary for them to imagine or be or do anything other than or in addition to what they were as jurors. In legitimate society, people have places and parts of dignity. They are covenant partners with God and each other. They are taken seriously and affectingly. There is mutuality—pledging of lives, fortunes, and honor—and the equality of participation in a common enterprise. The judicial process is an image of this society, an image of who we really are. Jurors are players in it.

In validation of his instructions to the jury, Judge Baldwin had made appeal "to the very nature of the social constitution."[18] This is the governing reality of both longboat and jury box. The jury judged Holmes by judging who we really are, a reality to which they were directed by the drama of which they were a part.

The subjects of a subsequent English lifeboat case, *Queen v. Dudley*,[19] were three men and a boy who had been adrift at sea. The three men were eventually rescued. They had been able to survive by eating the boy. The two who killed him were sentenced to death. The sentence was later commuted to six months. In the course of its opinion, the court said that it was generally a duty to preserve one's life but that it may be the plainest and highest duty to sacrifice it.

> It would be a very easy and cheap display of commonplace learning to quote from Greek and Latin authors—from Horace, from Juvenal, from Cicero, from Euripides—passage after passage in which the duty of dying for others has been laid down in glowing and emphatic language as resulting from the principles of heathen ethics. It is enough in a Christian country to remind ourselves of the Great Example which we profess to follow. . . . We are often compelled to set up standards we cannot reach ourselves.[20]

Holmes and *Dudley* expose the problem of blameworthiness that Hannah Arendt later perceived also in the trial of Adolf Eichmann in Jerusalem.[21] Administrative massacre, the extermination of Jews in which Eichmann was a participant, made it almost impossible, Arendt observed, to know or feel that one was doing wrong. Everyone around was doing the same thing. Eichmann did not appear monstrous; he was, she said, banal. That terrifies but does not cause judgment to be suspended.

If we could not judge because we were not there—in the lifeboat or Nazi Germany—or because we would have done the same thing if we had been there, then it would be impossible to administer justice. Judge Baldwin made it clear to the *Holmes* jury that decision could be rendered, *i.e.*, that those who had been in the longboat were to make their case in court, and that the jury's decision could be made without the reproach of self-righteousness, *i.e.*, fellow feelings might come into play resulting in mitigation of punishment but not in the first and threshold decision of guilt.[22]

Judge Baldwin referred to the "very nature of the social constitution," and the *Dudley* court referred to the "Great Example" to indicate what makes judgment necessary and possible. The reality which they sought to invoke is better accounted for, I argue, in terms of beginning. And, I argue further, the action of the courtroom is itself an indication of that reality, the reality of who we really are, which informs judgment. The process itself enables and instructs typological identifications, connections between the cases and the beginning.

Thus, for example, the Supreme Court noted in *Ashcraft v. Tennessee*,

> It is inconceivable that any court of justice in the land, conducted as our courts are, open to the public, would permit prosecutors serving in relays to keep a defendant witness under continuous cross-examination for thirty-six hours without rest or sleep in an effort to extract a "voluntary" confession. Nor can we, consistently with Constitutional due process of law, hold voluntary a confession where prosecutors do the same thing away from the restraining influences of a public trial in an open court room.[23]

What one is and is not, does and does not do within the judicial process, he is and is not, does and does not do without.[24]

❧ The Clarity of the Process

I place great emphasis upon courtroom action. But I do not deify it anymore than I deify the founders and founding of America. Much that happened at the beginning of this nation fails as a positive reflection of the biblical beginning. I have several times mentioned slavery as an example. The same is true of the judicial process. What the courts do may correlate with who we really are only negatively. The process is not an incorruptible source for the typology of judgment. Distortions, even radical distortions, occur. When they do, the image the process offers is not that of legitimacy, and it either gives no guidance or the wrong guidance to judgment and society.

A look at some illustrative, but by no means exhaustive, instances in which elements of theater can be or have been corrupted will help us to see how aspects of the judicial process do serve the imaging of who we really are.

JURY

Juries have a responsible function to fulfill in protecting citizens against inaccurate determination of fact and against aggressive, oppressive governmental prosecution.[25] These protections are by no means unimportant. But this kind of quality control of the judicial product, critical though it is, is not more important than the theatrical role of the jury. The jury's product is as much what it is and images as what it decides.

In the performance, the jury is an image of the makeup of the community, including minorities.[26] This role can continue effectively with a smaller jury than the standard twelve so long as there is a representative cross-section of the community. But the role is compromised by allowing less than unanimous verdicts.

The Supreme Court has held that states might allow criminal convictions on a less than unanimous vote.[27] However, Justice Stewart, in dissent, was correct to point out that unanimity is the complement to impartial selection of the jury inasmuch as unanimity prevents a majority from ignoring a minority of fellow jurors of a different race or class.[28] While majority rule may be a rule of necessity in society as a whole, unanimity witnesses to the full participation of minorities,[29] whether these minorities are identifiable groups or simply dissentient individuals.[30] The plurality and concurring opinions that composed the Supreme Court majority recognized the safeguarding function of juries but neglected to grasp their potential as images.

One explanation that was given for the unanimity rule was that it arose from the medieval concept that "'carried with it the idea of *concordia* or unanimity.'"[31] Jury unanimity mirrors the concord binding us together as the people we really are. To fracture it is to falsify the image, which only repeats our discord.

ADVERSARY TECHNIQUE

After his years of experience on the bench, Judge Marvin Frankel suggested that the present adversarial system may constitute less an expression of the sentiment of the Declaration of Independence than the ideology of that other document of 1776, Adam Smith's *The Wealth of Nations*.[32] Among other arguments he makes is that, rather than promoting communal equality, the system depends upon and promotes individual self-interest pursued through private enterprise and competitiveness. "The business of the advocate, simply stated," he says, "is to win if possible without violating the law."[33] His concern is that "the truth and victory are mutually incompatible for some considerable percentage of the attorneys trying cases at any given time."[34]

To the extent that the judicial process is simply another tool for satisfying the capitalistic instincts of the bar, then indeed Judge Frankel is right and his argument well taken. The process will not mirror legitimate society under those conditions. However, a mild caveat must be entered. If in fact the system has been savaged by plundering attorneys, the fault does not lie in the agonistic character of the judicial process, and the cure does not lie in removing the agonistic quality of trials and appeals (which, after all, are not always contests because of the attorneys but because of the precedent conflict of the parties).

It may well be that struggle is not necessarily the best way for "getting out all the facts."[35] But production of facts is not all that trials are about. They are not only to find truth; they are also, in the biblical phrase, to *do* truth.[36] Purification of the judicial process, while it certainly needs to take account of the corrupting intervention of the predatory self-interest of attorneys, should also take thought about the truth which the process does. And the truth which is done is less compromised by matches than by mismatches. Accordingly, it may be that there is less promise in the inquisitorial model than in an adversarial model, in which the quantity and quality of counsel does not depend upon the capacity of clients to pay and in which a private bar does not hold a monopoly on supplying representatives to the public drama of court.[37]

PLEA BARGAINING

Plea bargaining may account for as much as 90 percent of all convictions.[38] Plea bargaining is the practice, more accurately described as "sentence bargaining,"[39] whereby a prosecutor negotiates with a defendant, really defense counsel, for a guilty plea and sentence. The plea and sentence are achieved "through the best bargain their competitive skills, their undisclosed secrets, and the justice market conditions may combine to fashion."[40] Outside pressures are exerted by norms of efficiency associated with production lines.[41] Prosecutors and judges must show results. Overworked, underpaid, or uncaring defense counsels are under similar constraints. Guilt, but also frustration, fear of conviction-prone juries, the attractiveness of reduced charges, and protracted periods of waiting render the practice attractive to defendants. Although she later withdrew the confession, Joan of Arc first yielded to an ecclesiastical court's promise of leniency, thereby demonstrating "that even saints are sometimes unable to resist the pressures of plea negotiation." [42]

Plea bargaining not only threatens the trial process by supplanting it but also by perversion of what transpires in court. After prosecutor and defense counsel strike a bargain and secure the defendant's acquiescence, there follows "a solemn charade." [43] "A courtroom ritual more sham than real" proceeds according to the rubrics of a "litany of form questions." [44] In the course of it, the defendant tells the judge that no promise has induced his plea, prosecutor and defense counsel "mutely corroborate the defendant's false statement," and the court, which often knows of the negotiations, "plays its part in the rubric by asking the question about any promise, knowing that the answer will be false." [45] It serves as a commentary on the practice to note that one of the purposes of a North Carolina reform was to *allow* defendants to tell the truth in plea bargaining. [46]

There have been differing recommendations for reform of plea bargaining, which might be salvaged for continued use by opening the process to more courtroom-like processes and curing its subsequent ratification of the elements of masquerade. [47]

One recent study of the history of plea bargaining purported to find the lesson that the trial process itself contributed to the subversion. Thus it was concluded, "the more formal and elaborate the trial process, the more likely it is that this process will be subverted through pressures for self-incrimination. The simpler and more straightforward the process, the more likely it is that the process will be used." [48] But coincidence should not be mistaken for cause and effect.

Undoubtedly, those who are looking for productivity gains in the criminal process would welcome summary trials. A simpler, more efficient assembly line would allow prosecutors and defense attorneys to shift their business from the halls to the courtroom. But to make the court more the scene for copping pleas rather than making plea bargaining more courtlike would destroy exactly that dignity accorded to humans by trials, which must be rescued to stand as testimony against the inhumanity and excesses of the system.

To the extent that delays, congestion, poor administration, and limited resources contribute to pressure for negotiated pleas, steps could and should be taken to alleviate them and to make the system more efficient. However, the courtroom action cannot be made more efficient than a performance. The line at the ticket booth can be shortened, but the length of the play remains the same.

It may be thought that abolishment or radical reform of plea bargaining is a naive dream foreign to the realities of our resources, which could not cope with the resulting extra burden. Is it true that we cannot afford trials for all criminal defendants? Or is it true that we cannot afford not to provide trials? Those who think themselves realists and acquiesce in the present practice have yielded to a nightmare and commend abuse to our continued use. The problem is not one of resources. If there are so many criminals that the courts cannot cope with them, like our teeming prisons and jails which already cannot contain all the people we seek to stuff into them, then what is called in question is not the resources and efficiency for producing guilty pleas but our conception of criminality, our willingness to eliminate the causes of crime, and the criminal injustice of our criminal justice system. The hard problems of crime will not be solved by doing away with proper trials. Theater of justice is one of the few sources of real human guidance and of hope for redress of grievous social wrongs.

POSTTRIAL AND PRETRIAL: COUNSEL

There are events before and after trial whose significance so impinges upon the trial itself as to fall within concern for the capacity of the process to serve as a declaration of legitimate society. The assistance of counsel in criminal prosecutions is illustrative.

In *Gideon v. Wainwright*,[49] the Supreme Court held that an indigent criminal defendant accused of a felony must be supplied with counsel. Fair trials are a "noble ideal," the Court said, and "fair trials before impartial tribunals in which every defendant stands equal before the law cannot be realized if the poor man charged with crime has to face his accusers without a lawyer to assist him."[50]

Attorneys are integral to a criminal trial for the sake of promoting accuracy, for assuring the reality and appearance of "moral equality between the accused and his accusers,"[51] and for support of the dignity of the individual defendant. For any or all of these reasons, counsel may be necessary in both pre- and posttrial settings.

Before trial, there are critical stages in the process which, in the absence of counsel, may seriously compromise the trial because they would effectively foreclose the attorney's options for conduct of the defense. Thus, the Supreme Court has held that a lawyer is required at a police lineup.[52] Without the presence of an attorney to prevent, isolate, or expose causes for misidentification by witnesses, the trial might be no more than an appeal from the lineup.[53]

Oddly, although grand jury proceedings seem also to be a critical pretrial stage and although the right to counsel attaches both before and after them, counsel is not accorded suspects at grand jury examinations.[54] Grand juries and the departure from trial elements allowed them in the secrecy of their proceedings were designed to protect the integrity of the criminal justice process and to guard against oppressive prosecution.[55] Now, however, prosecutors can subpoena parties, grant them immunity from prosecution as a substitute for the privilege of silence against self-incrimination,[56] and extract testimony under threat of contempt for silence[57] and of perjury for lying.[58] Insofar as grand juries have become all sword and no shield, it would appear that there is little basis for excluding counsel and much reason for including them. Grand juries are an arm of the courts, but the image they give as they are presently allowed to operate in some instances is scarcely that of legitimacy.

There may be need for counsel after as well as before trial. Perhaps the need is even greater after than before a person has been found guilty of a crime and sentenced. The rights of defendants in the criminal process are not for the innocent only. Certainly trial rights, including the right to counsel, do support accuracy in fact finding and do, therefore, help to protect the innocent. But trial rights are not exhausted in promoting accuracy and protecting the innocent.[59] A finding of guilt does not, therefore, terminate the need for counsel.

A person remains a person whether guilty or innocent. As Justice Douglas reminded us, "[f]acts are always elusive and two-faced. What may appear to one to imply guilt may carry no such overtones to another. Every criminal prosecution crosses treacherous ground, for guilt is common to all men."[60] This commonality of guilt is a way of stating the commonality of our humanity, which is not forfeited by a court sentence. Human dignity continues after sentence, and the need for counsel may continue and may be required.[61] My point is that counsel may be required, besides other reasons,[62] in order to protect the integrity of the judicial process.

In *Gagnon v. Scarpelli*,[63] the Supreme Court rejected a general re-

78

THE PROMISE OF AMERICAN LAW

quirement of counsel at probation revocation hearings. Counsel would be required only if the probationer could show that the absence of an attorney was prejudicial. In effect, the Court held that a criminal prosecution, *i.e.*, the judicial process in which counsel is required, ended upon sentencing. From the point of view of the integrity of the trial process, the holding is unfortunate.

There must be a starting and a concluding point to the process. Lines must be drawn somewhere. However, there is little reason to draw them illiberally. The capacity of the process to image legitimate society calls for a safe margin. We could view a person who continues in the criminal justice system after trial (prison, parole, probation) as continuing in an extended denouement of the trial drama. Or we could view the carrying out of the sentence as a critical stage *after* trial just as there are critical stages *before* trial. Certainly the sentence impinges upon the trial itself because the horror of what may come after lends the trial a "special air of desperateness" with the "accused and his champion . . . fighting for the right to remain a member in the common society." [64]

In addition to protecting the judicial process, a more generous drawing of boundaries after trial would also allow for a greater affirmation of human dignity. The concern of the process with saying something positive about human life [65] is surely not brought to an end when a sentence brings a defendant within the control of the criminal justice system.

EXCLUSIONARY RULE

Under the exclusionary rule, evidence obtained by the police in violation of constitutional standards may be inadmissible at trial.[66] Cases in which the rule was applied so as to invalidate proceedings against "factually"[67] guilty defendants were among the most controversial decided by the Warren Court. The rule has been under attack by the Burger Court.

Various reasons have been offered for the exclusionary rule. Justice Rehnquist, writing for the court in *Michigan v. Tucker*,[68] listed four of them: to deter unlawful police conduct, to protect the courts from unreliable evidence, to place upon government the entire load of building its case, and to recognize the imperative of judicial integrity.[69] Justice Rehnquist classified the last—judicial integrity—as only an assimilation of the prior three reasons.[70] This is severely to limit the exclusionary rule and judicial integrity to narrowly empirical terms.

For example, Justice Powell believes that "the rule's prime purpose is to deter future unlawful police conduct."[71] It will be generally agreed that to deter violation of the law by the police is an admirable hope. The disagreement arises over making deterrence the prime purpose of the rule. If there is little deterrent effect upon the police or if the effect cannot be statistically demonstrated,[72] then there is little purpose to the rule, and it will be discarded. But this is anomalous, for it appears to mean that so long as the police disregard law and law courts enough, the courts will capitulate in their lawlessness.

Or, to take another example, Justice Burger believes that the test for exclusion is simply the reliability of the evidence.[73] If it is reliable, it is to be admitted; if unreliable, excluded. This is not an unattractive position to assume. False evidence should not be allowed, and its exclusion is a result of the application of the exclusionary rule. However, reliability of evidence is not the only purpose of the constitutional rights honored by the exclusionary rule. Thus, as Justice Stewart once wrote,

> the Fifth Amendment's privilege against self-incrimination is not an adjunct to the ascertainment of truth. The privilege, like the guarantees of the Fourth Amendment, stands as a protection of quite different constitutional values—values reflecting the concern of our society for the right of each individual to be let alone.[74]

Evidence taken in violation of the Constitution may well be reliable. This will frequently be so if the violation is of the Fourth Amendment, for tangible evidence of guilt, like possession of narcotics, will be reliable regardless of the method of seizure. If the only protection of the court's integrity sought is its integrity as a fact-finding or truth-producing mechanism, then the evidence will be admitted. But its integrity as a theater whose process reflects legitimacy will then be compromised.

Quite apart from its deterrent value or its insurance of accuracy in fact finding, the exclusionary rule prevents the court from becoming a party to and a reflecting of lawlessness. From the perspective of the courts' theatricality, Justice Brennan would appear to have made the more correct statement of the judicial integrity properly protected by the exclusionary rule as "enabling the judiciary to avoid the taint of partnership in official lawlessness and . . . assuring the people . . . that the government would not profit from its lawless behavior, thus minimizing the risk of seriously undermining popular trust in government."[75] Indeed, "it is impossible for a court to allow a finding of guilt to be based on constitutionally infirm evidence and simultaneously maintain its integrity as a court. The exclusionary rule then is nothing more and nothing less than a procedural expression of the court's interest in its own integrity."[76] The court's integrity, understood in this way as certified through the exclusionary rule, is its capacity for the authentic reflection of legitimacy.

REFORMATION

The judicial process may distort the image it gives of legitimate society in the ways I have discussed and in others. For example, the courts may turn in upon themselves, thereby creating too great distance from the human realities they are to mirror.[77] Or they may overemphasize the theatrical trappings so that dress and decorum become precious objects in themselves.[78] All of this is to say that judicial theater is corruptible.

Judicial proceedings must be acknowledged as vulnerable to this corruption of essence, which transforms them from judicial theater as the image of legitimate society—theater of beginning—into theater of cruelty or the ritualized sacrifice of scapegoats—theater of unjustice. Consequently, to welcome the theatrical character of courts is not to embrace all that judicial theater may become. Continual reformation is needed. So qualified, the assumption remains that judicial theater, as it exists, is preferable to possible alternatives.

One alternative, considerably more hypothetical than real, is the complete abandonment of the present court system. From the perspective of some like the Panther 21, American trials undoubtedly appear to be political pieces adjunct to an oppressive system.[79] But a court may prove to be the scene of acquittal even for Panthers.[80] This is not to say that the just outcome of a particular trial proves the justice of the system or excuses systemic injustice.[81] It is to say that, although trials are sometimes thought to be masks for enslavement, they may yet bear some humanizing potential. Corrupt as Russian courts were under Stalin (whom Aleksandr I. Solzhenitsyn calls the

"Chief Producer"),[82] control of the Soviet show trials ("these theatrical productions")[83] was exacting. Unless control was constantly exercised, which was impossible, human elements broke through the prepared scripts and predetermined outcomes.[84] Consequently, as Solzhenitsyn observed, "the NKVD could never have carried out its great assignment if they had fussed about with open trials."[85]

Another alternative is to replace or supplement judicial theater in the court system with more economically efficient means for deciding cases. Pressure for efficiency fails to understand that live performances are as much the end of courts as is the disposition of cases. When courts are converted from theaters to factories, from places of play to places of fabrication, then, as the National Advisory Commission on Civil Disorders discovered, poor people find themselves dispensed "assembly-line justice,"[86] which can scarcely be called justice at all.

Judicial theater as we experience it is a proper subject for reform. Reformation, however, is quite different from abandonment. Those who would quit judicial theater either overtly because of its injustices or covertly because of its economic inefficiencies have not reckoned its puissance: to give place to an expression of humanity wherein even the least member of the community may find "a local habitation and a name,"[87] i.e., to an expression of the way we are from the beginning. What we are called upon to do is not to abandon the judicial process as theater but continually to reform it so that it will conform to true theater of beginning.

Chapter 6

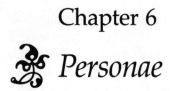 *Personae*

Turning from issues internal to the courts—the formation of decisions as well as the purity or clarity of the mirroring capacity of the judicial process—to the external consequences of judicial theater, I now shift focus from the process within courts to the world without. I shall not be examining something different, but shall only be following the process through to its outcome.

The Masks of Court and Society

PERSONAE JURIS

Seaman Holmes, the defendant in the lifeboat case I cited in the last chapter, was a right-and-duty-bearing person in court and was judged to have been one in the longboat. In the judicial process and according to the judgment that arose out of it, Holmes was an "artificial person." The term "artificial person" is not pejorative. It refers to the provenance of the word *persona*, which was a theatrical term and signified the mask worn by the actor. As Ernest Barker pointed out, this theatrical sense continued to be attached to the word when it was carried over into the law.[1] The *persona juris* is a creation just as the *dramatis persona* is. And just as *dramatis personae* are created by dramatists, *personae* in law are "juridical creations, or artifices, or fictions . . . . It is not the natural Ego which enters a court of law. It is a right-and-duty-bearing person, created by the law, which appears before the law."[2] And the public or political sphere as a whole may then be described as the scene of a legal drama played by legal actors.[3]

The courtroom is the locus for trying on, trying out, and proving *personae juris*. These *personae* are projected retroactively in guiding courtroom judgment. They are also projected prospectively to guide the society beyond the courtroom.

When judgment is rendered, there is an immediate consequence: a party is found guilty or innocent, liable or not liable. There is also a mediate consequence. The words and images of judicial theater "work on the world."[4] The courts not only show us who we really are but also nudge us toward fulfillment of the image, toward realization of the *persona*.

When seaman Holmes was convicted and sentenced for jettisoning the passenger Askin, the court spoke to Holmes but also addressed American sailors and the American public generally. The statement was about the social constitution, about the beginning, about who we are and will be held to be, and it took shape as the *persona*.

GOLDBERG VARIATIONS

The *persona* is the imaging in court and the becoming in the body politic of who we really are as citizens. What I must try to answer is the question about the nexus between *personae* in court and *personae* in society. Is the *persona* of court to be accorded the same treatment in society? Accompanied by the same theatrical paraphernalia? Is the judicial process to be projected onto the world outside of court? Must judge, jury, and attorneys become the complement of every lifeboat and every other social circumstance? If the answer is "obviously not," I must still work out a calculus of assimilation, which I can do on the basis of *Goldberg v. Kelly*[5] and *Goss v. Lopez*.[6]

The *Goldberg* decision in 1970 held that welfare benefits could not be terminated without a pretermination hearing. Until that opinion was handed down, cases involving the requirement of an opportunity to be heard took a kind of all-or-nothing approach.[7] Either a trial-type hearing was required or it was not. The primary question was whether the interest at stake was such as to call for this kind of elaborate procedure, *i.e.*, was the interest legally protected to that degree? In *Goldberg*, the Court analyzed trials into their constituent parts and listed a dozen of them.[8]

Then, in *Goss v. Lopez*, the Court held that public school students may not be suspended for as long as ten days without a hearing, consisting simply of notice of the charges against them coupled with an opportunity to be heard in response.

Kenneth Culp Davis has expressed knowledgeable enthusiasm for the *Goss* "principle" of an abridged hearing ("one of the most important legal developments that I have known in my lifetime").[9] In the course of an extensive study, Davis had found that the greatest injustice in the administrative process is in decision making involving the smaller interests. He believes that it is with respect to this vast majority of cases that *Goss* has the most potential for correction of injustice. An abridged hearing, he observes, can provide procedural protection in an almost limitless number of circumstances. A simple *Goss* procedure can be utilized wherein the evidence is stated and the party then listened to.[10]

I agree with Davis's assessment and wish to carry it a step further. Davis would add to the pre-*Goldberg* approach the flexibility of choosing an option at the other end of the spectrum from a full trial-type hearing, so that, instead of either a trial-type hearing or nothing, there may be a trial-type hearing, an abridged hearing, or nothing. I think that there is opportunity for even greater flexibility because the elements and formalities of trials are various, and the way is open for courts to exercise wider choice in calling them into play in extra-court circumstances.

Thus, the *Goss* Court was clear in stating that suspension of a student for a brief period may not require "even truncated trial-type procedures" but only "an informal give-and-take between student and disciplinarian." In the instance of long or "unusual" suspensions, the Court went on to say, more formal (or trial-like) procedures may be required.[11] In dissent, Justice Powell objected to this "constitutionalization"[12] of student-teacher relations because of, among other things, "its indiscriminate reliance upon the judiciary, and the adversary process, as the means of resolving many of the most routine problems arising in the classroom."[13]

Apparently for Justice Powell the appropriateness of "constitutionalizing" relationships—subjecting them to the image and review of the judiciary—depends upon their characterization as "faceless" or adversarial. He noted that, in many of the settings in which due-process hearings had been required by the Court, there was "a 'faceless' administrator dealing with an equally 'faceless' recipient of some form of government benefit or license; in others, such as the garnishment and repossession cases, there [was] a conflict of interest relationship."[14]

Justice Powell's analysis may be reworked into the present one by saying that when encounters between citizens take place in depersonalized settings or involve conflicting interests, then it is fitting that the courts require that "faces" or masks be given to the actors and require them to perform as suits their *personae*. That is to say, where there is likelihood that there will be an intrusion upon the person or a failure to listen to him, then the courts require a compensating "face," the *persona juris*.

I do not mean that every encounter between citizens and agents of the state or between citizens must be accompanied by robing, attorneys, and solemn oaths. My suggestion is that the action of the courtroom, as theater of beginning, is an image of the society in which people have significant, dignified roles and are taken seriously, with ceremonious, protective deference.

The more faceless or adversarial the encounter is likely to be, *i.e.*, the less suffused with the mutuality and human dignity of the beginning, the more exact and detailed the mask required. In the schoolhouse, as between school administrator and student, briefly stating the charge and allowing the student to respond before meting out punishment may suffice on some occasions. In the stationhouse, as between police officer and suspect, there is greater likelihood of facelessness and adversariness so that a set of prophylactic warnings is required and counsel may be necessary.[15]

The standard is the judicial process as it images the beginning. Therein is the model for treating people with the ceremonious deference that human dignity warrants. When participants in extra-court encounters prove prone to greater degrees of facelessness, then the more elaborate formalities required will thus, in general, shift toward the full complement of the courtroom.

This is not, as Justice Powell thought, to rely upon the adversary process as the *means* to resolving routine classroom problems. It is to look to the judicial process as the *source*. We find in judicial theater the models of *personae*.

🎭 *Personae* as Property

Players in the drama of court and of society have *personae juris*, the roles of right-and-duty-bearing persons. The *personae* of the judicial process are models for those of the political enterprise. When they mint *personae* in the judicial process and cause them to be circulated in the society at large, the courts create property.

Land and goods are not the only forms of property. The processes and products of the mind, goodwill, franchises, equities in corporations, status in organizations, and government largesse are among the many other forms of property besides land and goods.[16] In Chapter Three, I said that property is an expression of the spatial connotations of law. In all its howsoever diverse forms, property is best understood in the spatial rather than the possessory sense and in this sense is a means for taking part in the covenantal enterprise.

The most specific and individual form of property is a covering for the person, the animal skins which God tailored for Adam and Eve. Such coverings are not necessarily tangible or corporeal. Thus, the Christian is said to "put on" Christ in Baptism, *i.e.*, he receives the *persona* of Christ. The legal *persona* is such an individuated mask or covering or zone or enclave. And as one court has recently observed, "whether surrounded by palpable walls or not, zones of individual privacy are recognized as 'implicit in the concept of ordered liberty' and are constitutionally protected as such."[17] Like property generally, the *persona juris* is necessary to the equipping of citizens for the American experiment—implicit in the concept of ordered liberty. And also like property generally, it performs this function by both protecting and amplifying the person.

THE PROPERTY OF THE *PERSONA* AS PROTECTION

In the earlier discussion of property, I said that property sets off and protects a private sphere, an enclave. It protects the person. The *persona juris* has this function.

In the ancient theater, the mask or *persona* hid the actor's face. In the same manner, the *persona juris* masks the person. In doing so, it does not stifle or repress but protects the person. The state and other people may not intrude upon the person beyond the mask of legal rights and duties. The rights of the citizen are protective. Duties also contribute to the vindication of the human. They do so by making citizens responsible for their actions and the consequences of their actions so that citizens may be understood and understand themselves as responsible individuals and not as automatons in the machinery of corporation or state,[18] or in a storm-tossed lifeboat.

The requirement of a hearing, as developed after *Goldberg*,[19] is illustrative of one way of supplying a mask that safeguards the person and personal dignity. Allowing tenants the remedies of implied warranties and covenants [20] is another example of the protective covering of law. And the privilege against self-incrimination, in court and out, is a protective masking element; it is, as Judge Frank declared, part of the "right to a private enclave where [a person] may lead a private life. That right is the hallmark of our democracy." [21]

It may be thought that my suggestion about the property of the *persona juris* is, among other things, overly dependent upon and circumscribed by procedural safeguards, *i.e.*, that it lacks substance. Or it may be thought that it is substantial but only minimally so and that to send out persons from court with *personae juris* is no better than God's dismissal of Adam from Eden with a fig leaf, the merest qualification of naked exposure.

Procedural and substantive law are intertwined, however, so that seemingly procedural rights like the privilege against self-incrimination are also at the same time "a safeguard of the individual's 'substantive' right of privacy," [22] an enclave of privacy regarded by totalitarian regimes as "an offense against the state." [23]

Because it gives succor to privacy, independence, and diversity, this property, like any other, ought to be looked upon as worthy of increase, multiplication, and wide distribution in a free society. Charles Pinckney maintained that property was a foundation from which free men would be citizens on an equal footing. He thought that the expansion of the frontier and widespread property was therefore the complement to the exercise of freedom in the republic. [24] And Jefferson concluded that uncultivated land, although already owned, was subject to further apportionment as much for political good as for the relief of poverty. [25]

One-third of the nation's land remains in the hands of the federal government, but the expanding frontier which Pinckney thought likely to continue cannot. Moreover, the family farm system appears to be yielding to the economics of consolidation and agribusiness. [26] Limits to growth of property in land may thus serve to stimulate expansion of that other form of property, the *persona juris*. Of course, it is far from certain that legal masks can be enriched in such a way as completely to substitute for land, since a plot of land puts ground under one's feet literally as well as figuratively. [27] Nevertheless, it is a frontier to be explored.

THE PROPERTY OF THE
PERSONA AS AMPLIFICATION

Property sets off the private from the public sphere. The *persona juris* does this insofar as it designates a private enclave. In the earlier discussion of property in Chapter Three, I noted that the fruition of property was in politics, that it is a base for the citizen's participation in the government of affairs as well as a protection of privacy. This same double purpose is realized by the *persona juris*.

In ancient theater, the mask had two functions. First, it hid the actor; it gave him a dramatic face.[28] This function corresponds to the protective covering offered by the *persona juris*. Second, the mask acted as a resonator; it projected the actor's voice in the outdoor theater. Similarly, the *persona juris* not only protects the person but is also a relational vehicle. It amplifies the citizen's voice in community affairs.

In court, the *persona* allows the litigant to be heard. One of a party's rights is that of counsel, who is—and it is not just slang—a "mouthpiece." More than that, the right to bring grievances to court itself provides amplification. Individual voices are heard and acted upon. Even when an individual loses his case, he has still been listened to and been taken seriously.

Outside of court, right-and-duty-bearing persons are given influence through the ballot[29] and the polls.[30] These are only minimal rights for the citizen and, by themselves, may even lack efficacy.[31] In Aristotle's reckoning, humans are both political and, for that reason, speaking animals.[32] Minimal access to the public sphere in the form of elective office and voting is to be complemented therefore by the right that citizens may not only "think as [they] will" but also "speak as [they] think."[33] The citizen's voice is to be allowed to sound through the mask of legal rights in the public world of television,[34] the streets,[35] and shopping centers.[36]

If an increase in numbers of users or conflicting uses or, perhaps, inflammatory or obscene content threaten the continued viability of the various public fora, then it falls to the courts to devise "a set of Robert's Rules of Order for the new uses of the public forum."[37] This is not an easy assignment, but it is not an unfamiliar one since it calls only for extrapolation from the ordered sequences judges are accustomed to in the trial and appeal of cases. The amplification of citizen voices does not have to be reduced, just saved from cacophony.

In sum, like other forms of property spaces, the *persona juris* designates a protective, private enclave and is a means for taking part and being taken seriously in the public sphere of government action.

PUBLIC SPHERE AND PUBLIC VOICE

What I have said thus far about the political voice afforded by the property of the legal mask requires a further word. I have mentioned the citizen rights of access to and speech within public fora. These are necessary. But they are not sufficient. They are not a voice *in government*. Hannah Arendt went so far as to argue that the citizenry has no avenue for genuine participation in governmental affairs. She understood Jefferson's injunction to divide the counties into wards as an unsuccessful attempt to cure the defect of the Constitution's giving power to the people without giving them opportunity and structure to act as citizens.[38] We cannot all serve in Congress. Because there is no mode of participation but the ballot, she believed, citizens can have only their interests represented. Opinion and action are nondelegable. The result, in her estimation, is interest-group coercion of the governors in a government of and for the people but by, at best, an elite.[39]

The proliferation of surrogates for politics lends credence to her analysis. Public opinion polls and referenda abound, for example, but they are inimical to genuine opinion. Television programs like "Town Meeting of the Air," "Issues and Answers," "Face the Nation," "The Advocates," and groups like the Consumers' Union, Common Cause, the Sierra Club, along with numerous others, may support opinion and affect its climate, but they are still not a participation in the government of affairs. Moreover, in the most important cases where citizens have sought in recent years to engage in determining the external affairs of their lives in matters other than narrow self-interest—civil rights and Vietnam are instances—they were put to the streets and the expanse between the Washington Monument and the Lincoln Memorial, an indication of the absence of a suitable mode within government itself.[40]

Notwithstanding its power and impressive supporting evidence, Arendt's argument is not complete, for the courts are built into the structure of government.[41] And the courtroom is a place where a citizen's voice is heard and acted upon. It is true that the courts are meant as a place of last, not first, resort. It is also true that the heavy workload of the courts and the emergence of what Abram Chayes has identified as the model of "public law litigation" [42] indicate that other, primary avenues are not available. Nevertheless, the courts are a place in government where the citizen voice is given effect.

Too great or wrong demands can be made of the courts so that the press of business, delay, and expense could destroy their capacity to act even reflexively. It would be a denial of being rather than a solution to the problem to close the courthouse doors through a variety of procedural and substantive devices, an option favored at times by the Burger Court. [43] Instead, the solution would seem obviously to lie in taking the pressure off the courts by shifting the primary burden to the primary departments. Burgeoning resort to citizen suits is a testament to the remarkable public-spiritedness of citizens and their resilient determination to pursue happiness in public affairs notwithstanding the obstacles that have been placed in their way and the absence of suitable alternate fora in the other branches of government. Their frustration ought to be relieved and their residual will to govern themselves honored by creating or freeing means for authentic formation and expression of opinion through the other branches and levels of government. Only in this way can the joint enterprise of the beginning continue and grow.

The administrative process is an example of the potential for devising and implementing methods whereby citizens can fully participate in the covenantal action of government. Under the prodding of lower courts and especially in environmental matters, agencies have been working experiments in promoting participation by citizens. [44] Much of the experimentation has depended upon the introduction of procedural formalities, as is to be expected in the experimental theater of *personae juris*. However, in *Vermont Yankee Nuclear Corp. v. Natural Resources Defense Council*, [45] a unanimous Supreme Court limited to the minimum provisions of the 1946 Administrative Procedure Act the formalities that could be required by administrative agencies.

This freezing of development to the minima of the status quo ante will, one hopes, prove abortive or at least confined. [46] Certainly the decision is curious for a Court mindful of the judicial workload, for nothing promises more hope of relief than for agencies to become one of the preferred, first alternatives for citizens with a passion for governmental affairs. Deployment of the administrative processes to the service of widespread participation is certainly not free of enormous difficulty. But that is all the more reason to underwrite early, vigorous experimentation.

It bears repeating that the end in view is not to render government in general or agencies in particular more vulnerable to the pressure and clash of interests[47] and therefore prey to appetites for possession of property. The pursuit of interest through government agencies is not to be encouraged. It is not to be encouraged for the reason that I gave in the earlier discussion of property in Chapter Three: acquisitiveness—the desire to possess property and power—is exclusionary and monopolistic. It destroys politics. It is satisfied at the expense of, never with, others. Thus, Cain slew Abel and Romulus slew Remus.

To make governmental agencies media for the pursuit of interests would encourage that which is most to be discouraged. Moreover, it would force upon the agencies equally unacceptable, impossible alternatives: the aggregation of private interests so that they equal the public interest; or the partial satisfaction of all interests; or the complete satisfaction of a few but not most others.

The administrative process is not to be a mechanism that is either closed to the citizenry or only open to the attempted accommodation of interests. As I seek to describe them, agencies are fora for the expression of civic mutuality. It is especially critical at present that they be such fora. As resources shrink and demand grows, we are increasingly aware that what is longed for either suffices for none, or not for all. And we are tempted to follow a course equivalent to that chosen by Seaman Holmes in casting Askin out of the boat, *i.e.*, reducing the participants instead of multiplying the shares.

In order to say a further word about the administrative process as a forum for the expression of mutuality, I need to return momentarily to and elaborate in a slightly different way some of my earlier propositions.

The problem we encounter in the administrative process is a particular instance of the problem of politics generally, *i.e.*, the problem of authority. Rousseau described this problem as that of finding a form of government which places the law above man and so breaks the vicious cycle of internecine war. It is the problem of Romulus and Remus and of Seaman Holmes and Askin. It is the contemporary problem of exclusionary control of wealth, fossil fuel, land, hard minerals, water, and other natural resources that fall within the regulatory jurisdiction of governmental agencies.

The solution lies in shares that are less, but better. But this solution did not appeal to Romulus, and it will not appeal to us so long as we are governed by interests. There must be an alternative to interest. That is why Augustine rejected Cicero's definition of a people as "an assemblage associated by a common acknowledgement of right and a community of interests."[48] A community of interests is always subject to a centrifugal force that makes it finally impossible to hold the community together. Interest is ultimately self-destructive and renders a people ungovernable, a state allegedly reached already by the American people.

Augustine rejected the Ciceronian definition and assumed instead that "a people is an assemblage of reasonable beings bound together by a common agreement as to the objects of their love."[49] He saw that the prior question of a revolutionary, lasting politics is not interest but love.

Civic love requires a new beginning. It is not spontaneously generated and does not issue from our natality. Our beginnings come from the transcendent beginning, which intercepts the love of power with the power of love. This power is given in the adhesion of the human will to the *principium* which "gives to the 'object' world a wholly fresh complexion, thus 'making all things new.'"[50] When the power of love displaces the love of power, then people are freed from the destructive attachment to interests and freed for the politics of mutuality.

Governmental agencies properly serve such mutuality. They cannot cause us to want to seek the good of others. But they can be prevented from serving as tools for those who do not, and they can be made to serve as fora for those who do. They serve in this latter, positive fashion when they provide place for the public enjoyment and communication of opinion. Unlike interest, opinion is valueless if it is sole and despotic. Opinion requires rather than excludes others. Its formation and expression are a sharing in the common enterprise of the government of affairs. For this reason, it is important that the courts continue to prod the agencies to experiment with procedural formalities that allow for the widest possible participation by citizens who wish to share and develop opinion.[51]

Agency regulation is in bad odor presently, but it is highly desirable when it is the regulation of this passion to take part in government, what John Adams called the "passion for distinction,"[52] the passion to see and be seen by others engaging in "activity for the good of others."[53] Deployed to this end, agencies are not bureaus but places where citizens are esteemed for realizing the roles of *personae juris*. They are stages where citizens may employ their property—their masks—in expressing themselves as covenant partners in a joint venture.

✵ The Being and Action of Court

HOME

When the courts fashion *personae* in the judicial process and provide for their employment in the government and in society, they act consistently with their being. They do what they are.

This consistency is illustrated by Aeschylus' *The Eumenides*, the last of his trilogy centered on the cursed house of Atreus. The play tells the story of Orestes, pursued by the avenging Eumenides (Fates) because he had slain his mother, Clytemnestra. He had done so in revenge for Clytemnestra's murder of the king, Agamemnon, her husband and Orestes' father—the latest episodes in a primordial cycle of vengeance. Orestes finds his way to the hands of Athene and the justice of Athens. Upon trial before the Areopagus, the supreme judicial court, he is acquitted of blood-guilt. The outcome stops the vicious cycle. It also resolves the underlying conflict of the old order with the new, of Fate with Zeus. The reconciliation brought about by the court action is given expression in terms of intimately human place, home. Orestes responds to the judgment, "I was an exile; you have brought me home again."[54] And Athene promises the Eumenides a "house in Athens, where the gods most love to live,"[55] a "home"[56] which the Eumenides finally consent to share.

The Athenian court is the scene for a drama of reconciliation, and the consequence of its decree is room "in the midst of friends."[57] It is and makes a home.

There is a like consistency between the being and action of American courts. They are and they are to provide place for persons, room in a joint enterprise. *Personae juris* are a concrete form for the realization of this consistency.

THE PROMISE OF AMERICAN LAW

HOME FOR THE POWERLESS

The Eumenides was performed at the conclusion of the special pan-Athenaic festivities. As the play ended, a procession formed. The procession included a contingent of resident aliens. The play and the procession expressed the Athenians' belief that they were a people who welcomed strangers. The home which Athens provided was a home for outcasts, for even the despised and feared Eumenides.

I think that we Americans have an image of ourselves, our better selves, very like that of the Athenians. We believe ourselves to be those who protect the powerless.

The Athenian's self-portrait is attractive. It is a satisfactory picture of what that and all people are to be. Its definition is not to be faulted, but its description is. It did not describe accurately how a people is what *The Eumenides* portrayed them to be. Reconciliation is not effected by Athene or by any court. Reconciliation comes from the biblical beginning.

In the United States we view ourselves as those who welcome strangers, as providing the home for those who would be free. We have this picture and potential from the beginning. This is who we really are and what we shall do. This is the image that the courts authenticate and is the subject of the next chapter.

Chapter 7
Judicial Protection
of the Powerless

The courts create and deploy *personae juris*, which protect and amplify persons and so equip them for participation in the American experiment. When they expand the base of property in this form, the courts do so primarily for the benefit of the dispossessed, who need it most.

The Warren Court, Dick Gregory reported, "rendered so many decisions for the benefit of black folks that I used to call them 'our alternate sponsors.' And that was as it should be. The cats wearing the white sheets took our rights away from us, it's only natural that the cats in the black robes should give them back."[1] In addition to this happy connection between the vestments of Klan and Court, there is a primary connection between the biblical beginning and the contemporary action of courts in naturally giving rights back to blacks and other minorities.

Judicial solicitude for the weak is not a new theme in these pages. In Chapter Two, for example, I noted that the courts broaden participation in the story of beginning to include ever wider circles of citizens and that the recruitment of nondominant minorities enhances as well as arises from that story. I return to the theme now to elaborate its underlying rationale. I make this attempt because here is a specific instance, currently the most important one, of the bearing of the beginning upon the present: protection of the powerless inheres in the civic drama of the courts as theaters of beginning.

From the beginning we are committed to the cause of the dispossessed as necessary to the justice, strength, and survival of the body politic. This truth, like all basic truth, cannot be proved. It can only be performed. However, I can try to give it conceptual intelligibility. I shall be like the medievalists who sought to "prove" the

THE PROMISE OF AMERICAN LAW

existence of God, not so much seeking to prove anything as to make understandable for the faithful what was already believed to be true. I shall "prove" that nurture of the powerless inheres in the beginning, that protection of minorities is the recognition of the best interest of the majority, and that the judiciary is the branch of government especially designed to perform it. In the next chapter I shall then give an account of the *Carolene Products* theory of judicial review, a specific contemporary rationale for protection of "discrete and insular minorities."

 Why the Powerless?

MADISON

An argument for, or description of, American protection of the powerless was offered by James Madison. Minority rights were a concern of his both early and late in life. Madison knew well enough that the government might oppress the people. He was more acutely impressed by another possibility, one that he repeatedly turned to: a majority of the people might oppress a minority of the people. "Wherever there is an interest and power to do wrong," he said, "wrong will generally be done, and not less readily by a powerful and interested party than by a powerful and interested prince."[2]

He thought that "the invasion of private rights is *chiefly* to be apprehended" from acts in which "the Government is the mere instrument of the major number of the Constituents."[3] And he believed that such potential oppression by a majority rather than a minority "is a truth of great importance, but not yet sufficiently attended to."[4]

The root problem in Madison's view is man's factious spirit. He described a faction as a majority or minority of the citizenry "united and actuated by some common impulse of passion, or of interest, adverse to the rights of other citizens, or to the permanent and aggregate interests of the community."[5] He believed that, because factiousness belongs to man's nature, its causes cannot be removed.[6] But he also believed that its effects can be controlled and that the American form of government is designed to supply this control.[7]

The threatened effects of a factious *minority* are controlled by two devices. One is the division of governmental powers, "supplying by opposite and rival interests the defect of better motives."[8] The other is the vote, "which enables the majority to defeat [a factious minority's] sinister views."[9]

To guard minorities against the effects of a factious *majority* is the more critical and difficult task. Indeed, to secure minority rights "and at the same time to preserve the spirit and form of popular government" is in his view "the great desideratum, by which alone this form of government can be rescued from the opprobrium under which it has so long labored, and be recommended to the esteem and adoption of mankind."[10]

According to Madison, this preservation of minority rights, together with the spirit and form of popular government, is supplied by, again, two structural controls in the American design: representation and diversity. Representative government provides for passing public views through the medium of an elected body so that they will be refined, with consequent improvement of chances that more just considerations will prevail.[11] Diversity is the product of the greater extent of territory and larger number of people embraced by the American republic in comparison to a democracy like that of Athens, which could only be limited in size.[12] The greater the diversity, the less the danger of a factious majority.[13] Without diversity, there would be "a society under the forms of which the stronger faction can readily unite and oppress the weaker," which is anarchy.[14]

Madison was projecting into the political future the structure for progression of the American experiment. The assurance of minority rights is a condition for the continuation of political association. Otherwise, there would be anarchy, then despotism. Protection of the powerless is the practice of self-interest, "[t]aking the word 'interest,'" in this context, he once said, "as synonymous with 'ultimate happiness.'"[15] The protection of minorities is the pursuit of happiness.[16]

AFFECTION

In the Madisonian "proof," protection of minorities is a condition precedent to the survival of American politics and is, therefore, the practice of self-interest. This enlightened self-interest is to be safeguarded by the very structure of government, which provides for the controls of representation and diversity.

Diversity did not bear for Madison, as some have thought, the connotation of struggle, a cockfight of individuals and interests. The picture is one of the workings of mechanical counterpoise and balance.[17] Madison's metaphor is the machine. In the period, this was for him, as it was for Jefferson, the language of affection. What held the social machine together and drove it was love.[18] To structure the government to protect minorities was to formalize the bonds of affection in the "bands of government."[19]

Both earlier than Madison and later, the language of affection tended to the organic metaphor. So had John Winthrop exhorted the Puritans: "we must be knit together in this work as one man, we must entertain each other in brotherly affection, . . . we must delight in each other, make others' conditions our own, rejoice together, mourn together, labor and suffer together, always having before our eyes our commission and community in the work, our community as members of the same body."[20]

The organic is the biblical metaphor. The people created in and by the covenant is a body. In this body "there is neither Jew nor Greek, there is neither slave nor free, there is neither male nor female; for you are all one."[21] It is a body, not a pot; still less, a melting pot. And the body has diverse members. The oneness or equality of the body is not uniformity. The task requires preserving the diversity of members while activating them to function in concert, for the body is in movement. This end is accomplished by giving "the greater honor to the inferior part, that there may be no discord in the body, but that the members may have the same care for one another."[22] The oneness or equality of the performing body is a function of maturity, the coordination of the athletically graceful and efficient body, which comes about through "care for one another."

Equality was the pivotal statement of the American beginning for Lincoln, the proposition to which the nation is dedicated. This equality may be understood in the context of the biblical beginning as, not a rule or practice of reason, but an expression of affection: the bonds of sociability, the greater honoring of inferior parts producing the same care for one another. And justice, "the political form of love,"[23] may then be comprehended in the formula "the first shall be last and the last first" rather than in the formula "to each his due."

THE COURTS

Patent to Madison was the human capacity for abandoning affection—we do not always pursue happiness; we are not always eager to put the last first and the first last. Respect for character, conscience, honesty, in short, what he called all the "favourable attributes of the human character," will not withstand the power of factiousness.[24] The "basis and structure of the Government itself"[25] which curtails factiousness is the systematic defense of affection and thus minority rights against invasion.

It is at this point that the Madisonian program requires supplementation. As he explains it, the scheme limits dereliction but does not supply vigor; the structure guards affection against the incursions of factiousness but does not give motive encouragement to affection. It can be argued that government can do nothing actively to encourage affection, that such encouragement is the institutional responsibility of the religions and that the First Amendment does all that can be done structurally by prohibiting both the establishment of religion and the limitation of its free exercise. This is to argue that, while love is the dynamic power of American politics, the government is wholly dependent upon the private sphere to excite it.

This argument ignores the role of the courts. All branches of the government are to be constitutionally conscientious. All are, therefore, to protect the powerless. The courts are peculiarly equipped to do so. The singular characteristic of the judicial branch of the federal government is the confluence of permanent tenure and powerlessness. It is this characteristic which fits the courts to protect the powerless, thereby demonstrating love and stimulating us to go and do likewise—in Winthrop's words to the Puritans: "always [keeping] before our eyes our commission and community in the work."

Permanent tenure in office promotes the judges' independence, their distance from the majority and from temporary, passing opinions. They are put in position to see our better selves. Alexander Hamilton argued that independence would not be a source of frustration to the majority but would be an aid to their will. It would help the Supreme Court shield the will of the people, expressed in the Constitution, against legislative encroachment.[26] And, insofar as the Court did act in contravention of a given majority of the people, such action would only be to save the people from their own temporary ill-humors, an intermediate stop that would allow reason and justice to gather and reassert themselves.[27]

The complement to independence is the absence of coercive force. In Hamilton's famous phrase, the judiciary has "neither Force nor Will, but merely judgment."[28] The lack of force has a constraining effect; it prevents the Court from becoming autocratic. It also has a liberating effect. The courts are removed from the preoccupation of officeholders in the other branches. Denied power, they cannot engage in power politics and are insulated from its diversions.

This is not to say that the courts are apolitical. It is to say that they are freed alike from the necessities and from the temptations of power politics but freed for a different politics, more like that of Aristotle than that of Tammany Hall and Mayor Daley.

Aristotle thought of politics as the activity of the *polis*, doing and reflecting upon what is required for the *polis* to be the *polis*. The Greek word *polis*, generally translated "city-state," does not survive in our language. *Polis* "is to politics what athlete is to athletics. Politics, the abstract general characterization derived from the Greek survives, but *polis*, the concrete subject, does not."[29] However, if the *polis* was the now lost city-state, it was also always "the form of political community that [was] the best of all the forms for a people able to pursue the most ideal mode of life."[30]

Therefore, Aristotle's study of politics, whose concrete subject was the *polis*, was carried on in light of the question of the nature of man, for "every city-state exists by nature . . . and nature is an end, since that which each thing is when its growth is completed we speak of as being the nature of each thing . . . . From these things therefore it is clear that the city-state is a natural growth, and that man is by nature a political animal."[31] Although the *polis* has disappeared, politics has not.

The politics practiced by the courts[32] is the doing and reflecting upon what is required for America to be America, performing our nature from the beginning. It is our nature to be "knit together by [the] bond of love, and live in the exercise of it."[33] The judicial branch is designed to be free from the love of power to show us the power of love. The courts do so as they care for our least member, loving, like knowing us, better than we ourselves.[34]

🐛 The Cost: *De Funis, Bakke, Weber,* and *Fullilove*

Protection of minorities, our least members, can be effected only at some cost to the majority. When the cost is small, it may not be recognized or may not be provocative. As the cost grows, it becomes controversial. The commitment is that, although the majority share will be reduced to a lesser or greater extent, it will be made better. The commitment has been put to the test in four cases to come before the Supreme Court. They are sometimes referred to as "reverse discrimination" cases. That is a misleading label. The cases challenged efforts to advance the position of minorities. They are really cases about majority willingness to underwrite minority protection.

The first case was *De Funis v. Odegaard.*[35] De Funis was denied admission to law school. The school had a policy under which it admitted some minority applicants who would have been rejected had they been white, like De Funis. The Court did not decide the merits of the case on the ground that it had become moot. De Funis had been admitted to the school by order of a lower court and was completing his legal education when the Supreme Court considered his petition.

The second case, *Regents of the University of California v. Bakke,*[36] involved another denial of admission to a white person, in this instance to a medical school that had a minority admissions program. This time the Court decided the case and affirmed the state court's order requiring that the school admit Bakke. There was a complex alignment of votes making up the majority and a profusion of opinions. Justice Powell announced the Court's decision with the caveat, "I will now try to explain how we divided on this issue. . . . It may not be self-evident."[37] It was not.

While the order of Bakke's admission was upheld, a majority of the justices nevertheless agreed that government may "act affirmatively to achieve equal opportunity for all."[38] Thus, "[g]overnment may take race into account when it acts not to demean or insult any racial group, but to remedy disadvantages cast on minorities by past racial prejudice, at least when appropriate findings have been made by judicial, legislative, or administrative bodies with competence to act in this area."[39]

The third case was *United Steelworkers of America, AFL–CIO–CLC v. Weber.*[40] There an industry instituted an affirmative-action plan to

THE PROMISE OF AMERICAN LAW

eliminate the racial imbalance in an almost exclusively white skilled-craft work force. Seven blacks were among the 13 people selected for inclusion in a training program. Weber was not among them, although he had more seniority than one or more of the selected blacks. The Court upheld the company's plan and did not require that Weber be admitted as a trainee.

In the fourth case, *Fullilove v. Klutznick*,[41] the Court upheld an affirmative-action measure of Congress against the challenge brought by representatives of the construction industry. The act provided that 10 percent of certain federal funding of local public works projects be spent on goods and services supplied by minority-owned businesses. The 10 percent set aside was approved in an alignment of votes and opinions only slightly less elaborate than that in *Bakke*.[42]

One can try to fathom the opposite outcomes of *Bakke*, on the one hand, and *Weber* and *Fullilove*, on the other, in several ways. For example, in *Bakke* the affirmative-action plan was that of a governmental entity and was decided under the Constitution, whereas in *Webber* the plan was that of a private industry and was decided under a statute. But that would not account for the difference between *Bakke* and *Fullilove*, since the latter case was also decided under the Constitution.

Or it could be observed that Justice Stewart switched his vote from the group of Justices Stevens, Burger, and Rehnquist in *Bakke* to the group of Justices Brennan, White, Marshall, and Blackmun in *Weber*, thus making it a majority. Justice Stewart wrote no separate opinion in either case. Perhaps he simply changed his mind. Or, perhaps he thought there was some critical difference between Titles VI and VII of the Civil Rights Act of 1964. In *Bakke* he joined in the opinion, written by Justice Stevens, which would not have decided the case on the basis of the Constitution at all but on the basis of Title VI of the Civil Rights Act of 1964. The Stevens opinion then found that Title VI proscribed the use of racial criteria, even those of affirmative action, as the basis for excluding anyone as Bakke had been. *Weber*, on the other hand, was decided under Title VII, not Title VI, of the Civil Rights Act. Justice Stewart may have thought that Title VII, unlike Title VI, did not prohibit racially conscious affirmative-action plans. We do not know what he thought because he did not say.

Justice Stewart broke silence in *Fullilove*. He explained his vote against the affirmative-action plan there on the grounds that the 10 percent set aside in favor of minority business injured a nonminority class, that racial discrimination is invidious even when the race involved is that of a dominant majority, and that the Constitution "absolutely prohibits invidious discrimination by government."[43] He quotes twice from the Powell opinion in *Bakke* and cites that case once in a footnote. But he does not mention his vote or the opinion in which he joined in *Bakke*. Justice Stewart also makes footnote reference to *Weber* in support of the proposition that "nothing in the Constitution prohibits a private person from discriminating on the basis of race in his private or business affairs,"[44] a statement which is as insufficient as a statement of law[45] as it is unrevealing of how he reconciles his votes in the three cases.[46]

De Funis, Bakke, Weber, and *Fullilove,* taken together, mean that some carefully drawn affirmative-action plans can muster a majority of the Court as presently composed. They may also indicate a welcome Court trend in favor of affirmative action. Beyond that, they are not clear. They have determined little and invite further litigation.

The decisions in these cases are not wholly without redeeming social value. They do support thoughtful efforts to remove some of the detrimental results of years of racial prejudice. And they have left the judicial process open for further struggle with and consideration of the immensely difficult questions about remedies for the exclusion of minorities from preferred positions. In a way, the process and the opportunity to keep these matters in court is the decision. This is not an unimportant conclusion for the Court to have reached.

Were a temporary ill humor to harden into permanency, then no powerless minority would survive against it. The consent of the majority, over the long term, is necessary. One encouragement of such consent is the knowledge that the courts are available to all as a continuing forum for the argument of grievances. Insofar as the result of the cases is to invite the majority to join in the continuing process of decision—participation in the story which is the meaning of these things, as we learned from Deuteronomy—then the Court has done well.

On balance, however, the cases fail on two principal grounds. First, the openness of the process, which is one of their strengths, is seriously qualified by its partiality. The affirmative-action plans that were challenged were designed to eliminate some of the consequences that prejudice has forced upon minorities. These minorities had a huge stake in the litigation and its outcome. But they were not represented except in the form of amicus briefs.[47] Their exclusion was detrimental to the soundness of the decisions, an offense to the minorities, and a compromise of the authenticity of the judicial theater.

Second, insofar as it has spoken, the Court has spoken in tongues, only refracting popular confusion. Cases in which minority protection is an issue, whether brought by representatives of minorities or majorities, raise the question of equality. They put in issue our nature as a people.

Now it may happen that the majority will decide that we are not this people, will decide that affection, love, the equality of first last and last first, that all of this is talk and talk that has nothing to do with the real world of the twentieth and twenty-first centuries and that it is time to be done with such hoary nonsense. Such a decision would require fundamental revision of our perception of the fitness of things, but it may happen. So far, whenever the people have been faced squarely with the choice and made it, the decision has been to affirm and not to disaffirm our nature as we have known it from the beginning. That nature is to be a covenantal people in which even the least—especially the least—are full participating partners.

If resources and opportunities shrink and general need increases— *i.e.*, if we approach the limits of a social equivalent to Seaman Holmes's lifeboat in a rising sea—then the decision to protect minorities will increase in complexity in the most individually and corporately painful ways. This decision belongs to the people. It has been ours from the beginning. We are embarked on a joint venture. It is not for the courts to make or revise our decision. If fundamental revisions are to be made, the decision about them is ours. We cannot make that decision or even know that that is the decision to be made if the Court equivocates and allows us to believe that protection of minorities is not costly or that it will not be required when it is costly or that it is not the subject being decided. Our decision is not to be denied us by the obfuscation of the very body which we created only and always to give illumination and which has the greater obligation for clarity the more counsel is darkened at large.

The proposition about equality, about our nature as a people, is, said Jefferson, a truth which is "self-evident." Had this truth been self-evident in the sense that it was irresistibly compelling politically,

Jefferson would not have prefaced his recitation of truths in the Declaration with the words, "We hold." With this introduction Jefferson conceded, grammatically if in no other way, that these truths in the political arena stand

> in need of agreement and consent—that equality, if it is to be politically relevant, is a matter of opinion, and not of "the truth." . . . We hold this opinion because freedom is possible only among equals, and we believe that the joys and gratifications of free company are to be preferred to the doubtful pleasures of holding dominion. Such preferences are politically of the greatest importance, and there are few things by which men are so profoundly distinguished from each other as by these. . . . Their validity depends upon free agreement and consent, they are arrived at by discursive, representative thinking, and they are communicated by means of persuasion and dissuasion.[48]

The truth of the biblical beginning is relational and quite opposed to totalitarian force. Even truth is a communal, humanizing enterprise. Because "the perverse can deny anything, . . . 'self-evident' truth demands good faith [candor] in the hearer."[49] Either the story of beginning will have purchase among the people or it will not.

However, if self-evident truth requires good faith in the hearer, it also requires "distinct exposition in the speaker."[50] Accordingly, Jefferson said that he had undertaken "to place before mankind the common sense of the subject in terms so plain and firm as to command their assent."[51]

It is the labor of the Court to place before us in performance our nature in terms commandingly plain and firm, howsoever painful. Formally, court judgments are delivered to us as "opinions." The courts do not hold dominion. They hold opinion. They are freed from the necessities and temptations of power for clarity of vision and voice in opinion. They have neither force nor will, only judgment. But they must have that. When they do not have judgment, they have nothing, least of all authority. And then they do not declare the law; they declare that they are bankrupt in heart and in politics. Instead of beginning, there is an end.

Chapter 8

🕉 *Carolene Products*

In my exploration of the judicial affinity for powerless minorities and in earlier chapters, I have been largely concerned with the protection afforded persons in and through courtroom action, its procedure and projections. I will now shift emphasis to the judicial protection given by judicial review. This will not be an exclusive or new emphasis. It will be more particular and technical. It will focus upon decisional theories, that element of the judicial process which lawyers generally single out for the most attention.

I want to lay out in detail the specifics of one legal theory that can be utilized by judges and lawyers who are mindful of the necessity of protecting the powerless. In the last chapter I shall then offer a nontechnical assessment of how the teaching of law, animated by beginning, might proceed. I do not wish to squander your patience before the last chapter, but I am under compulsion to state as carefully and concretely as I can how one, moved by the biblical beginning to defend the weak, may frame a conceptual legal argument on their behalf using the materials at hand.

🕉 The Footnote Four Theory

Recent discussion of the courts' solicitude for minorities has centered upon a doctrine proposed by Justice Harlan Fiske Stone and familiarly identified with footnote four of *United States v. Carolene Products Co.*[1] It provides a conceptual vehicle for the courts to carry into effect concern for and care of the powerless.

The *Carolene Products* proposal for judicial protection of powerless minorities has spawned a considerable literature. Curiosity, if nothing else, bids us examine closely the source of this uncommon jurisprudence of a footnote.[2] The footnote is divided into three paragraphs. The first proposes that the courts will presume that the challenged act of a legislature is constitutional but that they will give narrower scope to this presumption when the legislation on its face violates a specific constitutional prohibition.[3] It is the second and third paragraphs, especially the third, which are germane to the present analysis.

The second paragraph raises the possibility that, when it is challenged, "legislation which restricts those political processes which can ordinarily be expected to bring about repeal of undesirable legislation" may warrant, because of this frustration of the political process, "more exacting judicial scrutiny under the general prohibitions of the Fourteenth Amendment than . . . most other types of legislation."

The final paragraph entertains the prospect of close judicial scrutiny also of challenged legislation that affects certain minorities. It proposes that "prejudice against discrete and insular minorities may be a special condition, which tends seriously to curtail the operation of those political processes ordinarily to be relied upon to protect minorities."

In sum, the footnote proposes that there are three instances in which an exacting, close judicial scrutiny of legally challenged legislation may be invoked: Those in which legislation violates specific constitutional provisions, especially the Bill of Rights (paragraph one); those in which legislation restricts the political processes and so limits the potential for subsequent self-cure (paragraph two); and those involving "prejudice against discrete and insular minorities" (paragraph three).

It is important to see that the footnote in fact delineates three instead of only two classes of challenged legislation possibly subject to strict judicial scrutiny. This distinction is often overlooked.[4] The first class, that within the scope of specific constitutional prohibitions, is clear enough. The difficulty lies in distinguishing the classes of the second and third paragraphs, especially since both paragraphs refer to political processes.

The error generally made is to subsume the third class under the second so that judicial protection of minorities would then depend upon a given minority's chances of winning its way through the legislative process. Courts will be more forthcoming, accordingly, the less chance the minority has of political victory.[5] This is not what the footnote proposes.

The second paragraph of the footnote treats *restrictions* of (or restrictions of access to) political processes. If legislation restricts political processes, then the possibilities for repealing undesirable legislation through the ordinary channels are reduced, and the need for judicial attention is correspondingly increased. The appropriateness of close judicial review of this second class of legislation should be gauged by the openness of political processes and the opportunity for the vindication of rights through them.

The third paragraph refers to the *operation* of political processes in the context of prejudice, which tends to curtail the desire of some and the capacity of all to protect minorities. Prejudice may issue in legislation that restricts a minority's access to political processes, in which case the legislation will also fall within the class set out in the second paragraph of Stone's footnote.

But prejudice against a discrete and insular minority may give rise to other forms of legislation. Strict judicial scrutiny is appropriate in these instances also, and it is appropriate whether or not the prejudiced minority in question has sought to vindicate its rights through political processes. Minorities do not have to exhaust political remedies. They do not have to play the majority's game. Judicial attention is appropriate because of the assumption that prejudice may have prevented those within the political processes from protecting those without. The critical factor is protection of minorities and not necessarily the openness of the political processes or the chances of vindication by real or prospective participation in them.[6]

Such a reading draws support from Justice Stone's later dissent in *Minersville School District v. Gobitis*.[7] In *Gobitis*, the majority upheld a statute that made it compulsory for public school pupils to salute the national flag.[8] A father who was a Jehovah's Witness and whose two children had been expelled for failure to make the salute challenged the statute.[9] Stone, dissenting alone, was "not persuaded that we should refrain from passing upon the legislative judgment 'as long as the remedial channels of the democratic process remain open and unobstructed.' This seems to me no less than the surrender of the constitutional protection of the liberty of small minorities to the popular will."[10]

Justice Stone goes on to discuss the importance of the Court's previously having made "a searching judicial inquiry into legislative judgment" in two situations. One concerned prejudice against "discrete and insular minorities" that curtails political processes.[11] The other concerned legislation which restricts "the civil liberty of racial and religious minorities *although no political process was affected.*" [12] Since Justice Stone cited his own *Carolene Products* footnote and cases employed in its third paragraph to support this contention,[13] it is clear that he contemplated such a distinction.

If a distinct third class of "discrete and insular minority" cases is allowed, then the doctrine might be plausibly elaborated as follows: legislation which is the product of a democratic process representing and governed by a majority decision will ordinarily be upheld. Such legislation, however, is subject to judicial review and may be struck down when it transgresses specific constitutional provisions, especially those of the Bill of Rights. In addition, legislation may be invalidated, even though it does not violate specific constitutional prohibitions, when it restricts political processes either by frustrating majority decision or by giving inadequate play to minority voices.[14] Finally, legislation may be submitted to strict judicial scrutiny, not only when it violates specific constitutional provisions, and not only when it restricts political processes, but also when powerless[15] minorities have been prejudiced.

I must enter two caveats about this statement of the *Carolene Products* doctrine. First, although it involves a slight extension at most, I do not claim that Justice Stone would subscribe to this formulation of his footnoted doctrine.[16] Second, the three classes of cases may overlap. The aggrieved parties in *Gobitis* were members of a discrete and insular minority (class three) whose First Amendment rights (class one) had been violated. Not infrequently, a discrete and insular minority will also be the object of restriction of the political process (class two). The three different classes do, however, establish characteristics that bear separate emphasis even though there may be a confluence of them in particular cases. The point is that powerless minorities, as such, qualify for special judicial attention.

By way of a further cautionary note, it should be observed that my focus on minorities is not to be construed as meaning that oppressed *individuals* should not be protected by the courts. Nor should it be taken to mean that individuals must first be classified as members of a minority before they qualify for strict judicial scrutiny. The theory adumbrated hereinafter would complement or expand instead of replace or restrict the possibilities for safeguarding individual rights.

For example, if a person is treated as something other or less than a right-and-duty-bearing person because he is a black, then to supply correctives where prejudice against blacks exists is to provide the conditions in which the person is to be treated with the dignity and respect which personhood deserves and prejudice had denied. I note the point because Justice Powell's opinion in *Bakke* evidences confusion on the point and seems wrongly to play off concern for persons against concern for protection of minorities, as though the two were in conflict.[17]

🎜 The Decisional Shape of the Theory

In *Graham v. Richardson*,[18] the Court was presented with an equal-protection challenge to state statutes which predicated entitlement to welfare aid upon the potential recipient's possession of American citizenship or American residence for a specified minimum number of years.[19] The equal-protection claim was upheld.[20] In the course of his opinion for the court, Justice Blackmun said,

> Aliens as a class are a prime example of a "discrete and insular" minority for whom . . . heightened judicial solicitude is appropriate. Accordingly, it was said in [another case] that "the power of a state to apply its laws exclusively to its alien inhabitants as a class is confined within narrow limits."[21]

Graham, and inferentially its reliance upon the *Carolene Products* footnote, was followed in the two further alienage cases of *Sugarman v. Dougall*[22] and In re *Griffiths*.[23] Justice Rehnquist dissented to both decisions and objected to the use of footnote four.

> The mere recitation of the words "insular and discrete minority" is hardly a *constitutional* reason for prohibiting state legislative classifications such as are involved here, and is not necessarily consistent with the theory propounded in that footnote. The approach taken in *Graham* and these cases appears to be that whenever the Court feels that a societal group is "discrete and insular," it has the constitutional mandate to prohibit legislation that somehow treats the group differently from some other group.
>
> Our society, consisting of over 200 million individuals of multitudinous origins, customs, tongues, beliefs, and cultures

is, to say the least, diverse. It would hardly take extraordinary ingenuity for a lawyer to find "insular and discrete" minorities at every turn in the road. Yet, unless the Court can precisely define and constitutionally justify both the terms and analysis it uses, these decisions today stand for the proposition that the Court can choose a "minority" it "feels" deserves "solicitude" and thereafter prohibit the States from classifying that "minority" differently from the "majority." I cannot find, and the Court does not cite, any constitutional authority for such a "ward of the Court" approach to equal protection.[24]

Justice Rehnquist's objections would be well taken were the words "discrete and insular minority" a thaumaturgic refrain, mere recitation of which substituted for exposition or which concealed arbitrary selection of groups "felt" to deserve solicitude.[25] I have taken pains to demonstrate that the phrase "discrete and insular minority" (or, "powerless minority") is not a verbal diversion, but the description or name for people designated by the beginning as having an original claim upon the republic's and the courts' supportive attention. But, granted that certain groups are to be given special consideration, how are these groups to be identified? Justice Rehnquist worriedly hypothesizes that a lawyer might find "insular and discrete" minorities at every turn, while Professor John Hart Ely, for his part, suffers the opposite puzzlement: "I'm not sure I'd know a discrete and insular minority if I saw one."[26] Either way—finding minorities everywhere or nowhere—once protection of powerless minorities is established as a function of the courts, there remains the problem of defining or recognizing those who are to be protected.

CRITERIA OF IDENTIFICATION

"Minorities" have customarily been racial, religious, national, political, and business groups that are smaller and less powerful than other competing groups. In recent years, groups that are not readily placed within any of these traditional categories have nevertheless described themselves and have been acknowledged as minorities, *e.g.*, homosexuals, women, and prisoners. Doubtless, other minorities will continue to emerge into recognition. Determination of who is a minority will be largely contextual. Obviously, a minority is determined at the threshold by some characteristic, such as a shared interest or physical attribute, which serves as a basis for classifying a number of people as a distinct group. It might be added that a minority is determined also by its number; the minority is smaller than the controlling group against which it is measured. Number, however, may not be a dispositive indicator of a minority.

Those minorities who are the special subject of judicial protection are "powerless minorities." I use "powerlessness" in the place of "discreteness and insularity" since the well-being of minorities is the end sought. A minority may flourish in chosen isolation or insularity. What engages judicial protection is a minority's impotence in protecting itself, whether insular or not. Three comments on powerlessness as a criterion are in order.

First, powerlessness rather than size is decisive. A group may be small in number but, like the very wealthy, possessed of the power to protect itself. By the same token, a group may be very large but as women's liberation has taught us, may conceive of itself as and in fact be a minority because it lacks power to protect its rights.[27]

Second, powerlessness or vulnerability is relative. Those who are powerless in one setting may be powerful in another.[28] A group may rank high on a hypothetical, absolute scale of power, whereas in a given situation and with respect to an opposing group, it may be sufficiently powerless to warrant invocation of judicial solicitude. In the *Carolene Products* footnote,[29] Justice Stone, intriguingly, cited *McCulloch v. Maryland*[30] and *South Carolina v. Barnwell Brothers, Inc.*[31] to his proposition about discrete and insular minorities. Comparative powerlessness helps to explain the sense of the citations. In *McCulloch*, the power of the national bank and of the Congress in creating it was relatively weak in comparison to the power of a state to tax. Similarly, in *Barnwell*, the out-of-state trucking interests which the South Carolina legislature sought to regulate were relatively powerless as against intrastate interests.[32] Clearly then, the requisite powerlessness is a question of the comparative interests in issue.

The relative powerlessness which is of concern to the courts is the inability of a minority to defend itself against: (*a*) denial of those things which are fundamental to its life and identity as a minority (*e.g.*, an Amish sect's own schooling of its high-school-age children), and/or (*b*) denial to its members of those things fundamental to their life and identity as individuals because of their membership in the minority (*e.g.*, denial of the franchise to blacks because they are blacks).

Third, powerlessness in this context is not to be equated with political impotence. Minorities powerless in other ways will generally also lack political power. However, except when the controverted issue revolves around political processes, political powerlessness is not necessarily the factor to be singled out. Justice Stone's footnote expressed his belief that prejudice would prevent the political process from protecting minorities.[33] It was not so much that prejudice would close the processes to a minority's participation—although it would do that also—as it was that prejudice would affect the outlook of those already within the processes and close their capacity to act justly with respect to the prejudiced minority. An excluded minority might undertake to vindicate its own interests through the political processes and thus have its political impotence confirmed. And an excluded minority might not seek vindication through the processes but still be said, hypothetically, to be politically impotent because political failure could reasonably be projected.

To focus on political powerlessness, however, would mean that a minority, regardless of the nature of the right it sought to vindicate, would be expected to seek vindication in the political processes. Judicial review would be withheld as long as the avenues to the political marketplace remained open. If a minority could or would not sell its wares politically, it might repair to the judicial forum. But then it would come to court pejoratively cast in the role of a failure and with a failure's burden of demonstrating why judges should accept that which the political majority turned down. If it is in the interest of all to protect minorities, and if it is the majority's and/or government's failure to do so that has led a minority to the Court, then activation of judicial scrutiny should not be colored by this kind of reckoning. To do otherwise, as Justice Stone said, "seems to me no less than the surrender of the constitutional protection of the liberty of small minorities to the popular will."[34]

In addition to powerlessness, the other mark of a qualifying minority, obviously, is a shared characteristic such as race, sex, or religion. The characteristic may be the cause of the minority's powerlessness; this would be the case in the instance of indigency.[35] Or there may be no causal relation between the characteristic and the group's powerlessness; a racial minority's powerlessness would not be caused by an inherent quality in its race. The bearing of the two upon decision making will be taken up in conjunction with the discussion of judicial response to abuse of the shared characteristics.

OCCASIONS FOR REVIEW

Judicial protection of powerless minorities may be given expression under four rubrics.

Specific Constitutional Rights

Strict scrutiny is engaged when a minority brings its claim within the scope of specific constitutional provisions. Two examples are *Wisconsin v. Yoder*[36] and *Furman v. Georgia*.[37] In *Yoder*, Amish parents successfully demonstrated that refusal to send their children to school beyond the eighth grade was religiously motivated and protected by the free-exercise clause.[38] The religious basis of the Amish resistance was certainly determinative, but Chief Justice Burger, writing for the Court, was mindful of the fact that vindication of the religious practice was vindication also of a minority whose "mode of life has . . . come into conflict increasingly with requirements of contemporary society exerting hydraulic insistence on conformity to majoritarian standards"[39] and whose "idiosyncratic separateness exemplifies the diversity we profess to admire and encourage."[40]

In *Yoder* there was a direct connection between the Constitution and a minority, between the free-exercise clause and the Amish respondents whose shared characteristic was religion. That so clear a line between text and minority is not a prerequisite to invocation of specific constitutional provisions is demonstrated by *Furman*. Imposition of the death penalty in the cases before the court in *Furman* was held to violate the Eighth Amendment's ban on cruel and unusual punishment.[41] Prejudice against a minority was not proved as motivating capital punishment, but suspicion that it did was warranted[42] and appears to have been a strong undercurrent to the decision[43] since the identity of petitioners as members of a powerless minority was highlighted in the opinions of three of the five justices who formed the majority.[44]

Abuse of a Shared Characteristic

When a transgression of the rights of a minority is not also transgression of a specific constitutional provision, judicial protection may be invoked under the equal-protection clause if a legislative classification's basis on a shared characteristic is suspect.[45]

Classifications based upon shared characteristics which historically have been the foci of prejudice are immediately suspect. Prejudice curtails the capacity of the majority and the political processes to secure a minority's rights. When history has borne out a likelihood of prejudice, then a close look is in order. Characteristics which fall into this category, and the use of which makes for classifications judicially recognized as inherently suspect, include race,[46] nationality,[47] and, arguably, illegitimacy[48] and sex.[49]

A classification based upon alienage was also numbered, in *Graham v. Richardson*,[50] among the inherently suspect. Prejudice has not been historically associated with alienage, but there is another explanation for its inclusion: causation. Alienage is a shared characteristic that is causally related to powerlessness. An alien, by definition, does not enjoy the privileges of citizenship which, like the vote, may provide power to be heard and reckoned with. There is no causal connection between race and powerlessness; history has taught us to expect a relation nonetheless. One is not left to wait upon the lessons of history where there is a causal link. When a shared characteristic that is the basis for a legislative classification is, like alienage, causally related to powerlessness, careful judicial examination is fitting to guard against oversight. The out-of-state truckers in *Barnwell*[51] were, by the circumstance of their shared characteristic, powerless intrastate.[52] Poverty, about which more will be said later,[53] is another shared characteristic causally related to powerlessness and should bring into question a classification based upon it. Those who are absent or who are present but effectively invisible or voiceless are presumptively vulnerable.

In addition to those classifications about which either history or cause (or both) raise automatic suspicions, there is one other that deserves attention: the classification which creates a powerless minority.[54] This occurs when a benign or latent characteristic, like redheadedness, not heretofore perceived as demarcating a minority (and therefore unlike the characteristics already noted), is employed legislatively to deny something fundamental. For example, a statute might provide that only nonredheads may vote.[55] The minority (redheads) in this event is brought into being and simultaneously rendered powerless. The wrong may be described as one of classification. After all, the classification is capricious, arbitrary, and presumably not reasonably related to any legitimate end sought to be achieved,[56] and is under- (or over-) inclusive.[57] However, the wrong lies more in what is done to the minority than in creating it. The invidiousness of the classification turns on the fundamentality of the right denied. The problem is not really one of classification, and such instances and their kindred are best remitted to discussion under the heading of fundamental interests. Reserved for consideration as presenting classification issues are only those "pure" problems in classification where history or causation teach that the use of certain shared characteristics is to be greeted with judicial circumspection.[58]

Of course, any given case may include both problems of classification and fundamental interests. The point is that in analysis of whether or not a classification is suspect, issues impinging on interest analysis may helpfully be kept out of classification analysis.[59] Wealth classifications have proved troublesome in this regard. The characteristic of poverty is neither benign nor latent, and classifications based upon poverty or whose effect is to discriminate against the poor might be judged inherently suspect on the grounds of history,[60] or of cause,[61] or both. But findings about the suspicion attaching to particular wealth classifications have come in conjunction with analysis of the fundamentality of the interest denied.[62] Justice Powell's opinion for the Court in *San Antonio Independent School District v. Rodriguez*,[63] upholding the Texas public school financing system which relied on local property taxation, did not maintain that wealth classification was permissible. Instead, he found that a class of disadvantaged poor had not been identified.[64] For one thing, according to Justice Powell, there had been no establishment of "any class fairly definable as indigent, or as composed of persons whose incomes are beneath any designated poverty level."[65] Additionally, the class was not identified because there was no absolute deprivation.[66] That is to say, the classification was not suspect because there was no deprivation of a *fundamental* right. In the light of *Bullock v. Carter*,[67] which Justices White and Marshall noted in dissent did not require exactitude in definition,[68] the finding with reference to the interest was probably decisive. But its inclusion here served only to confuse classification analysis.

Perhaps analysis of wealth classifications will have to continue to make use of interest analysis. In his dissent in *Rodriguez*, Justice Marshall offered an explanation of why.[69] "While the 'poor' have frequently been a legally disadvantaged group, it cannot be ignored that social legislation must frequently take cognizance of the economic status of our citizens."[70] Given the society as it is, so the argument runs, it would be impossible to protect the poor in every circumstance, therefore, the occasions have to be selected by coupling the invidiousness of wealth classifications with the fundamentality of interests involved. Thus, says Professor Michelman:

> We do better by the Court to regard it, not as nine (or seven, or five) Canutes railing against the tides of economic inequality which they have no apparent means of stemming, but as a body commendably busy with the critically important task of charting some islands of haven for economic disaster in the ocean of (what continues to be known as) free enterprise.[71]

Practicality may argue against the elevation of poverty to the status of a shared characteristic warranting heightened judicial skepticism, but the poor are a powerless minority in need of judicial protection. And the Court's authoritative responsibility is not to be surrendered to the exigencies of a society that has for the time being taken the marketplace as its definitive model.[72] Rhetoric about the per se invidiousness of wealth classifications along with action where fundamental interests are at stake may be a temporarily expeditious compromise. However, this compromise should not obscure the preference for separating interest from classification analysis, and for preserving to the latter shared characteristics about which history and cause rightfully raise judicial suspicion. Nor should it obscure the need for scrutiny of legislation that discriminates against the poor.[73]

It is surely right to say that the problem that justice "confronts in America, today and for the next decades, is poverty—hydra-headed, hundred-handed poverty—poverty that has even come to be the ugliest facet of racism."[74] One commentator believes that "courts very plainly have no means, material or intellectual, for effecting that major allocation of all our resources, that restructuring of all our priorities, that change in our values and even in our perceptions of the world, which the conquest of poverty will require."[75]

The old biblical alliance between judging and defense of the poor and meek,[76] however, indicates that the political function of judgment implies a more robust role for the courts in confrontation with poverty. To talk about strategic innovation in the distribution of wealth is

to talk about a change of heart, the prerequisite to reallocation of resources and priorities. By describing, continually returning to, and
augmenting our communal beginnings, the courts can be instrumental in a change of heart that will bring about redress for the poor. At
least poverty is one of the subjects for that action, which is according
to and empowered by the constitutive reality of the beginning.

Denial of Basic Needs

Denial to a minority of satisfaction of a want shared by all or most
may be remedied under a specific constitutional provision if, as has
been seen, the thing denied, like the free exercise of religion, is
textually guaranteed. Further, minorities may be protected against
deprivation of rights that the Court has found to be implicitly guaranteed by the Constitution, including the franchise,[77] equal access to
appellate review in criminal cases,[78] interstate travel,[79] privacy,[80] pro-
creation,[81] and marriage.[82] Redress may be granted under the due-
process clause,[83] or may be forthcoming under the equal-protection
clause.[84]

The present Court has not been eager to extend the list of fundamental interests.[85] Qualms have been expressed about subjective selection of what is and what is not fundamental.[86] However, lines of
inquiry may be brought to bear on the subject which, although not
altogether objective, are judgmentally appropriate.

A minority's susceptibility to oppression or its oppression in fact
may be effected through the denial of something the fundamentality
of which is a constant (food, freedom). But the opportunities for and
types of deprivation increase as the majority's power and resources
increase. Thus, what and how much is fundamental to the protection
of a minority is constant with respect to some things but variable with
respect to others, and will be functions of what the majority gathers
to itself.[87] In order for minorities to sustain themselves or for members
of minorities to make a way, if they choose, into a majoritarian society,
they must be adequately equipped according to contemporaneously
realistic standards.

Determination of the variable fundamentals, those which are to be
added to the list as the majority acquires them and their denial to a
minority trenches upon the minority's capacity for fruitful survival,
does not have to be abandoned to judicial subjectivity and guess-
work. It will require contextual judgment and will derive from a

monitoring of the majority in the commanding interest of protecting minorities. Questions to be raised in discharging this responsibility of authority are: What has the majority arrogated to itself and thereby indicated as essential? Does its enjoyment by the majority but not by a minority erode a powerless minority's position in a balance of power? What share is necessary to maintain a minority's integrity?[88] Finally, what does the minority advance as necessary? A minority's own understanding of its felt needs must be attended to, for what is weal to one minority—or a majority—may be woe to another. The Amish respondents in *Yoder* believed it necessary to remove their children from the public school system at a certain stage; they wanted less. The Mexican-American parents in *Rodriguez* wished their children to continue in a more uniformly financed system; they wanted more and better.

Public education may be a variable fundamental which has become necessary to minorities. The majority in *Rodriguez* was unpersuaded that it is. Those challenging the Texas school finance system argued in that case that education was implicitly guaranteed by the Constitution because it is necessary to effective exercise of First Amendment freedoms and to intelligent utilization of the franchise.[89] Justice Powell, writing for the Court, responded that neither the most effective exercise of free speech nor the most informed use of the franchise were guaranteed,[90] and that, even if an identifiable quantum of education is a fundamental right, the Texas system was not charged with failing to provide the requisite minimum.[91] Additionally, he could not distinguish appellees' argument for the implicit guarantee of education from arguments which would also establish as implicitly guaranteed rights to public welfare and housing which *Dandridge v. Williams*[92] and *Lindsey v. Normet*[93] found were not constitutionally protected fundamental rights.[94] Societal significance is not necessarily to be translated into constitutional significance.

The concession that appellees' argument might have merit if a state financing system occasions an absolute denial of education and the determination that the Texas system was saved because it produced only relative disparities seem to add up to the conclusion that equal education is not a fundamental right but that some education may be. That would be to reverse the correct analytical order. The Court should decide whether the interest in issue is fundamental as a step in determining whether it should be equally available. Here the Court found that the interest was not fundamental because it was only un-equally available.[95] Of course, once a right has been found funda-mental for equal-protection purposes, precise uniformity may be out of the question. Even so, permissible latitude in variance does not stretch from a maximum to some quantum just shy of absolute denial. And permissible latitudes in variance should not be involved in a threshhold determination of whether the right is fundamental.[96] It should be the other way around; the fundamentality of the interest should be one of the critical factors in concluding whether variation is allowable.

Establishing education as a right that has become fundamental squarely confronts the Court's reservations about determining what is constitutionally fundamental on the basis of current views about what is socially important.

> It is not the province of this Court to create substantive consti-tutional rights in the name of guaranteeing equal protection of the laws. Thus, the key to discovering whether education is "fundamental" is not to be found in comparisons of the relative societal significance of education as opposed to subsistence or housing. Nor is it to be found by weighing whether education is as important as the right to travel. Rather, the answer lies in assessing whether there is a right to education explicitly or im-plicitly guaranteed by the Constitution.[97]

It was to meet the need for making such an assessment that Justice Marshall, in his *Rodriguez* dissent, formulated a test, approved also by Justice Brennan in his dissent,[98] whereby fundamentality would be determined by the right's importance to the effectuation of rights guaranteed by the Constitution.

> Although not all fundamental interests are constitutionally guaranteed, the determination of which interests are funda-mental should be firmly rooted in the text of the Constitution. The task in every case should be to determine the extent to which constitutionally guaranteed rights are dependent on in-terests not mentioned in the Constitution. As the nexus between the specific constitutional guarantee and the non-constitutional interest draws closer, the nonconstitutional interest becomes more fundamental and the degree of judicial

scrutiny applied when the interest is infringed on a discriminatory basis must be adjusted accordingly.[99]

By Justice Marshall's test, education is fundamental; public welfare
and housing are not.

> There can be no question that, as the majority suggests, consti-
> tutional rights may be less meaningful for some without
> enough to eat or without decent housing. . . . But the crucial
> difference lies in the closeness of the relationship. Whatever
> the severity of the impact of insufficient food or inadequate
> housing on a person's life, they have never been considered to
> bear the same direct and immediate relationship to constitu-
> tional concerns for free speech and for political processes as
> education has long been recognized to bear . . . . Education, in
> terms of constitutional values, is much more analogous, in my
> judgment, to the right to vote in state elections than to public
> welfare or public housing. Indeed, it is not without significance
> that we have long recognized education as an essential step in
> providing the disadvantaged with the tools necessary to
> achieve economic self-sufficiency.[100]

The application of Justice Marshall's test to food and housing produces the wrong result,[101] but his test does provide a judicial method
for determining the fundamentality of other rights such as education.

However, application of the test must be undertaken with the un-
derstanding that the well-being of minorities is itself an imperative.
Perhaps expression might be given this concern by amending Justice
Marshall's test to read:

> The task in every case should be to determine the extent to
> which constitutionally guaranteed rights and/or the survival of
> minorities are dependent on interests not mentioned in the
> constitution. As the nexus between the specific constitutional
> guarantee or the particular minority's capacity to sustain itself
> and the nonconstitutional interest draws closer, the non-
> constitutional interest becomes more fundamental and the
> degree of judicial scrutiny must be adjusted accordingly.

Use of this test would inevitably require the Court to confront the societal significance of litigated activities because a minority's ability

to survive varies in some instances according to what a majority has and does. The Court would do so, not in order to read extraneous views of what is important into the Constitution, but to carry out the original mandate to protect minorities dictated by "the historic experiences with oppression of and discrimination against discrete, powerless minorities which underlie that document." [102]

Denial of Special Needs

In the discussion about relief for deprivations of minority rights, attention has thus far been confined to those things which, either as constants or as variables, are generally shared. When a minority has a need peculiar to itself, the equal-protection clause as traditionally construed will not protect it, regardless of how essential to the minority the need may be. [103] Indeed, traditional equal protection might even be thought to prohibit the government from undertaking positively to satisfy a special want belonging only to a particular minority and not generally shared. [104] Unless the right is one specifically enumerated in the text of the Constitution, the range of possibilities for a remedy will be narrow. This is not to say that they are nonexistent. A Court instructed by its mandate to protect minorities can safeguard a minority whose integrity is seriously compromised by abridgment of a need sui generis.

The much-maligned *Abortion Cases* [105] may be read as helpfully exemplifying vindication of an interest unique to a minority. Such vindication was the effect of the Court's finding that a right of privacy encompassing a pregnant woman's decision to have an abortion was guaranteed by the due-process clause. [106] Women are a powerless minority. [107] Abortions are patently unique to them. The right to choose an abortion does not impinge upon the survival of women as a minority, but it is closely associated with their identity and integrity as individuals who are members of a minority. Legislative proscription of abortion presents a fit opportunity for exercise of judicial protection.

Also involved, however, was another powerless minority, or so we may describe fetuses. The presence of this second minority led Ely to the conclusion that *Wade* and *Bolton* cannot be rationalized [108] as proceeding from the rationale of the *Carolene Products* footnote (or any other value traditionally inferable from the Constitution). [109] *Carolene Products* was inapposite, in his view, because women, although a minority in comparison with men, are not a minority in comparison to the unborn.[110] It may be agreed that the unborn are a powerless minority. But their presence neither dissolves women's status as a powerless minority nor makes the *Carolene Products* rationale inapplicable. There are two minorities, or, more accurately, a minority (women) and a subminority (fetuses).[111] An analogous situation existed in *Yoder*, which involved a minority (Amish) and a subminority (Amish children).[112] In both cases, legislatures may be said to have acted on behalf of the powerless by forbidding the abortion of fetuses in one case and by providing for the education of children in the other. But the protection extended these subminorities conflicted with the interests of the minorities of which they were a part.

In this type of situation, it may be that a legislature truly bent upon aiding a subminority could find alternate means for supplying protection in ways that did not penalize the related minority. For example, proscription is not the sole means for contending with abortions. Abortions might be eliminated or reduced by eliminating or reducing those things which make them necessary, *e.g.*, by improving health care of pregnant women, by doing away with the poverty and hopelessness which encourage abortions, by increasing respect for life (as by eliminating the death penalty), and by making birth control information and devices more freely available.

If there is no way to protect a given subminority except at the expense of a related minority,[113] then the unavoidable conflict ought at least be kept to a minimum. An example of a means for doing so is to be found in Justice Douglas's dissent in *Yoder*. Justice Douglas would apparently have protected the Amish minority against enforced secondary public education, but he would also have taken account of the best interests of individual Amish children.

> On this important and vital matter of education, I think the children should be entitled to be heard. While the parents, absent dissent, normally speak for the entire family, the education of the child is a matter on which the child will often have decided views. He may want to be a pianist or an astronaut or an oceanographer. To do so he will have to break from the Amish tradition.
>
> It is the future of the student, not the future of the parents, that is imperiled by today's decision. If a parent keeps his child out of school beyond the grade school, then the child will be

forever barred from entry into the new and amazing world of diversity that we have today. The child may decide that that is the preferred course, or he may rebel. It is the student's judgment, not his parents', that is essential if we are to give full meaning to what we have said about the Bill of Rights and of the right of students to be masters of their own destiny. If he is harnessed to the Amish way of life by those in authority over him and if his education is truncated, his entire life may be stunted and deformed. The child, therefore, should be given an opportunity to be heard before the State gives the exemption which we honor today.[114]

Justice Douglas sought to protect a neglected subminority, but in neither the *Abortion Cases* nor in *Yoder* can it be said that a subminority's vital interests were adequately insured against abuse. Some justification for the failure can be offered. Courts are to protect minorities when their interests have been overlooked or overridden by majorities or legislatures, and the interests of subminorities also require judicial protection. But parents and prospective mothers, it may be supposed, are less likely as classes to abuse the interest of those within their keeping than are legislatures and majorities. In the *Abortion Cases* and *Yoder*, the Court did protect the interest of a primary minority, perhaps at the expense of a subminority. But at least the subminorities were not abandoned to indifferent or hostile majorities. And it may be that the *Abortion Cases* can be read as a commendable effort to protect a singular right held as necessary by a particular minority.

Conclusion

One immediate and concrete effect of judicial review may be to strike down a particular discriminatory statute or practice. A minority will have been protected in this case from the hardships inflicted by the offending measure. Less immediately but no less importantly, the fact that the courts have scrutinized or may scrutinize and invalidate their acts may lead legislators and administrators to give greater sympathetic attention to minority needs. Or, in consequence of court opinion, the public may be led to remember and encourage minority rights. In these instances, minorities will have been protected against their own despair of finding vindication. In a word, judicial protection is that constellation of immediate as well as long-range, specific as well as broadly educative, symbolic, and hortatory possibilities of judicial review. Fragile though they may be, these possibilities have their best chance of realization when the courts, sensitive to minority interests, give strict scrutiny[115] to challenged measures.

My habit of using "judicial protection" and "strict judicial scrutiny" interchangeably may be a dispensable one dating from the days when "[s]ome situations evoked the aggressive 'new' equal protection, with scrutiny that was 'strict' in theory and fatal in fact; [while] in other contexts, the deferential 'old' equal protection reigned, with minimal scrutiny in theory and virtually none in fact."[116] Although I seriously doubt it, the Burger Court, at the prompting of Justice Marshall,[117] may yet teach us that there are better choices than either heightened judicial skepticism or enlarged judicial credulity.[118] My virtual equation of protection with strict scrutiny is not intended as an endorsement of a double standard of judicial review. It is intended as an indication that protection of minorities educes judicial review with bite, howsoever described or practiced.

I have tried in this chapter to elaborate the *Carolene Products* theory as a conceptual legal argument for invocation of active judicial protection. I have done so in order to state, in lawyers' terms, a theory that can be utilized in espousing the cause of the weak, whom the biblical beginning commends for their own sake to the strong.

Chapter 9

Law, Language, Death, and Life

Law School

The source of authority is the beginning, the American beginning judged in the environment and economy of the transcendent biblical beginning. The legitimacy of law depends upon the performance of beginning within the judicial process in which persons have significant, dignifying roles, and without the judical process when these roles are realized in government by, of, and for the people. The people are equipped for the exercise of citizenship by the protecting, amplifying property of *personae juris*. In casting *personae*, the courts take as their special constituents the powerless, who are placed first in care by the power of love which is structurally and dynamically necessary to the body politic.

The beginning is also to be found in the teaching of law. This happens in the classroom just as it happens in the courtroom, when there is no disjunction between the process and the substance of law. It occurs, that is to say, when one finds the reality and experience of a partnership which is the better the more inclusive it is. Thus, if property outfits the participants in an expansive covenantal enterprise, then a course on property must itself somehow equip students for the mutuality and respect of a joint venture directed at gathering others. I think this happens when the class becomes expeditionary. At the least, it requires the avoidance of stultification and ennui. At the most, it requires embarking on a journey, with possibilities of pilgrimage. Legal education of this order is the subject of this, the concluding chapter.

🦋 Diagnoses

Chief Justice Burger has leveled powerful criticism at the law schools. He accuses them of escapism from "the foul antiseptic odor of the jail house and the depressing atmosphere surrounding the short and simple annals of the poor."[1] He finds that "young law school graduates are well-trained to write a fine appellate brief but not trained to recognize concealed usury in the sale of a television set on installments."[2]

The Chief Justice is right. His assessment of the result of legal education is well taken. It was also taken to heart. His criticism was instrumental in the formation of a Task Force, under the auspices of the American Bar Association, which issued a report, *Lawyer Competency*.[3] Unfortunately, its recommendations were limited from the outset by the decision to appraise "programs, experiments, and trends currently visible in law schools" rather than to compare present legal education to what it might or should be.[4] Accordingly, the recommendations "do not call for law schools to abandon areas of traditional strength, but to build upon them."[5]

While the Chief Justice's assessment of results is correct, his diagnosis of causes is not. He indicates that the cause is the appellate case method, the basic method of teaching in use in the law schools. The problem runs deeper than the Chief Justice believes and deeper than the Task Force was prepared to probe. The problem is one of ideology. It is the ideology of technocracy. The Chief Justice indicates his own adherence to this ideology when he speaks of society as "organized society."[6] Efficiency and order are hallmarks of such a society, and, in it, lawyers are viewed as providing "solvents and lubricants which reduce the frictions."[7]

Some years ago, Myres McDougal made what still stands as a more adequate diagnosis of causes. He saw that the conception of law as a body of rules

> underlies the over-all organization of curricula and the detailed patterning of most particular courses in Anglo-American law schools; the organizing principle of both whole and part is that of legal technicality, with particular subject matters purportedly

128

demarcated and arranged in terms of highly ambiguous, over-
lapping and contradictory concepts of authoritative myth.[8]

Legal education on this model produces, at best, lawyers tech-
nically accomplished in rules. The Chief Justice said that lawyers
are—and he meant it positively—"important cogs in the machinery
of . . . society."[9] If cogs are sought, cogs will be manufactured. Lawyers who are motivated by and able to remedy the odor of the jail-
house and the short and simple annals of the poor are not cogs. They
are more likely troubled and troubling persons with heart. For such
persons, law is metaphor. And metaphor is "pure adventure."[10]
The real challenge to legal education is how to get students going
on the adventure. I think it is done by leading them to confront the
possibilities for life and death in the law.

The Legal Imagination

There are some challenging, experimental textbooks and
courses currently available in legal education. One of them is James
White's *The Legal Imagination*.[11] I shall not here review his book, but
I shall use it as a medium for discovery of the nature of legal education as pure adventure and the linkages of law, language, dying, and
living.
The book is intended for use in law schools. The author describes it
as a kind of "advanced course in reading and writing."[12] It is composed of groups of selected readings, commentary, questions, and
writing assignments. The readings that precede and color the assignments and make up the bulk of the volume are drawn from literature
and the classics as well as law. The range of selections is unusual for a
law casebook,[13] and its organizing principle is more than unusual.
The book is a fresh departure, involving the reader in a companion-
able, systematic venture of the mind. White seeks to define and animate a legal imagination, hitherto thought nonexisting, by relating it
to other kinds of imagination.
This sort of comparison might seem alien to legal thinking. The
supposed incapacity of the legal mind for relational thinking was
fixed in a notorious dictum of Thomas Reed Powell, who alleged that
when "you can think about something which is attached to some-

thing else without thinking about what it is attached to, then you have what is called a legal mind."[14] It is not that lawyers have been thought incapable of making any connections at all; connections, even creative ones, are of course the coinage of the common law. It is, rather, that the range of comparison has appeared circumscribed within a discrete, closed universe of discourse, the world of *stare decisis*. Other worlds intrude only to be transmuted into the terms of the legal one; outside connections are processed into a cash-and-case nexus.

One example of this reductionist conversion is an advertisement for the *Medical Atlas for Attorneys* that appeared in the *Journal of the American Bar Association* and that read in part:

> More than 2000 drawings expose the entire anatomy—structure by structure from skin surface to skeleton. Brief marginal text notes alert you to the *possibilities* of your client's case; you see at a glance the potential implications.
>
> Every part of the body is keyed with citations to cases, awards, ALR annotations, and other references which take you directly to the relevant law.[15]

The lawyer translates the human body from the world of nature into the world of courts just as Linda Lovelace translated it into the world of pornography: the body is made to seem incredible but is actually divested of mystery; it is seemingly opened to illimitable *possibilities* but is in fact reduced to an object denuded of wonder. The body loses the referents of a human world, to be analyzed into cases. Such is the paradigmatic fate of things and acts brought within the processes of law.

It is therefore singular that White stimulates the reader to discover comparisons to worlds outside of law. Legal education should not grind those other worlds through the wheels of law but define the law by looking at it from the outside. The law thus defined can be controlled; one can invest the law, and one's life within it, with more deliberate, more creative responsibility. As White observes, "For some people, law leads to an ever duller and more restricting life, to drudgery and routine; for others, to a life by comparison free and self-expressive, which seems to yield and form itself to the controlling intelligence or imagination."[16] The point is to have law render a life of choice.

Legal education has been inching toward this kind of experience for as long as we have reckoned with the truth that law is neither self-enclosed nor self-sufficient. Thus, casebooks have dressed their cases with ever more generous dollops of economic theory and even theology.[17] Law schools have been developing courses like "Law and Literature" and "Law and Psychiatry"; the Harvard Law School together with the National Endowment for the Humanities experimented with a program in law and the humanities.

Books and courses on "law and" various other disciplines are analogical. They compare law to something else basically different from it. *The Legal Imagination* and kindred courses are metaphorical. For example, there is a lot of literature in White's book, but it is not simply a law-and-literature book; it is rather a book about law *as* literature. There is a lot of imagination in this book, but it is not simply a book about law and the imagination; it is rather a book *of* legal imagination. There is an affirmation of a basic likeness between law and imagination. The relation is univocal rather than equivocal.

❧ Teaching Law and Teaching Its Meaning

Most of the students I have encountered in recent years have come to law school willing to work. They do not always appreciate in advance how much work of what kind is involved, and they have not always been prepared for it, but they want to succeed. Good teaching nourishes this desire and helps it develop into a technical command and a respect for craftsmanship. Although this is a great, difficult, and rewarding job in and of itself, there is a more complex and demanding responsibility: to seek the meaning of the rules, of the law, of success in the law.

A JOINT VENTURE

The meaning of law is a subject not often raised in law school classrooms by either teachers or students, except perhaps sardonically. One of the more intriguing reasons advanced for this omission is that teachers themselves are uncertain about the meaning of law, its significance *sub specie aeternitatis*. The uncertainty is in turn perceived as symptomatic of a more general loss of direction, a pervasive loss of a sense of transcendence.

The uncertainty may actually be turned to advantage and serve as a clue to the form and content of a renewed search for meaning. If one does not know the answers, he cannot teach them to students. But he is then free to seek answers with students. Uncertainty becomes an occasion, not for abandonment of the study of the meaning of law, but for a fresh approach to it. It becomes an occasion for a joint enterprise, and the collegial, relational form of such an undertaking itself has substantive importance.

A collegial class is an artistic achievement impossible without technique. To speak of legal education as a joint endeavor, therefore, is to speak of it not as abandoning structure but as adopting a common, thoughtful discipline.

This discipline does not have to be static, although it is traditionally conceived this way. Even the nontraditional mind thinks of contracts and torts as "blocks." [18] The casebooks, too, are blocks, tablets of stone that pile up until the student has constructed a base on which to erect a career. White notes about legal education so conceived, the "implication is that there is in the world an identifiable thing or body of knowledge called 'law' which is transferred from teacher to student. . . . 'I teach them law' is parallel to 'I give them soup.'" [19] ("Soup" is a polite substitute for what some of my students think I give them.)

There is another order of legal education, however—the kind that allowed Archibald MacLeish to discover that by no study better than that of law could one envision "the interminable journey of the human mind." [20] White's book is predicated on such a vision. Law and legal education are, for him, in movement: if they may be expressed in terms of relations, the relationships are dynamic.

White creates in his book a sense of movement from the start. The first reading in the book is taken from Mark Twain's *Life on the Mississippi*,[21] and it is followed by other selections on the Mississippi and adventure. Throughout the book, this suggestion of flow and exploration is never far below the textual surface. The book is summarized at one point as an attempt to enable the reader to look back at his life, to take a position from which to survey his education and to address the question, "Where do I go now?"[22] The final chapter then begins by advising, "You have been pushed off, as it were, to make your own way."[23] The reader is encouraged to make a new beginning, "to pull together what you have done in this course, and in law school, to put it into some sort of order, and move on."[24] Thus, the author engages the reader in a journey; the book is a passage, the way all legal education should be.

As a teacher, White achieves a sense of movement through the surprisingly simple device of the weekly writing assignment. The student, in the process of writing, becomes what the lawyer is: a creator of literature, a translator of human activity and experience. The student creates the real subject matter of the course. His writings are subjected to case analysis: cross-examination and the drawing out of nuances, contradictions, and limitations.

This is clinical education in the best sense and should not be overlooked as such. My own students are anxious to plunge into the real mind. I do agree, however, that law school is not the real world. Indeed, law schools are never so unsuccessful, it seems, as when they pretend that they are. Law school is really more like play, an analogy that does not at all assail its seriousness or importance. Like play, law school "is not life and affords . . . more of a chance for experimentation, a wider scope for the realization of . . . imagination than life itself."[25] My point is not to denigrate traditional clinic-in-law programs, but only to call attention to the value of those academic clinics that honor the spirit of play by inviting students to experiment in the creation of utopias. A student in White's course is asked, for example, to create an insanity defense.[26] That is a utopian exercise. Law school needs more utopias.

It has been said that whenever "the utopia disappears history ceases to be a process leading to an ultimate end. The frame of reference according to which we evaluate facts vanishes"[27] and we are at last brought "to a 'matter-of-factness' which ultimately would mean the decay of the human will."[28] In short, without utopias and some opportunity to engage in creating them, a law student will simply not be equipped for either judgment or improvement of the world.[29] The ABA Task Force tilted toward this conclusion: "much that otherwise might appear to be 'speculative' or 'theoretical' in a law school curriculum . . . deserves to be thought of as vital, useful, and practical training. [It] may help lay the theoretical or conceptual base for forty years or more of continuing self-learning."[30]

THE METHOD: CASES, POLICIES, AND FUNDAMENTAL QUESTIONS

"How odd it may seem," White remarks almost casually at one point, "that law school does not begin with, or perhaps consist of, a course on the subject of justice: what it is and how it can be achieved."[31] However, as he knows[32] and as another has observed, the "beginning is not what one finds first: the point of departure must be reached, it must be won."[33] In law school, the beginning of justice and meaning is won by wrestling with the cases.

These make for a good start. There are ancient appeal, fascination, and fun in them; they are rich in tragedy, antagonism, and high as well as low comedy. No student would want to miss the fertile octogenarian[34] and the unborn widow[35] of the Rule Against Perpetuities. Nor, in studying rescission, the mistake about the infertility of the cow, Rose 2d of Aberlone.[36] Nor the pleasurable words themselves: feoffors and feoffees, the assize of novel disseisin, and fee tail female specials. Such gifts are to be accepted when and as they are given. They prevent the aggressive error of always hard driving the fundamental questions and nothing but the fundamental questions.

Soon after the cases come the policies and purposes that offer provisional explanations for the way rule and precedent are deployed in given settings. Discussion of policy is an established trend. But policy is not the final stage. The ultimate question is "how an intelligent and educated person can possibly spend his life working with the law, when life is short and there is so much else to do."[37] It is not a separate inquiry. It is part and parcel of the law school curriculum.

White's treatment of the insanity defense illustrates specifically the way fundamental questions may be pursued in the midst of the curriculum.[38] After a brief introduction to the subject about to be traversed, White opens carefully by setting out the Modern Penal Code proposals for formulation of the insanity defense.[39] It is straightforward material, which is then drawn through a series of cases and questions in the received case-method style. But while the method itself is conventional, its application and results are not.

One innovation is White's treatment of the insanity defense as a label or caricature to be analyzed, case-method style, as language: Is the defense as generally articulated an adequate description of the person or phenomenon sought to be described? What is its function in the institution that employs it, and what does it intimate about that institution? What does it imply about the people on the jury to whom it is addressed, and what does it tell us about those (judges, psychiatrists, and lawyers) who invoke it? Because the reader himself has spoken or may in the future speak in the tongue of the insanity defense, the question finally becomes: What do you mean when you talk that way, and what do you say about yourself? Why? White thus exposes rule, policy, and fundamental meaning by subjecting the insanity defense—as a case of language—to traditional case-method analysis. As a result, he opens up a new line of questions about the insanity defense, about the law, and about us.

The other innovation is his selection of "cases" that draw out the insanity defense or are played against it and that precipitate his questions. Some are the standard fare of judicial opinions. Others are not. The latter include Marais on the "well-known yellow South African weaver bird," baboons, otters, Namaqua partridges, and blindfolded men and boys;[40] and Lévi-Strauss as a "note case."[41] If judicial opinions on the insanity defense can be characterized as cases of language, then other cases of language, though nonlegal, may be set down helpfully alongside them.

For one example, *Ferrin v. People*[42] is followed by Emily Dickinson's "A Bird Came down the Walk."[43] *Ferrin* concerned a child who inexplicably shot his younger brother to death. The poem begins,

> A Bird came down the Walk —
> He did not know I saw —
> He bit an Angleworm in halves
> And ate the fellow, raw,
> And then he drank a Dew
> From a convenient Grass —
> And then hopped sidewise, to the Wall
> To let a Beetle pass—[44]

The juxtaposition of the two selections suggests an answer to the question that precedes them: "Is it perhaps only a failure of imagination that makes us believe that the man in the dock has a mind that is directly comprehensible, that it has workings that can be measured and tested?"[45] The reader is made to realize how much the label of insanity may conceal, not unmercifully, and he is ultimately better equipped to understand and use the insanity defense.

A second example of this unconventional "case" method is found in White's discussion of the *M'Naghten* rule.[46] There he introduces, as though it were effortlessly natural to do so, a luminous paragraph on Marlowe's *Doctor Faustus*. The *M'Naghten* rule would prevent the punishment of a person who, through mental illness, does not know that what he is doing is wrong; in *Doctor Faustus*, the protagonist is condemned to eternal punishment.

> [H]e blasphemes a God he knows to exist and to be omnipotent. He is presented as knowing as fully as one could that what he is doing is wrong; and at the last moment before death he is offered a chance to repent, which he rejects. Is this the criminal or the insane mind? The theological answer is damnation. The answer of the play seems to be that such a damnation is a hideous wrong. This is not a play in which the author says he disbelieves in God, but that he hates him.[47]

This is not only a striking way to teach the *M'Naghten* rule but also a fruitful, artful introduction to prior, fundamental issues. The *M'Naghten* rule cannot thereafter be viewed as simply a legal rule.

White's book is composed, then, of cases, albeit some unorthodox ones. It is basically, I submit, a casebook. It does not ask that students study anything but cases by any means other than the case method. It teaches law, not some other subject, and it seeks to educate lawyers and not some other professionals—literary critics, say, or philosophers. It makes its appeal to the possibility—important to my success-oriented students—that it may assist the student to become a more authentic lawyer, better at what he or she chooses to do. It moves through rules and policies toward fundamental questions and back again, not in order to discard the rules and policies, but to illuminate them and enlighten those who would use them.

The Legal Imagination leads one to consider—to engage in, really—the interaction between, on the one hand, law and one's practice of it, and on the other hand, the theory, as it were, of one's life. To say the same thing in a different way, I find in this book encouragement to study, to practice, and to teach in three dimensions: that of rules and cases and their sometimes inherent fascination; that of rules and cases in relation to policies; and, most notably, that of rules, cases, and policies in relation to what one imagines his life ultimately to be about.

✣ Law as Metaphor

As I noted in the preface, lawyers speak a reductive language. They do so necessarily, for the disposition of cases requires it. Tort litigation, for example, is possible only if the human body is analyzed into parts keyed to cases. Paradoxically, this alchemy that reduces life to the immediate needs of courtroom judgment is meant ultimately to augment and humanize life. As Archibald MacLeish has said, the "business of the law is to make sense of the confusion of what we call human life—to reduce it to order *but at the same time* to give it possibility, scope, even dignity."[48] The law is marked by a pull in opposite directions, a simultaneity of reduction and augmentation. This is the very stuff of metaphor.[49]

If law is a metaphor, what is it a metaphor of? What is the other thing meant when we talk in terms of law? White notes how "one has the feeling about a legal argument that it involves everything."[50] When we speak the language of law, we may mean *everything*: law may be a metaphor of life and death.

Law is a metaphor of death when the practice of it is dull, restrictive, a routine drudgery, despairing.[51] In this event, it is a metaphor of the attorney's death. Law is a metaphor of death, too, when it crushes the troubled and the troubling or oppresses the powerless. In this circumstance, it is a metaphor of the society's death.

We are not often willing to recognize death in law. From the point of view of most of us, law appears viable. It seems just, protective. But it will seem quite different to someone like George Jackson, who was convicted of a theft of $70 and died in San Quentin after twelve years' imprisonment. The legal system has dealt with blacks in the same manner that it disposed of Jackson, says William Stringfellow; "[t]here is no other honest way to describe the relation between the law in America and American blacks . . . than in terms of the aggressions of the legal system against human life." And if the legal system is not viable for blacks and others, then how, Stringfellow asks, "in the name of humanity, can it be affirmed as viable for me or for any human being?"[52]

Law may mean death but does not have to. It can be made a metaphor of life. It becomes a metaphor of life for the lawyer when it is an enterprise of the imagination, a language which, controlled, is a vehicle of deliberate commitment. This is to claim that the lawyer, with law as the given term of the metaphor, can define the meaning of the other term, without having to accept such meaning as may be assigned by the law itself, by any institution, or by default. In White's vision, the lawyer works out an identity. "You define a mind and character, very much as the historian or poet or novelist might be said to do. At the end of thirty years you will be able to look at shelves of briefs, think back on negotiations and arguments . . . and say, 'Here is what I have found it possible to say.'"[53]

In writing those briefs and conducting those negotiations and arguments, one will experience, White notes, "the central frustration of writer and lawyer, the perpetual breaking down of language in your hands as you try to use it."[54] No language, he adds, "can bear the stresses of our demands for truth and order and justice."[55] To make law mean life will be, accordingly, a continual struggle with words, an ongoing exploration of language.

In the course of this exploration, the lawyer does work out an identity, en route, and so gives expression to his life. However, identity and life are not self-bestowed any more than the beginning of America was autogenetic. The lawyer's self is not the only or primary self involved. In the Reformation doctrine of the priesthood of believers, each is priest for the other. In modern legal practice, what the lawyer says, he says on behalf of clients. His struggle with words is an attempt to translate their grievances into judicially cognizable terms. Finding, as a lawyer, "what it is possible to say" is finding words that work for others. The more such words the lawyer finds, the more he will have made law mean life, for his clients and therefore also for himself.

This translation which constitutes the most essential but humble task of the legal profession requires two faculties. The lawyer must be able to use legal language, the medium of translation, competently and creatively.[56] But another capacity is of equal, even more critical, importance. The lawyer must not only conjure legal arguments; he must also be able to hear the poor and blacks and others whose grievances cry out to be translated. These faculties, insofar as they require more than imagination, may be said to depend upon conscience, or heart. White has taught us to animate the imagination. How to in-spirit the heart is another question.

Its answer will come from legal education that ventures the risk of a pilgrimage undertaken with as well as for others. The pilgrimage will be rare even though it follows a circular course, seeking to achieve that which gives it origin. Such education, like life, will be filled with amazement, always starting from and always on the way to the New Beginning.

Notes

 Introduction

1. FELIX FRANKFURTER ON THE SUPREME COURT 203 (P. Kurland ed. 1970).
2. Lehmann, *The Logos in a World Come of Age*, THEOLOGY TODAY, Oct. 1964, at 274, 284. John Calvin begins the *Institutes* with the observation that wisdom consists of the knowledge of God and of ourselves, two branches of knowledge "so intimately connected, which of them precedes and produces the other, is not easy to discover." J. CALVIN, I INSTITUTES OF THE CHRISTIAN RELIGION 47 (J. Allen trans. 1949). The decision about whether to begin with theology or anthropology has served as a watershed among theologians. Karl Barth, for example, chose the former, Friedrich Schleiermacher the latter. Calvin himself concluded that the proper order of instruction required first treating the knowledge of God. To start at the God end, as Barth and Calvin do, is not at all to diminish the role and significance of man but is really to commit one to giving the human truest and greatest significance. As Calvin said, "no man can arrive at a true knowledge of himself, without having first contemplated the divine character." *Id.* at 48. The anthropological significance of Barth's theology is still overlooked by some. In American theology, Jonathan Edwards attempted to place man and human history in a trinitarian context. It seems to me that this aspect of Edwards's work has yet to be fully explored. Paul Lehmann has been this country's foremost modern expositor of the pursuit christologically of the knowledge of man. I have tried to discover whether law, as a human enterprise, is not to be understood and practiced most authentically when one is given a theological starting point.
3. N. CHIAROMONTE, THE WORM OF CONSCIOUSNESS AND OTHER ESSAYS 148 (1976).

 Chapter I. Beginning and Authority

1. *See, e.g.*, L. HAND, THE BILL OF RIGHTS (1958); Wechsler, *Toward Neutral Principles of Constitutional Law*, 73 HARV. L. REV. 1 (1959).
2. Taylor, *H. L. A. Hart's Concept of Law in the Perspective of American Legal Realism*, 35 MOD. L. REV. 606, 611 (1972).
3. Both James Madison and John Marshall spoke of the people as providing the validating authority for the Constitution. In both instances, however, "the people" were being distinguished from the states as the authorizing agency. THE FEDERALIST No. 43, at 296–97 (J. Cooke ed. 1961) (J. Madison) [hereinafter cited as THE FEDERALIST]; McCulloch v. Maryland, 17 U.S. (4 Wheat.) 316, 402–04 (1819).

140

Notes to Chapter One

4. T. Paine, Political Writings 45 (1837), *quoted in* Corwin, *The "Higher Law" Background of American Constitutional Law*, 42 Harv. L. Rev. 149 (1929).
5. Marbury v. Madison, 5 U.S. (1 Cranch) 137, 163 (1803) (Marshall, C.J.).
6. *See* Corwin, *supra* note 4, at 152; R. Cover, Justice Accused: Antislavery and the Judicial Process 34 (1975).
7. There is a vast literature, sometimes forbidding, on natural law. Sherpa guides into the Himalayas of natural law upon whom I have relied and who are not elsewhere cited in the notes are H. Cairns, Legal Philosophy From Plato to Hegel (1967); F. Flückiger, Geschichte des Naturrechtes (1954); E. Troeltsch, The Social Teaching of the Christian Churches (O. Wyon trans. 1931). *See also* E. Bodenheimer, Jurisprudence (1974); and W. Friedmann, Legal Theory (1967).
8. *See* Corwin, *The "Higher Law" Background of American Constitutional Law* Part II), 42 Harv. L. Rev. 365, 396 (1929); Address by John Dickinson, Committee of Correspondence in Barbados, Philadelphia, 1776, *quoted in part in* B. Bailyn, The Ideological Origins of the American Revolution 187 (1967). In addition to the laws of nature and nature's God, Jefferson also invoked "self-evident truths." These "opinions and beliefs of men [which] depend not on their own will, but follow involuntarily the evidence proposed to their minds," Jefferson, *Preamble to the Virginia Bill for Establishing Religious Freedom*, in 2 The Papers of Thomas Jefferson 545 (J. Boyd ed. 1950), may be a restatement of the already enumerated laws of nature and of nature's God.
9. H. Arendt, On Revolution 196 *passim* (1963).
10. Adler & Gorman, *Reflections: The Gettysburg Address*, The New Yorker, Sept. 8, 1975, at 42, 42–43. The Greek word *politeia* can be translated to mean "constitution," in the sense, for example, of the constitution of the body or soul. It was in this sense that John Adams likened a political constitution to "the constitution of the human body," with "certain contextures of the nerves, fibres, and muscles, or certain qualities of the blood and juices," some of which "may properly be called *stamina vitae*, or essentials and fundamentals of the constitution; parts without which life itself cannot be preserved a moment." J. Adams, 3 Works 478–79 (C. Adams ed. 1850–1856).
11. *See* L. Strauss, Natural Right and History 136 (1953). As Strauss noted, "The *politeia* is more fundamental than any laws; it is the source of all laws. . . . No law, and hence no constitution, can be the fundamental political fact, because all laws depend on human beings." *Id.*
12. Address by Abraham Lincoln, Springfield, Ill., June 26, 1857, in 2 The Collected Works of Abraham Lincoln 398, 406 (R. Basler ed. 1953). "Matthew Arnold, who prided himself on his ability to discern touchstones of great style, is reported to have said that he stopped reading when he came to the phrase about the dedication to a 'proposition.' Lincoln's instinct for style caused him no qualms over the use of that word to designate an object to which men can be dedicated. In traditional logic, a

proposition is a sentence setting forth something judged ('held') to be either true or false. In the first line of the second paragraph of the Declaration, that men are equal is held to be true and so is declared in a proposition." Adler & Gorman, *supra* note 10, at 43. Wilbur Samuel Howell traces the form of the Declaration and the term "self-evident" to Duncan's *Logick*. Howell, *New Insight into Declaration of Independence*, PRINCETON ALUMNI WEEKLY, Dec. 9, 1975, at 8, 10. Thus, Lincoln's logic may simply reflect Jefferson's logic, which is simply a reflection of Duncan's logic.

13. Letter from Thomas Jefferson to Joseph C. Cabell, Feb. 2, 1816, in THE LIFE AND SELECTED WRITINGS OF THOMAS JEFFERSON 660, 661 (A. Koch & W. Peden eds. 1944).

14. *See* H. ARENDT, *supra* note 9, at 128. As John Rawls noted, "Taking part in political life does not make the individual master of himself, but rather gives him an equal voice along with others in settling how basic social conditions are to be arranged." J. RAWLS, A THEORY OF JUSTICE 233 (1971).

15. Whether the passengers on the *Mayflower* landed outside the jurisdiction of the Virginia Company by design or by the accident of a contrary headwind is not clear. *Compare* G. WILLISON, SAINTS AND STRANGERS 81–82 (1965), *with* S. MORISON, THE OXFORD HISTORY OF THE AMERICAN PEOPLE 55 (1965), and AN AMERICAN PRIMER 1–2 (D. Boorstin ed. 1966). It seems certain that the threat of mutiny by some of the Strangers in consequence of the landing at a point beyond the company's jurisdiction was not the principal or only ground for the Compact. *But see* G. WILLISON, *supra* at 20. *See also* H. ARENDT, *supra* note 9, at 166.

16. *The Mayflower Compact*, in AN AMERICAN PRIMER, *supra* note 15, at 3.

17. H. ARENDT, *supra* note 9, at 214.

18. *Id.*

19. *Id.* at 215, *quoting* THE FEDERALIST No. 1, *supra* note 3, at 3 (A. Hamilton).

20. *Id.* at 213.

21. H. ARENDT, *supra* note 9, at 212.

22. AUGUSTINE, THE CITY OF GOD, bk. x, ch. 24, at 328 (M. Dods trans., 1950).

23. C. COCHRANE, CHRISTIANITY AND CLASSICAL CULTURE 384 (1957).

24. AUGUSTINE, *supra* note 22, at 328.

25. *Id.* (footnotes omitted).

26. *Id.* at 328.

27. C. COCHRANE, *supra* note 23, at 501.

28. *Cf.* P. Lehmann, Ethics in a Christian Context 97 (1963).

29. H. ARENDT, *supra* note 9, at 172.

30. *Id.* at 308.

31. C. COCHRANE, *supra* note 23, at 512.

32. *Id.*

33. *See* J. MCNEILL, UNITIVE PROTESTANTISM, at 57 (1964); P. LEHMANN, *supra* note 28, at 63–73 *passim*.

34. J. MCNEILL, *supra* note 33, at 129.

35. *Id.* at 93–94.

36. *See* T. HOBBES, LEVIATHAN pt. 1 (M. Oakeshott ed. 1947). Hobbes gives a

sobering account of the war of every man against every man:
> In such condition, there is no place for industry; because the fruit thereof is uncertain: and consequently no culture of the earth; no navigation, nor use of the commodities that may be imported by sea; no commodious building; no instruments of moving, and removing, such things as require much force; no knowledge of the face of the earth; no account of time; no arts; no letters; no society; and which is worst of all, continual fear, and danger of violent death; and the life of man, solitary, poor, nasty, brutish, and short.
>
> *Id.* at 82.

37. J. LOCKE, TWO TREATISES OF CIVIL GOVERNMENT, bk. 2 (W. Carpenter ed. 1966). According to Locke, this disorder is caused by the "strange doctrine" that "in the state of Nature every one has the executive power of the law of Nature." *Id.* at 123.
38. T. HOBBES, *supra* note 36, pt. 1, at 82–84; pt. 2, at 109, 113.
39. J. LOCKE, *supra* note 37, at 180, 228.
40. Some have raised the question whether there may have been two separate contracts: a compact to be a society (*the pactum unionis*) and a compact to be subject to a government (*the pactum subjectionis*). *See generally* O. GIERKE, NATURAL LAW AND THE THEORY OF SOCIETY (E. Barker trans. 1957); L. STRAUSS, *supra* note 11, at 232. For Hobbes and Locke, the contracts are identical.
41. T. HOBBES, *supra* note 36, pt. 2, at 12.
42. J. LOCKE, *supra* note 37, at 158–63.
43. *Id.* at 228–29.
44. *See* L. STRAUSS, *supra* note 11, at 232.
45. G. WILLS, INVENTING AMERICA: JEFFERSON'S DECLARATION OF INDEPENDENCE, 315 *passim* (1978).
46. *Id.* at 195.
47. *Id.* at 292.
48. *Id.* at 291.
49. *Id.* at 319.
50. *Id.* at 312–13.
51. H. ARENDT, *supra* note 9, at 66.

Chapter 2. Story in Law

1. G. VON RAD, STUDIES IN DEUTERONOMY (D. Stalker trans. 1953). *See also* J. BRIGHT, A HISTORY OF ISRAEL (1959); G. WRIGHT, GOD WHO ACTS (1952).
2. "In this book, the result of my inquiries into history, I hope to do two things: to preserve the memory of the past by putting on record the astonishing achievements both of our own and of the Asiatic peoples; secondly, and more particularly, to show how the two races came into conflict." HERODOTUS, THE HISTORIES (A. de Selincourt trans. 1954).
3. *See* H. ARENDT, ON REVOLUTION 222 *passim* (1963).

4. I shall count my country lost in the loss of the Primitive Principles, and the Primitive Practices, upon which it was at first Established: But certainly one good way to save that Loss would be to do something . . . that the Story of the Circumstances attending the Foundation and Formation of this Country, and of its Preservation hitherto, may be impartially handed unto Posterity.
    C. MATHER, MAGNALIA, bk. II, 8–9, *quoted in* H. ARENDT, ON REVOLUTION, *supra* note 3, at 319.

5. *See, e.g.,* Lincoln, *Address Delivered at the Dedication of the Cemetery at Gettysburg*, Nov. 19, 1863, in ABRAHAM LINCOLN: HIS SPEECHES AND WRITINGS 734 (R. Basler ed. 1969). *Cf.* Adler & Gorman, *Reflections: The Gettysburg Address*, THE NEW YORKER, Sept. 8, 1975.

6. Johnson, *Special Message to the Congress: The American Promise*, Mar. 14, 1965, in I PUBLIC PAPERS OF THE PRESIDENTS OF THE UNITED STATES: LYNDON B. JOHNSON: 1965, at 281 (1966).

7. "[T]he Court is the only public and official institution consciously and continuously concerned with relating past, present, and future in American life." C. MILLER, THE SUPREME COURT AND THE USES OF HISTORY 193 (1972). In the course of his fruitful work on the Court's uses of history, Miller also notes, "Along with the constitutional text, constitutional doctrine, precedent, and social facts, history is a category of legal reasoning which contributes first to deciding a case and then to explaining the decision in an opinion." *Id.* at 189. The suggestion made hereinafter is that history is something more than one among several categories of legal reasoning and explanation. It would be overstated but would be closer to the position taken here to say that the Court is more used by than using of history. For other points of view, see J. NOONAN, PERSONS AND MASKS OF THE LAW 152–67 (1976) ("The Alliance of Law and History"); Wyzanski, *History and Law*, 26 U. CHI. L. REV. 237 (1958). *See also* F. STRENG, UNDERSTANDING RELIGIOUS MAN 123 (1964) ("Only in such disciplines as theology and law is there a self-conscious effort to determine truth in the light of the value decisions made by one's past religious or social community.")

8. J. WIGMORE, A KALEIDOSCOPE OF JUSTICE 487 (1941), *quoted in* Estes v. Texas, 381 U.S. 532, 570 (1965) (Warren, C.J., concurring).

9. HERODOTUS, *supra* note 2, at 13.

10. Aeschylus, *The Persians* (S. Bernadete trans.), in AESCHYLUS II, at 45 (D. Green & R. Lattimore eds. 1967). The text follows the interpretation of N. CHIAROMONTE, THE WORM OF CONSCIOUSNESS AND OTHER ESSAYS 131–33 (1976). *See also* Arendt, *Reflections: Truth and Politics*, THE NEW YORKER, Feb. 25, 1967, p. 44.

11. *See* text after note 1 *supra*. *See also* Deuteronomy 5:3.

12. P. LEHMANN, THE TRANSFIGURATION OF POLITICS 24 (1975).

13. *See* p. 18 *supra*.

14. THE FEDERALIST No. 14, at 83, 89 (J. Cooke ed. 1961).
    There is, as Hannah Arendt perceived, "a kind of necessary 'augmentation' by virtue of which all innovations and changes remain tied back to

the foundation, which at the same time, they augment and increase."
ARENDT, *supra* note 3, at 203.

15. In E. CORWIN, THE CONSTITUTION AND WHAT IT MEANS TODAY 3 (1958)
(quoting Woodrow Wilson). *But see* Katz v. United States, 389 U.S. 347,
373 (1967) (Black, J., dissenting) ("It never meant that this Court have
such power, which in effect would make us a continuously functioning
constitutional convention"); L. LUSKY, BY WHAT RIGHT? 5 (1975) ("it raises
a serious question as to whether the Court has shaken itself free from all
external restraint and begun to function as a continuing constitutional
convention").

16. Baker v. Carr, 369 U.S. 186, 259 (1962) (Clark, J., concurring).

17. *Id.*

18. The "one-person, one-vote" formula arose out of Reynolds v. Sims, 377
U.S. 533 (1964).

19. Powell v. McCormack, 395 U.S. 486 (1960).

20. LUSKY, *supra* note 15, at 314.

21. *See, e.g.,* Chamber of Commerce v. Department of Agriculture, No.
78–1515, 8 ELR 20754 (D. D.C. Oct. 10, 1978) (agency funding of views of
otherwise unrepresented parties) ("[T]he court considers it in the public
interest to allow all possible views to be placed before the agency." 8 ELR
20757). But see Greene Co. Plan. Bd. v. Federal Power Comm., 559 F.2d
1227 (2d Cir. 1977) (*en banc*), *cert. denied*, 98 S. Ct. 1280 (1978). *See generally,*
Stewart, *The Reformation of American Administrative Law*, 58 HARV. L. REV.
1669 (1975); Note, *Federal Agency Assistance to Impecunious Intervenors*, 88
HARV. L. REV. 1815 (1976).

22. *See* Javins v. First National Realty Corp., 428 F.2d 1071 (D.C. Cir.), *cert.
denied*, 400 U.S. 925 (1970); Williams v. Walker-Thomas Furniture Co., 350
F.2d 445 (D.C. Cir. 1965); Weaver v. American Oil Co., 257 Ind. 458, 276
N.E.2d 144 (1971); Seabrook v. Commuter Housing Co., 72 Misc.2d 6, 338
N.Y.S. 2d 67 (Civ. Ct. 1972).

23. W. Auden, *Elegy for J.F.K.*, ABOUT THE HOUSE 57–58 (1965).

24. Wofford, *The Blinding Light: The Uses of History in Constitutional Interpretation*, 31 U. CHI. L. REV. 502, 506 (1964), at 506 (citing Max Farrand).

25. Young, *Afterword*, THE AMERICAN REVOLUTION 449, 453 (A. Young ed.
1976). The extent of participation in and support of the revolution continues to be a matter of historical interest and debate. For a survey and
assessment of some of the extensive literature on the subject see Morgan,
The American Revolution: Was There "A People"? N.Y. REV. OF BOOKS, July
15, 1976, at 14 (pt. 1); N.Y. REV. OF BOOKS, Aug. 5, 1976, at 29 (pt. 2)
("[T]he probability remains that a majority of adult [white] males in the
colonies owned the property on which they supported their families and
were qualified to participate in the political process, that the national government, in other words, did have a popular base." *Id.* at 30).

26. Young, *supra* note 25, at 460 ("We will do better if we attempt to set the
American Revolution within the larger and longer frame of reference of
the history of Indians, blacks, and women, rather than force their history

into the framework of American political history and its periodization.").

27. After noting that revolutions require a story to hold them together, Lehmann adds that the "word *story* in this context, refers to the way in which one generation tells another how the future shapes the present out of the past." P. LEHMANN, *supra* note 12, at 7.

28. *See* R. DWORKIN, TAKING RIGHTS SERIOUSLY, 40 (1977).

29. HERODOTUS, *supra* note 2. *See* C. COCHRANE, CHRISTIANITY AND CLASSI-CAL CULTURE (1957). Herodotus' attempt to discover why the Greeks and barbarians had fought each other was a search after the *logos* which governed history. What he discovered was a cycle. As Charles Cochrane notes,

> To the Ionian physicists "souls" were nothing more or less than combinations of cosmic matter, destined as such to follow the upward and downward path ordained for nature as a whole. From this standpoint their "motion" could be explained as a result of what Herodotus calls a divine urge . . . . This urge he identifies with desire . . . which thus envisaged as the human counterpart to physical "attraction," becomes the dynamic of life. Desire demands fulfillment and this, appropriately enough, is designated by the word *eudaemonia* or *happiness*. But the self-same law which dictates the urge to *eudaemonia* also puts a limit upon it. In the language of theology the god seldom grants to men more than a "taste" of happiness and then only to snatch it from their grasp.

Id. at 462.

Caught as they are in the oscillations whereby "successive agglomerations of potential *eudaemonia* are shattered and destroyed," *id.* at 468, humans are left in the conscious impotence described in words attributed by Herodotus to a Persian: "That which is destined to come to pass as a consequence of divine activity, it is impossible for man to avert. Many of us are aware of this truth, yet we follow because we cannot do otherwise. Of all the sorrows which afflict mankind, the bitterest is this, that one should have consciousness of much, but control over nothing." *Id.*

Augustinian Christianity maintained that the discovery of Herodotus and his successors was no discovery at all but was in fact a failure of their search after causes. Faced with such "barren ideologies" as those of the classical historians, the Christians substituted "the *logos* of Christ for that of Classicism." *Id.* at 480, 474.

30. The preserving and clarifying services of story have ancient origins and have gathered importance with time. The narrative mind is not immature or pre-Socratic. The contemporary power of story has been laid bare by many and by none more movingly than Paul Fussell in a book about World War I, which provides an example of that "process by which life feeds materials to literature while literature returns the favor by conferring forms upon life." P. FUSSELL, THE GREAT WAR AND MODERN MEMORY ix (1977). He makes the case that the past, the unspeakable horror of the war in particular, contains "our own buried life" and that its study "leads

to a recognition scene, a discovery in which we see, not our past lives, but the total cultural form of our present life." N. Frye, Anatomy of Criticism 346 (1957), *quoted in* P. Fussell, *supra*, p. 335.

31. The Federalist No. 6, *supra* note 14, at 32 (Hamilton).

32. Jefferson, *Notes on Virginia*, The Life and Selected Writings of Thomas Jefferson, 265 (A. Koch & W. Peden eds. 1944). It has been said that "no other American generation has been so deeply immersed in or preoccupied with history. Indeed, we might say with considerable justice that the Founding Fathers thought history too serious a business to be left to the historians. It was the concern of all, but especially of statesmen." H. Commager, *Leadership in Eighteenth-Century America and Today*, in Freedom and Order: A Commentary on the American Political Scene 160 (1966).

For a review of what has happened to the production of history textbooks for the public schools, see Fitzgerald, *Onward and Upward with the Arts: History Textbooks*, The New Yorker, Feb. 26, 1979, at 41 (pt. 1); *id.*, Mar. 5, 1979, at 40 (pt. 2); *id.*, Mar. 12, at 48 (pt. 3).

33. *Id.*

34. *See* note 30 *supra*. James White has noted how lawyers fashion stories when they present their clients' cases in the courtroom. The judge hears two versions and then offers his own account with a conclusion "in legal language, with words that work on the world." J. White, The Legal Imagination 859 (1973). The various possibilities for retelling the story "come to an end at last with a characterization of experience in the terms of the law." *Id.* The judge speaks. "So it is," he concludes, "that one story, one set of experiences, can be connected with others; so it is that the law is made." *Id.*

Notwithstanding this observation of the role of story in the making of law, White draws a distinction "between the mind that tells a story and the mind that gives reasons," between the storyteller and the lawmaker. *Id.* at 801–02, 777. But if there is such a distinction, it is one which makes no essential difference. The legal words that work on the world are of the same order as the language of story.

35. *See* Hutcheson, *The Judgment Intuitive: The Function of the "Hunch" in Judicial Decision*, 14 Cornell L. Q. 274, 282–83 (1929). *See also* J. Frank, Courts on Trial 170–85 (1950).

36. *See, e.g., Romans* 5:17, 19 (Adam and Christ); *Hebrews* 7:12ff. (Melchizedek and Christ); *Matthew* 4:2ff. (Israel's 40 years in Sinai and Jesus' 40 days in the wilderness); *Matthew* 1:22, 2:14–18 (parallel events in Israel's history and Jesus' life). *See generally* G. Lampe & K. Wollcombe, *Essays on Typology*, in Studies in Biblical Theology No. 22 (1957); Miner, *Preface*, Literary Uses of Typology ix (E. Miner ed. 1977).

37. *See* Zwicker, *Politics and Panegyric: The Figural Mode from Marvell to Pope*, in Literary Uses of Typology, *supra* note 36, at 115, 116, 144–46.

38. *See, e.g.,* Winthrop, *A Modell of Christian Charity*, in An American Primer 8 (D. Boorstin ed. 1966).

39. Keller, *Alephs, Zahirs, and the Triumph of Ambiguity: Typology in Nineteenth-Century American Literature*, in LITERARY USES OF TYPOLOGY, *supra* note 36, at 274, 282.
40. Id., 274–314.
41. von Rad, *Typological Interpretation of the Old Testament*, in ESSAYS IN OLD TESTAMENT HERMENEUTICS, 17 (J. Bright trans., C. Westermann ed. 1963).
42. *Cf.* R. DWORKIN, *supra* note 28, at 110–15.
43. Wagner v. International Ry. Co., 232 N.Y. 176, 133 N.E. 437 (1921) (Cardozo, J.). Plaintiff and his cousin, Herbert Wagner, boarded a crowded train. Herbert was thrown from the car in the darkness. Plaintiff was injured when he went looking for Herbert. The jury should have been allowed to decide whether plaintiff's action was reasonable.
44. I do not argue that rules and principles do not figure importantly in common law adjudication. I do argue that they are penultimate. *Cf.* J. NOONAN, *supra* note 7.
45. *Cf.* R. DWORKIN, TAKING RIGHTS SERIOUSLY, *supra* note 28, at 107–10.
46. *Id.* at 109–10.
47. The common law has roots deep in English history. The *Mayflower* passengers, like their successors, evidently adopted and adapted it. *See* L. FRIEDMAN, A HISTORY OF AMERICAN LAW 14–25, 29–33, 93–100 (1973). The "reception" of the common law was a source of no little political controversy. *See* P. MILLER, THE LEGAL MIND IN AMERICA, *supra* note 7. The "snake of Americanization" of the common law was scotched but not eradicated. *Id.* at 119. The adoption of the common law was qualified by subjection to postrevolutionary legislative modification. Jefferson, among others, was emphatic: "The common law did not become, *ipso facto*, law on the new association; it could only become so by a positive adoption, and so only as they were authorized to adopt." *Letter from Thomas Jefferson to Edmund Randolph*, in THE LIFE AND SELECTED WRITINGS OF THOMAS JEFFERSON, *supra* note 4, at 552. *See also id.* at 249 (Notes on Virginia). Madison was equally explicit. The common law, he maintained, was declared as the law of the land "merely to obviate the pretexts that the separation from G. Britain threw us into a State of nature, and abolished all civil rights and obligations. Since the Revolution every State has made great inroads and with great propriety in many instances on the *monarchical* code." *Letter from James Madison to George Washington*, Oct. 18, 1787, in M. FARRAND, 3 THE RECORDS OF THE FEDERAL CONVENTION OF 1787, at 130 (1966). *See also* THE FEDERALIST No. 42, *supra* note 14, at 281 (Madison).
48. Justice Harlan believed that the Court's interpretation of the due-process clause, for example, has regarded "what history teaches are the traditions from which it developed as well as the traditions from which it broke. That tradition is a living thing" and had led the Court

> to perceive distinctions in the imperative character of Constitutional provisions, since that character must be discerned from a particular

provision's larger context. And inasmuch as this context is one not of words, but of history and purposes, the full scope of the liberty guaranteed by the Due Process Clause cannot be found in or limited by the precise terms of the specific guarantees elsewhere provided in the Constitution.

Poe v. Ullman, 367 U.S. 497, 542–43 (1961). For recent citation to Justice Harlan's views and discussion about history and tradition in adjudication, see Justice Powell's plurality opinion and Justice White's dissenting opinion in Moore v. East Cleveland, 431 U.S. 494, 501–04 & n. 12, 549–50 (1977).

The textual discussion should not be read as favoring abandonment of attention to specific passages or the constitutional text as a whole. As Charles Black says, the "question is not whether the text shall be respected, but rather how one goes about respecting a text." C. BLACK, STRUCTURE AND RELATIONSHIP IN CONSTITUTIONAL LAW 30 (1969). He argues for "the method of inference from political structure," *id.* at 13, which he alternately describes as the method of inference from "the structures and relationships created by the constitution in all its parts or in some principal part," *id.* at 7, or "the logic of national structure, as distinguished from the topic of particular textual exegesis." *Id.* at 11. I would look to the story of the beginning rather than the logic of national structure. Or, I would say that the story of beginning is the logic of national structure. On the subject generally, *compare, e.g.*, Grey, *Do We Have An Unwritten Constitution?*, 27 STAN. L. REV. 703 (1975); [*and*] *id.*, *Origins of the Unwritten Constitution: Fundamental Law in American Revolutionary Thought*, 30 STAN. L. REV. 843 (1978), *with* H. BLACK, A CONSTITUTIONAL FAITH (1969). And *see* P. BREST, PROCESSES OF CONSTITUTIONAL DECISION-MAKING (1975); C. MILLER, *supra* note 7.

49. *Compare* Wofford, *supra* note 24, at 509. ("Only the document itself bound the nation, both then and now.")

50. 384 U.S. 436 (1966).

51. *Id.* 458–60 & n. 27.

52. Ely objects "that tradition does not really generate an answer." Ely, *The Supreme Court 1977 Term: Foreword: On Discovering Fundamental Values*, 92 HARV. L. REV. 5, 39–40 (1978). But he acknowledges that objections predicated upon indeterminacy are not entirely satisfactory "if only because the implications of *any* nontrivial theory will be open to debate." *Id.* at 42. Justice Powell has noted that "an approach grounded in history imposes limits on the judiciary that are more meaningful than any based on [an] abstract formula." Moore v. East Cleveland, 431 U.S. 494, 504 n. 12 (1977).

53. James Dickey quotes the French poet Pierre Reverdy: " 'Insofar as the juxtaposition of entities be separated by the greater distance, and yet be just, the metaphor will be thereby stronger,' " J. Dickey, *Metaphor as Pure Adventure, A Lecture Delivered at the Library of Congress*, Dec. 4, 1967, at 4 (1968). Dickey adds that, if we could figure out and apply the word "juste"—just or apt—in this aphorism, "we would be a lot nearer know-

ing how the poetic metaphor lives." *Id.* We would also be nearer knowing how the law lives.

54. 217 N.Y. 382, 111 N.E. 1050 (1916).
55. *See, e.g.*, E. LEVI, AN INTRODUCTION TO LEGAL REASONING 20–27 (1949); R. DWORKIN, *supra* note 28, at 111, 116, 118–19.
56. Thomas v. Winchester, 6 N.Y. 397 (1852).
57. Losee v. Clute, 51 N.Y. 470 (1882).
58. Devlin v. Smith, 89 N.Y. 470 (1882).
59. Dyett v. Pendleton, 8 Cow. (N.Y.) 727 (1826).
60. East Haven Associates v. Gurian, 64 Misc. 2d 276, 313 N.Y.S. 2d 927 (Civ. Ct. 1970).

   For a *juste* juxtaposition of events separated by great distance, Lord Mansfield's opinion in *Moses v. Macferlan*, 2 Burr. 1005 (King's Bench 1760), surely takes a top prize. There, upon default of a debtor, an endorsee of debtor's note required payment from the endorser notwithstanding the endorsee's express agreement that he would not require the endorser so to pay. The payment in the hands of the endorsee was viewed by the court as though it were a debt accompanied by an obligation to repay. The court found that the endorsee had to make restitution to the endorser *quasi ex contractu*. By such a connection was the modern law of quasi-contract conceived. *See generally* DAWSON, UNJUST ENRICHMENT (1951).

61. J. NOONAN, *supra* note 7, at 30 (attributed to John Randolph).
62. *See id.* 54–64.
63. The reference is to Palsgraf v. Long Island R.R., 248 N.Y. 339, 162 N.E. 99 (1928), and to A.L.I., Restatement of Law of Torts Preliminary Draft No. 20, sec. 165 illustration under (f) (1928), Restatement of the Law of Torts (1934), sec. 281, illustration under (g), as the episode is recounted and commented upon in J. NOONAN, *supra* note 7, at 54–64.
64. 397 U.S. 337 (1970).
65. *Id.* at 346–47.
66. *Cf.*, Tigar, *The Supreme Court 1964 Term: Foreword: Waiver of Constitutional Rights: Disquiet in the Citadel*, 84 HARV. L. REV. 1, 26 (1970).
67. Lowance, *Typology and Millennial Eschatology in Early New England*, in LITERARY USES OF TYPOLOGY, *supra* note 36, at 228, 264 (quoting Jonathan Edwards).
68. *Id.* (quoting Jonathan Edwards).
69. *See* J. NOONAN, *supra* note 7, at 167; Ely, *supra* note 35, at 39.
70. Selection is not undertaken in order to edit out or forget the evil in our past but for the purpose of determining what of all that we remember is to be a positive ground of present action and aspiration. On the importance of not forgetting the folly and horror of our past, including our recent past, see Fussell, Untitled, N.Y. TIMES, Friday, Nov. 11, 1977, at 29, col. 2. Elsewhere Fussell has said that the irony of hope abridged is the dominant form of modern understanding. Fussell, *supra* note 11, at 35. My only question is whether "innocence savaged and destroyed," *id.* at 335,

Notes to Chapter Two

     is the complete pattern. The affirmation of the biblical story, cited later in the text, is that the pattern is one of birth-death-resurrection.

71. Dworkin, *Seven Critics*, 11 Ga. L. Rev. 1201, 1249 (1977).

72. Arendt, *Reflections: Truth and Politics*, supra note 10, at 84. Arendt noted that Herodotus had been the first to undertake the task consciously. *Id.* at 49. She provides a helpful analysis of story and judgment, and I have relied upon it. Myth also seeks to express basic reality. But myth is not bound to the corrective realities of the past and is more subject than history to political abuse.

73. *See, e.g.*, H. Cox, Turning East: The Promise and Peril of the New Orientalism (1977); R. Bly, The Kabir Book (1977).

74. C. Cochrane, *supra* note 29, at 456.

Chapter 3. Law in Place

1. *See* text *supra* at ch. 2, note 1.

2. *Deuteronomy* 6:31 (RSV).

3. Or, law was a place. I am indebted to Steven Friedell of the Rutgers-Camden Law School for calling my attention to the saying on the law from the Babylonian Talmud: "Since the day that the Temple was destroyed, the Holy One, blessed be He, has nothing in this world but the four cubits of *Halachah* alone." The Babylonia Talmud 41 (I. Epstein trans. 1948) (Berakoth 8a) (saying of R. Hiyya b. Ammi in the name of 'Ulla).

4. Lincoln, *Address Delivered at the Dedication of the Cemetery at Gettysburg*, Nov. 19, 1863, in Abraham Lincoln: His Speeches and Writings 734 (R. Basler ed. 1969).

5. F. Cornford, From Religion to Philosophy 30 (1957).

6. *Id.*

7. *Quoted in* S. Morison, The Mayflower Compact, An American Primer 19, 20 (D. Boorstin ed. 1968).

8. The Federalist No. 14, at 88 (J. Cooke ed. 1961) (Madison).

9. S. Lessard, *Reflections: The Suburban Landscape: Oyster Bay, Long Island*, The New Yorker, Oct. 11, 1976, at 44, 48.

10. L. Tribe, American Constitutional Law 15 (1978).

11. *See* H. Arendt, On Revolution 123 (1964) ("To the men of the eighteenth century . . . it was still a matter of course that they needed a constitution to lay down the boundaries of the new political realm and to define the rules within it, that they had to found and build a new political space within which the 'passion for public freedom' or the 'pursuit of public happiness' would receive free play for generations to come").

12. On Jefferson's notion of the pursuit of happiness, its background and public character, see G. Wills, Inventing America 247, 252, 254–55 (1978).

13. Montesquieu, The Spirit of the Laws, bk. XI, para. 4, at 69 (T. Nugent trans. 1952).

14. *Id.* at bk. XI, paras. 1, 6. "An *elective despotism* was not the government we fought for, but one which should not only be founded on free principles, but in which the powers of government should be so divided and balanced among several bodies of magistracy, as that no one could transcend their legal limits, without being effectually checked and restrained by others." T. Jefferson, *Notes on Virginia*, in THE LIFE AND SELECTED WRITINGS OF THOMAS JEFFERSON 237 (A. Koch & W. Peden eds. 1944).

15. United States v. Nixon, 418 U.S. 683, 704 (1974).

16. *Id.* On the power and the limits of the power of the three branches, see, e.g., Marbury v. Madison, 1 Cranch 137 (1803), and Cooper v. Aaron, 358 U.S. 1 (1958) (Court's role as interpreter of the Constitution); Powell v. McCormack, 395 U.S. 486 (1960) (House of Representatives without authority to exclude duly elected person who meets constitutional requirements for membership; excluded person's claim justiciable, not barred by political question doctrine); Youngstown Sheet & Tube Co. v. Sawyer, 343 U.S. 579 (1952) (President Truman's seizure of steel mills an unconstitutional usurpation of legislative authority); United States v. United States District Court, 407 U.S. 297 (1972) (no inherent authority in Executive to conduct warrantless surveillance in domestic security case); United States v. Curtiss-Wright Export Corp., 299 U.S. 304 (1936) (President alone has power to speak in foreign affairs as national representative).

17. On the overlap between separation of power and federalism, see L. TRIBE, *supra* note 10, at 17–18.

18. *See, e.g.,* Wickard v. Filburn, 317 U.S. 111 (1942).

19. *See* National League of Cities v. Usery, 426 U.S. 833 (1976).

20. *See, e.g.,* C. BLACK, STRUCTURE AND RELATIONSHIP IN CONSTITUTIONAL LAW 13 (1964); Bell, *Some Concluding Reflections*, 9 TOL. L. REV. 871 (1978). *See also* M. BALL, LAW OF THE SEA: FEDERAL-STATE RELATIONS, Dean Rusk Center Monograph No. 1, at 59–71 (1978).

21. Writing for the Court in National League of Cities v. Usery, 426 U.S. 833 (1976), Justice Rehnquist proposed that there are "attributes of sovereignty attaching to every state government," *id.* at 845, which limit the exercise of Congress's power to regulate commerce and which invalidate the application of federal minimum wage and hour provisions to state and local public employees as an impermissible interference "with the integral governmental function" of the states. *Id.* at 851.

In dissent, Justice Brennan averred that the majority had chosen the Bicentennial year "to repudiate principles . . . settled since the time of Chief Justice John Marshall" according to which the only restraints on Congress's commerce power "lie in the political process and not in the judicial process." *Id.* at 857. He thought that the states' political power was of such dimension as to raise the question whether concern for federalism "might better focus on whether Congress, not the States, is in greater need of this Court's protection." *Id.* at 878.

For other recent commentary on federalism, including discussion of National League of Cities, see the excellent symposium on federalism dedicated to Justice Brennan, *Symposium: Federalism*, 86 YALE L. J. 1018

Notes to Chapter Three

(1977). The relation between the national government and the states is a central and recurrent theme of both G. GUNTHER, CONSTITUTIONAL LAW 82–83 *passim* (1975), and TRIBE, *supra* note 10, 17–18 *passim*. For a bouquet of Supreme Court cases on the reach and restraints upon federal power in various contexts, see, *e.g.*, Younger v. Harris, 401 U.S. 37 (1971) (federal judicial intervention in state court proceedings as a failure to respect "our federalism"); Zschernig v. Miller, 389 U.S. 429 (1968) (barring application of state alien inheritance law as intrusion upon foreign affairs); Wickard v. Filburn, 317 U.S. 111 (1942) (Congress has power under commerce clause to regulate acts which are nationally significant in the aggregate); Cooley v. Board of Wardens of the Port of Philadelphia, 53 U.S. (12 How.) 299 (1851) (states free to regulate activities only local as compared to national in nature). *See generally*, Wechsler, *The Political Safeguards of Federalism— The Role of the States in the Composition and Selection of the National Government*, in PRINCIPLES, POLITICS, AND FUNDAMENTAL LAW 49 (1961). *See also*, M. BALL, LAW OF THE SEA: FEDERAL-STATE RELATIONS, The Dean Rusk Center Monograph No. 1 (1978).

22. THE FEDERALIST NO. 10, *supra* note 8, at 63–64 (Madison); *id.* No. 51, at 351–52 (Madison).

23. *Id.* No. 51, at 351–52.

24. *Id.* No. 10 at 60.

25. Rice v. Foster, 4 Del. (4 Harr.) 479, 487 (1847).

26. MONTESQUIEU, *supra* note 13, at bk. XI, para. 6, at 70.

27. It has been argued that the sovereignty of the people is a political fiction which it would be dangerous to take literally and consistently. Morgan, *The Great Political Fiction*, N.Y. REV. OF BOOKS, Mar. 8, 1978, at 13. Thus, Madison, who drafted the Bill of Rights, "initially considered them to be inconsistent with popular sovereignty. And so, in a sense they were and are. Indeed, they have generally operated at the insistence of that branch of government whose members are appointed for life." *Id.* at 18.

28. J. Madison, *Memorial and Remonstrance Against Religious Assessment*, in THE COMPLETE MADISON 299, 300 (S. Padover ed. 1953).

29. MONTESQUIEU, *supra* note 13, at bk. XI, para. 4, at 69.

30. THE FEDERALIST NO. 14, *supra* note 8, at 88. "The preservation of a free government requires not merely, that the metes and bounds which separate each department of power may be invariably maintained: but more especially that neither of them be suffered to overleap the great Barrier which defends the rights of the people." J. Madison, *supra* note 28, at 300.

31. E. GELLHORN, ANTITRUST LAW AND ECONOMICS IN A NUTSHELL (1976). *See also* L. SULLIVAN, ANTITRUST 14 (1977).

32. D. BONHOEFFER, LETTERS AND PAPERS FROM PRISON 105 (E. Bethge ed. 1967).

33. Warren & Brandeis, *The Right to Privacy*, 4 HARV. L. REV. 193 (1890).

34. C. GREGORY & H. KALVEN, TORTS 884 (1959). *See* PROSSER, TORTS, Ch. 20 (1955).

35. MONTESQUIEU, *supra* note 13, at bk. I, para. 1, at 1.

36. *Id.* at bk. XI, para. 6, at 74.
37. With respect to both federalism and the separation of powers, "it is *institutional interdependence* rather than *functional independence* that best summarizes the American idea of protecting liberty by fragmenting power." L. Tribe, *supra* note 10, at 17.
38. H. Thoreau, Walden 138 (1962).
39. "[B]oundaries around the self are not isolating, but can actually encourage communication with others." R. Sennett, The Fall of Public Man 10 (1978). *See also id.* at 15; A. Hollander, Seeing Through Clothes (1979) (in Western tradition, clothes are a mode of revelation, not concealment).
40. *Id.*
41. *Id.* at 6.
42. *Id.* at 6–7.
43. *See id.* at 195–96, 212, 221, 261, 264.
44. J. Matthews, *What Are You Doing There? What Are You Doing Here? A View of the Jesse Hill Ford Case,* 26 The Georgia Review 121, 135 (1972).
45. O. W. Holmes, *The Path of the Law,* 10 Harv. L. Rev. 457, 477 (1897).
46. *See* Ardrey, The Territorial Imperative (1966).
47. W. Blackstone, 1 Commentaries 138–39 (W. Lewis ed. 1898).
48. J. Bentham, Theory of Legislation 112–13 (R. Hildreth ed. 1864).
49. *Quoted in* C. Donahue, T. Kauper & P. Martin, Cases and Materials on Property 195 (1974).
50. C. Cochrane, Christianity and Classical Culture 46 (1957). *See* Cicero, 1 De Oratore para. I, 1, at 3 (E. Sutton trans. 1967) ("those men always seem to me to have been singularly happy who, with the State at her best, and while enjoying high distinctions and the fame of their achievements, were able to maintain such a course of life that they could either engage in activity that involved no risk or enjoy a dignified repose").
51. W. Lippmann, The Method of Freedom 101–02 (1934).
52. According to Cicero,

    The man in an administrative office . . . must make it his first care that everyone shall have what belongs to him and that private citizens suffer no invasion of their property rights by act of the state . . . . For the chief purpose in the establishment of constitutional state and municipal governments was that individual property rights might be secured. For, although it was by Nature's guidance that men were drawn together into communities, it was in the hope of safeguarding their possessions that they sought the protection of cities.

    2 De Officiis ch. XXI, para. 73, at 249 (W. Miller trans. 1968). According to Locke, "[t]he great and chief end . . . of men uniting into commonwealths, and putting themselves under government, is the preservation of their property." J. Locke, Two Treatises of Government, bk. II, ch. 9, para. 124.
53. C. Cochrane, *supra* note 50, at 45 (commenting on Cicero).
54. Those in the Constitutional debates who favored a property qualification

for electors believed that "[n]o one could be considered as having an inter-est in the government unless he possessed some of the soil." M. FAR-RAND, 1 THE RECORDS OF THE FEDERAL CONVENTION OF 1787, at 209 (1966) (John Dickinson). Even Madison, who opposed the property qualifica-tion, let fall that in "a certain sense the Country may be said to belong to [the owners of the soil]. If each landholder has an exclusive property in his share, the Body of Landholders have an exclusive property in the whole." Madison, *Note to His Speech on the Right of Suffrage*, 3 M. FARRAND, *supra* at 452. His compromise conceptual solution to the extension of the franchise to free men as well as freeholders was to propose that "it is bet-ter that those having the greater interest at stake, namely that of property and persons both, should be deprived of half their share in the Govern-ment; than, that those having the lesser interest, that of personal rights only, should be deprived of the whole." *Id.* at 454–55.

Harrington had maintained that "without an Agrarian law, govern-ment, whether monarchial, aristocratical, or popular, has no long lease. . . . [T]o property producing empire, it is required that it should have some certain root or foothold, which, except in land, it cannot have, being otherwise as it were upon the wing." J. Harrington, *The Commonwealth of Oceana*, in IDEAL COMMONWEALTHS 187 (J. Hawthorne ed. 1901).

Thomas Paine, it has been observed, broke with "the tradition that linked the right of voting with ownership of property. Yet he still remained tied to the idea that some sort of guarantee of personal inde-pendence was necessary in voters . . . . He insisted that property qualifi-cations were inherently unfair, since property 'makes scarce any, or no difference, in the value of the man to the community.' It seems clear that in line with his general antifederal attitudes, it was *personal* rather than economic independence which he perceived as a necessary qualification for voting." E. Foner, *Tom Paine's Republic: Radical Ideology and Social Change*, THE AMERICAN REVOLUTION 189, 210–11 (A. Young ed. 1976).

55. Sennett refers to "the effacement of the *res publica* by the belief that social meanings are generated by the feelings of individual human beings. This change has obscured for us two areas of social life. One is the realm of power, the other is the realm of the settlements in which we live." SENNETT, *supra* note 39, at 339.

56. W. BLACKSTONE, 2 COMMENTARIES 1–2 (3 Tucker ed. 1) (1803).

57. Reinhold Niebuhr spoke of "the problem of arranging some kind of armi-stice between various contending factions and forces." R. NIEBUHR, AN INTERPRETATION OF CHRISTIAN ETHICS 45 (1958). And he thought law a reflection of this political armistice: "To establish justice in a sinful world is the whole sad duty of the political order. There has never been justice without law; and all laws are the stabilization of certain social equilibria, brought about by pressures and counterpressures in society, and ex-pressed in the structures of government." REINHOLD NIEBUHR: HIS RE-LIGIOUS, SOCIAL, AND POLITICAL THOUGHT 180 (C. Kegley & R. Bretall eds. 1961). *Cf.* J. CARTER, WHY NOT THE BEST? 106 (1975). The present en-

deavor diverges from the Niebuhr-Carter position in that the proposal here begins from reconciliation, not a mere armistice. Law then springs from and serves this reconciliation and is not just the reflection of a stabilization brought about through the play of forces.

58. AUGUSTINE, THE CITY OF GOD, at bk. XVIII, ch. 2, at 610 (M. Dods trans. 1950).

59. *Id.* bk. XV, ch. 4, at 881.

60. *Id.*

61. *Id.*

62. *Id.*

63. Lessard, *supra* note 9, at 47.

64. The complement to suburban homesites are suburban business areas, which, Ada Louise Huxtable observes, are usually labeled "centers" apparently without ironic intent. These "centers," which are not centers, also have no focal center. There is about them, as Huxtable says, "no sense of place." Huxtable, *Shlockton Greets You,* N.Y. TIMES, Nov. 23, 1976, at 33, col. 2 (N.J. ed.).

65. Lessard, *supra* note 9, at 60 *passim.*

66. *Cf.* R. SENNETT, *supra* note 39 (public man has become passive spectator).

67. 426 U.S. 668 (1976).

68. *Id.* at 673.

69. Sager, *Insular Majorities Unabated*: Warth v. Seldin *and* City of Eastlake v. Forest City Enterprises, Inc., 91 HARV. L. REV. 1373, 1425 (1978).

70. Cochrane observes that "whereas the Greek *polis* had carried with it the suggestion of 'one big family' or an all-in partnership, the term *res publica* could hardly be used without an implied reference to its counterpart, *res privata. Res privata,* although distinct from, was not in conflict with *res publica,* but rather its correlative, indissolubly linked to it by what may be called 'a principle of polarity' and, in a precisely analogous sense, the object of right." C. COCHRANE, *supra* note 1, at 46.

71. AUGUSTINE, *supra* note 58, at bk. XV, ch. 5, at 482.

72. G. WILLS, *supra* note 12, at 195, 231, 234–37.

73. Madison, *Property, National Gazette,* Mar. 29, 1792, in THE MIND OF THE FOUNDER 243 (M. Meyers ed. 1973).

74. *Id.* at 244.

75. *Letter from Thomas Jefferson to Joseph Cabell, supra* note 14, at 660. *See generally* H. ARENDT, *supra* note 11, at 252 *passim.*

76. *Id.,* Jefferson, *supra* note 14.

77. *Id.*

78. *See* text at note 51 *supra.*

79. *See* C. MILLER, THE SUPREME COURT AND THE USES OF HISTORY 187 (1969); W. MURPHY, CONGRESS AND THE COURT 1 (1962). It is possible that the aura of some courtrooms is a vestige of the ancient practice of setting apart from the ordinary world a sacred spot for the pronouncement of judgment. *See* J. HUIZINGA, HOMO LUDENS, A STUDY OF THE PLAY-ELEMENT IN CULTURE 76–77 (1949). *See also* F. CORNFORD, FROM RELIGION TO PHILOSO-

Notes to Chapter Three

PHY 31–33 (1912). But many lower state courtrooms evoke profane responses; on their inadequate condition and undesirable effects, see N.
DORSEN & L. FRIEDMAN, DISORDER IN THE COURT 239–40 (1973); Tigar,
*The Supreme Court 1969 Term: Foreword: Waiver of Constitutional Rights: Dis-
quiet in the Citadel*, 84 HARV. L. REV. 1, 5–6 (1970).
80. COURTHOUSE (R. Pare ed. 1978).
81. Reardon, *The Origins and Impact of the County Court System*, in *id.* at 19.
82. *The Center of the Community*, THE N.Y. TIMES BOOK REV., July 23, 1978, at
15.

✺ Chapter 4. Judicial Theater

1. *See* note 46 *infra* and accompanying text; Griswold, *The Standards of the
Legal Profession: Canon 35 Should Not Be Surrendered*, 48 A.B.A.J. 615, 616
(1962) ("A courtroom is not a stage; and witnesses and lawyers, and
judges and juries and parties, are not players. A trial is not a drama, and
it is not held for public information").
2. For recent, helpful commentary on the law as drama, especially with respect to its relation to religion, see H. BERMAN, THE INTERACTION OF LAW
AND RELIGION 31–37, 74, 148–50 n. 12 (1974).
3. *See* W. BAUMOL & W. BOWEN, PERFORMING ARTS—THE ECONOMIC DI-
LEMMA 161–72 (1966), which explores the relationship of productivity
gains and the technology of live performance. The idea advanced in this
paragraph is a pale, partial reflection of their suggestive formulation.
4. The development of a "consumer perspective" among some lawyers has
led them to accept certain streamlining of appellate court procedures,
e.g., providing full court procedures only where basic interests are at
stake. *See* Weaver, *Lawyers in Favor of Court Revision*, N.Y. TIMES, Dec. 2,
1974, § 1, at 36, col. 3.
5. In the course of a discussion of the crime control and due-process models ventured by Herbert Packer, John Griffiths noted that both models
"are concerned only with the relationship of trials and pleas to the end
of the process—punishment of the guilty. But if a trial can be seen as
a goal in itself—a lesson in legal procedure, dignity, fairness and justice, for the public and for the accused (whether he is convicted or
acquitted)—we would not want to lose its potential for good by encouraging shortcircuits. Because of the constraints imposed by our ideology
about criminal procedure, speculation in this direction has been almost
entirely neglected." Griffiths, *Ideology in Criminal Procedure or A Third
"Model" of the Criminal Process*, 79 YALE L. J. 359, 398 (1970).
6. *See* AESCHYLUS, THE EUMENIDES.
7. *See* W. SHAKESPEARE, THE MERCHANT OF VENICE, act IV, scene 1; KING
LEAR, act III, scene 6.
8. *See* D. BERRIGAN, THE TRIAL OF THE CATONSVILLE NINE (1970).
9. Eric Bentley has observed,

To begin with, the theatre is a place. This place, in all known forms, sets up such a vibration in those who frequent it that certain properties roughly suggested by the term magic are invariably attributed to the building itself. In our epoch, for example, how many journalists, and even college freshmen, have mentioned the expectant lull when the lights dim, and the thrill when the curtain rises! This, you say, may be partly a matter of audience psychology. It remains true that the paraphernalia of the theatre has of itself remarkable suggestive power. Even when no audience is present, even when the stage is bare of scenery and the brick wall at the rear is exposed, the curious machine retains an insidious attraction.

E. Bentley, The Theatre of Commitment 55 (1967).

10. On the judicial robe, see J. Frank, Courts on Trial 254–61 (1950) (criticizing the robe); A.B.A. Project on Standards for Criminal Justice, Standards Relating to the Function of the Trial Judge § 1.3, at 29–30 (Approved Draft 1972).

11. There are, for example, the "Oyez" and the response of rising at the judge's entrance.

12. See J. Huizinga, Homo Ludens, A Study of the Play-Element in Culture 76–77 (1949). See also F. Cornford, From Religion to Philosophy 31–33 (1912). But many lower state courtrooms evoke profane responses; on their inadequate condition and undesirable effects, see N. Dorsen & L. Friedman, Disorder in the Court 239–40 (1973); Tigar, *The Supreme Court 1969 Term: Foreword: Waiver of Constitutional Rights: Disquiet in the Citadel*, 84 Harv. L. Rev. 1, 5–6 (1970). See ch. 3, n. 86.

13. 346 F. Supp. 401, 402, 404 (W.D.N.C. 1972).

14. *Id.* at 404.

15. *Id.*

16. 100 Neb. 199, 158 N.W. 930 (1916). The defendant's conviction of murder in the first degree was reversed because of, among other reasons, its staging.

17. 100 Neb. at 203, 158 N.W. at 931–32 (1916), *quoted in* Estes v. Texas, 381 U.S. 532, 573 (1965) (Warren, C. J., concurring).

18. 381 U.S. 532, 552 (1965).

19. *Id.* at 561 (Warren, C. J., concurring) (citation omitted). *See id.* at 572–73.

20. *Id.* at 557, 565, 573–84.

21. *Id.* at 571.

22. *Id.* at 573.

23. J. Bentham, *Rationale of Judicial Evidence*, in 6 Works of Jeremy Bentham 353, 354 *passim* (J. Bowring ed. 1838–1843). Bentham referred to the courtroom as "the main theatre of justice" and the judge's chambers as the "little theatre of justice." *Id.* at 354.

24. *See, e.g.*, P. Brook, The Empty Space 127 (1968).

25. *In re* Oliver, 333 U.S. 257 (1948). *See* U.S. Const. amend. VI: J. Wigmore, 6 Evidence §§ 1834–35, pp. 332–44 (1940); Annot. 49 A.L.R. 3d 1007 (1973). *But cf.* Radin, *The Right to a Public Trial*, 6 Temp. L. Q. 381 (1932).

Notes to Chapter Four

When the "public" involved are news media, then there is a constellation of problems on which there is extensive and developing case law
and literature. *See, e.g.,* Richmond Newspapers, Inc. v. Virginia, 65
L.Ed. 2d 973 (1900); Sheppard v. Maxwell, 384 U.S. 333 (1966).

26. *See, e.g.,* Estes v. Texas, 381 U.S. 532, 588 (1965) (Harlan, J., concurring);
In re Oliver, 333 U.S. 257, 270 (1948). For other grounds supporting pub-
lic trials, see *In re* Oliver, 333 U.S. 257, 270 n. 24 (1948); United States v.
Kobli, 172 F.2d 919 (3d Cir. 1949); J. WIGMORE, *supra* note 25, § 1834.

27. Oxnard Publishing Co. v. Superior Ct., 68 Cal. Rptr. 83, 95 (2d Dist.
1968) (hearing granted in California Supreme Court was dismissed as
moot due to change of venue).

28. *Id.* at 97.

29. Mueller, *Problems Posed by Publicity to Crime and Criminal Proceedings,* 110
U. PA. L. REV. 1, 6 (1961).

30. *Id.* at 6–7. *But see* Friedman, *San Benito 1890: Legal Snapshot of a County,*
27 STAN. L. REV. 687, 698 (1975), which draws a darker picture of early
justice in rural America: "The newspapers seemed totally innocent of
any notion of the majesty and awesomeness of law. No doubt citizens
had ideas about fair trials and fair play and some pride in their legal system; at the same time, they knew it cynically as a powerful weapon of
social control, a magnificent instrument for insuring power and wealth."
Concludes Friedman, "Legal process was a game, a weapon, and an entertainment." *Id.* at 700.

31. U.S. CONST. art. III, § 2; amend. VI; amend. VII.

32. *See, e.g.,* Taylor v. Louisiana, 419 U.S. 522, 530; McKeiver v. Pennsylvania, 403 U.S. 528, 554–56 (1971) (Brennan, J., concurring in part, dissenting in part) (juvenile proceedings); Duncan v. Louisiana, 391 U.S.
145, 151–56 (1968); THE FEDERALIST No. 83, at 562–65 (Cooke ed. 1967)
(A. Hamilton). *But see* H. KALVEN & H. ZEISEL, THE AMERICAN JURY 296
(1966).

33. *See* Fed. R. Crim. P. 23(a); Fed. R. Civ. P. 38(d). See also Singer v. United
States, 380 U.S. 24 (1965) (defendant may not waive "right" to jury trial
without consent of government).

34. In criminal cases, juries are not required for the trial of "petty" offenses.
See, e.g., Frank v. United States, 395 U.S. 147 (1969); Dyke v. Taylor Im-
plement Mfg. Co., 391 U.S. 216 (1968); Cheff v. Schnackenberg, 384 U.S.
373 (1966). Nor are juries required in juvenile proceedings. McKeiver v.
Pennsylvania, 403 U.S. 528 (1971). As a rule, juries are not utilized in equity. *See* Katchen v. Landy, 382 U.S. 323 (1966); James, *Right to a Jury Trial
in Civil Action,* 72 YALE L. J. 655 (1963); O'Neil, *Law or Equity: The Right to
Trial by Jury in a Civil Action,* 35 Mo. L. REV. 43 (1970). *Cf.* Chesin & Hazard, *Chancery Procedure and the Seventh Amendment: Jury Trial of Issues in
Equity Cases Before 1791,* 83 YALE L. J. 999 (1974), *with* Langbein, *Fact
Finding in the English Court of Chancery: A Rebuttal,* 83 YALE L. J. 1620
(1974). *See also* Note, *Congressional Provision for Nonjury Trial under the
Seventh Amendment,* 83 YALE L. J. 401 (1973).

The Supreme Court is expanding those occasions when a jury may be required but contracting the size and voting requirements of the jury when it is employed. On the expansion of the jury right in criminal cases, see Bloom v. Illinois, 391 U.S. 194 (1968). On the same in civil cases, see Pernell v. Southall Realty, 416 U.S. 363 (1974); Curtis v. Loether, 415 U.S. 189 (1974); Ross v. Bernhard, 396 U.S. 531 (1970); Dairy Queen, Inc. v. Wood, 369 U.S. 469 (1962); Beacon Theaters, Inc. v. Westover, 359 U.S. 500 (1959). On the matter of nonunanimous votes, see Johnson v. Louisiana, 406 U.S. 356 (1972); Apodaca v. Oregon, 406 U.S. 404 (1972). On the issue of juries of less than 12, see Colgrove v. Battin, 413 U.S. 149 (1973); Williams v. Florida, 399 U.S. 78 (1970).

35. For a description of the historical transformation whereby jurors became triers of fact instead of witnesses, see Estes v. Texas, 381 U.S. 532, 557–58 (1965) (Warren, C. J., concurring).
36. The dominant role of the judge is that of director. *See* text accompanying note 40 *infra*. Even when a case is tried to a jury, however, the judge is also an audience.
37. J. GROTOWSKI, TOWARDS A POOR THEATRE 32 (1968).
38. An accused has the right to be "confronted with the witnesses against him." U.S. CONST. amend. VI. The dramatic potential of the right is underlined by the fact that its purpose is

> to prevent depositions or *ex parte* affidavits . . . being used against the prisoner in lieu of a personal examination and cross-examination of the witness in which the accused has an opportunity, not only of testing the recollection and sifting the conscience of the witness, but of compelling him to stand face to face with the jury in order that they may look at him, and judge by his demeanor upon the stand and the manner in which he gives his testimony whether he is worthy of belief.

Mattox v. United States, 156 U.S. 237, 242–43 (1895). The two-fold content of the right—both cross-examination of accusers and the observation of their demeanor by the jury—was reaffirmed in Barber v. Page, 390 U.S. 719, 725 (1968). However, more recent cases have emphasized cross-examination that can occur prior to trial, with the consequence that the dramatic possibilities are eliminated. *See* Dutton v. Evans, 400 U.S. 74 (1970); California v. Green, 399 U.S. 149 (1970); Griswold, *The Due Process Revolution and Confrontation*, 119 U. PA. L. REV. 711 (1971).
39. Simonett, *The Trial as One of the Performing Arts*, 52 A.B.A.J. 1145 (1966).
40. See Sheppard v. Maxwell, 384 U.S. 333 (1966) ("The carnival atmosphere at trial could easily have been avoided since the courtroom and courthouse premises are subject to the control of the court." *Id.* at 358); Dagnello v. Long Island R.R., 289 F.2d 797, 805 (2d Cir. 1961); Moore v. State, 46 Ohio App. 433, 437, 188 N.E. 881, 883 (1933) ("The test in determining whether the absence of the judge from the courtroom during the progress of the trial calls for a reversal of the judgment is whether, by his absence, he loses control of the proceedings").

41. It should be noted, however, that even within the small play alone, the roles of the judge and jury may shade over into participation as actors. In the judge's case, this is most likely to happen when the judge exercises his prerogative to call and question witnesses, *see* Jackson v. United States, 329 F.2d 893 (D.C. Cir. 1964), or to comment upon the evidence, *see* Patton v. United States, 281 U.S. 276, 288 (1930) (dictum); *but see* H. KALVEN & H. ZEISEL, *supra* note 32, at 420 (state courts). The jury assumes the role of actor in the small play when it renders the verdict. It may also be permitted to participate in the small play's action by asking questions. *See* Sparks v. Daniels, 343 S.W.2d 661, 667 (Mo. Ct. App. 1961); State v. Martinez, 7 Utah 2d 387, 389, 326 P.2d 102, 103 (1958). For a suggestion that the jury ought to be encouraged to assume a greater role, see Tigar, *supra* note 12, at 27. In fact, judges and counsel seldom raise the possibility of participation by the jury.

42. The French word for performance, *representation*, aptly suggests the theatrical role of appellate counsel.

> A representation is the occasion when something is represented, when something from the past is shown again—something that once was, now is. For representation it is not an imitation or description of a past event, a representation denies time. It abolishes that difference between yesterday and today. It takes yesterday's action and makes it live again in every one of its aspects—including its immediacy. In other words, a representation is what it claims to be—making present.

P. BROOK, *supra* note 24, at 139.

The right to counsel applies both to criminal trials, Gideon v. Wainwright, 372 U.S. 335 (1963), and to the first appeal as of right, Douglas v. California, 373 U.S. 353 (1963), but not to discretionary appeal, Ross v. Moffit, 417 U.S. 600 (1974). For recent concern about the quality of advocacy, see Burger, *The Special Skills of Advocacy: Are Specialized Training and Certification of Advocates Essential to Our System of Justice?*, 42 FORDHAM L. REV. 227 (1973); Bazelon, *The Defective Assistance of Counsel*, 42 U. CIN. L. REV. I (1973); Palmer, *Implementing the Obligation of Advocacy in Review of Criminal Convictions*, 65 J. CRIM. L. & C. 267 (1974).

43. Dewey, *Logical Method and Law*, 10 CORNELL L. Q. 7, 27 (1924).
44. *Id.* at 26.
45. Dewey, *supra* note 43, at 23.
46. Radin, *supra* note 25, at 395.
47. F. FERGUSSON, THE IDEA OF A THEATER 166 (1949).
48. *Id.* at 147.
49. J. Grotowski, *supra* note 37, at 63.
50. *Id.* at 63–64.
51. McCarthy, *Nicola Chiaromonte and the Theatre*, N.Y. REV. OF BOOKS, Feb. 20, 1975, at 29.
52. *Id.*
53. Chiaromonte, *On Pirandello's "Clothing the Naked,"* N.Y. REV. OF BOOKS, Feb. 20, 1975, at 31.

54. *Id.*
55. Ms. McCarthy notes, for example,
    The actor, willing or unwilling, in each of us perceives his prototype on the stage, a walking shadow, the shade of a shade . . . . Now in so far as we are all actors or doers (it comes to the same, for doing, as exposed on the stage, is mere feinting, shadow play), the mask we put on is only a metaphor for the illusion we project whenever we appear among others . . . . The incomprehensible mixture of reality and unreality that we are aware of in the acts we perform is dramatically present in the situation of the actor, who consents for our pleasure to be someone both real and unreal.
    McCarthy, *supra* note 50, at 29.
56. Judge Frank labored to make it clear that "[t]he actual events, the real objective acts and words of [litigants], happened in the past. They do not walk into court. The court usually learns about these real, objective, past facts only through the oral testimony of fallible witnesses. Accordingly, the court, from hearing the testimony, must guess at the actual, past facts." J. FRANK, *supra* note 10, at 15–16. He saw that the proving of facts "is at the mercy of such matters as mistaken witnesses, perjured witnesses, missing or dead witnesses, mistaken judges, inattentive judges, biased judges, inattentive juries, and biased juries." *Id.* at 27. Although he rightly referred to these matters as "imperfections," *id.* at 27 n. 16, there is a more fundamental mix of illusion and reality in the presentation of facts in court.
    This mix is part of the human condition and is not the consequence of defaults in the way the "facts" of a case are "proved." Indeed, the impossibility of presenting literal reality in court may be due to human physiology itself. Structuralists such as Claude Lévi-Strauss (anthropology), Jean Piaget (psychology), Noam Chomsky (linguistics), and Gunther Stent (biology) have contended that the reality we perceive and respond to is largely determined and confined by the structure of our nervous system. As Stent explained,
    structuralism recognizes that information about the world enters the mind not as raw data but as highly abstract structures that are the result of a preconscious set of step-by-step transformations of the sensory input. Each transformation step involves the selective destruction of information according to a program that preexists in the brain. Any set of primary sense data becomes meaningful only after a series of such operations performed on it has transformed the data set into a pattern that matches a preexisting mental structure.
    Stent, *Cellular Communication*, SCIENTIFIC AMERICAN, Sept. 1972, at 43, 50–51. *See also* Arnheim, *Perceptional Abstraction and Art*, in TOWARD A PSYCHOLOGY OF ART 27 (1972).
57. L. FULLER, LEGAL FICTIONS 24 (1967).
58. *Id.* at 24–26.
59. H. FOWLER, A DICTIONARY OF MODERN ENGLISH USAGE 558 (2d ed. 1965).
60. It is arresting, but unnecessarily pejorative, to refer to the attorney's case

as a "lie" simply because he must proceed by substitution. Although F. S. Cohen refers to the lawyer's presentation as "lying," he apparently intends no moral condemnation by the term.

> In a certain sense, it is true that lawyers are liars. In the same sense, poets, historians, and map-makers are also liars. For it is the function of lawyers, poets, historians, and map-makers not to reproduce reality but to illumine some aspect of reality, and it always makes for deceit to pretend that what is thus illumined is the whole of reality. None of us can ever possibly tell the whole truth, though we may conscientiously will to do so and ask divine help towards that end. The ancient wisdom of our common law recognizes that men are bound to differ in their views of fact and law, not because some are honest and others dishonest, but because each of us operates in a value-charged field which gives shape and color to whatever we see. The proposition that no man should be a judge of his own cause embodies the ancient wisdom that only a many-perspectived view of the world can relieve us of the endless anarchy of one-eyed vision.

Cohen, *Field Theory and Judicial Logic*, 59 YALE L. J. 238, 242 (1950).

61. The exclusionary rule is discussed in ch. 5.
62. In a review of Mary McCarthy's WATERGATE PORTRAITS, Richard Goodwin proposed that, as distinguished from the view that truth is immanent in facts, "our tradition of criminal justice assumes we are more likely to approach correct knowledge by imposing news [*sic*—views?] about character, probability and feeling on the external evidence and on the competing logics of analysis." Goodwin, *Watergate Observed: The Mask of State*, N.Y. TIMES, June 30, 1974, § 7 (Book Review), at 5. Similarly, with respect to the criminal process, Packer spoke of the "tyranny of the actual" that may obscure value choices. H. PACKER, THE LIMITS OF THE CRIMINAL SANCTION 152 (1968).
63. Patterson v. Colorado, 205 U.S. 454, 462 (1907).
64. *Id. Cf.* Irvin v. Dowd, 366 U.S. 717, 729–30 (1961) (Frankfurter, J., dissenting).
65. Even *raising* all the questions involved in a discussion of the relationship between truth and justice would require us to range far afield. But a brief word on the subject may be ventured.

It is possible to begin with the premise that "truth" and "the facts" are roughly equivalent and then proceed to different conclusions about the relation of truth and justice in trials. On the one hand, it could be argued that all the facts ought to be admitted into evidence at trials because all the truth is necessary in order for justice to be done (and the exclusionary rule, for example, therefore offends both truth and justice). On the other hand, it could be concluded that there are circumstances when all the facts should not be allowed as evidence because truth must sometimes be sacrificed to other valued ends for justice to be done (and the exclusionary rule is consequently viewed as serving justice but not truth).

A fresh approach to the relation between truth and justice at trial is made available by calling the initial premise into question. Is truth to be equated with the facts? Possibly not. For suggestive exploration of truth as something other than "optimal verbal veracity," see P. Lehmann, Ethics in a Christian Context 124–30 (1963); D. Bonhoeffer, Ethics 326–34 (E. Bethge ed. 1955). If truth and facts are not readily subject to equation, then it is possible that truth may be arrived at without the consideration of all the facts. Thus, trials which do justice, notwithstanding the omission of some facts, may also arrive at truth. (The exclusionary rule could then be said to serve both truth and justice.)

66. Different views have been expressed about the relationship between trials and truth. For example, Berman maintained that "[a] judicial proceeding is primarily a method of deciding what ought to be done in a given situation and only secondarily a scientific investigation of the truth. It is concerned with what happened only insofar as what happened is thought to be relevant to a possible decision, a possible outcome of the case." Berman, *Introduction* to The Trial of the U2 at xxvii–xxviii (1960). Lord Devlin expressed a somewhat different view. "Trial by jury is not an instrument of getting at the truth; it is a process designed to make it as sure as possible that no innocent man is convicted." H. Kalven & H. Zeisel, *supra* note 32, at 190.

On the other hand, Justice Stewart writing for the Court in Tehan v. United States *ex rel* Shott, 382 U.S. 406, 416 (1966), said, "The basic purpose of a trial is the determination of truth." However, he went on to note that "the Fifth Amendment's privilege against self-incrimination is not an adjunct to the ascertainment of truth." *Id. See* note 65 *supra.*

67. Aristotle, Poetics 25 (G. Else trans. 1965); F. Fergusson, *supra* note 47, at 246; McCarthy, *supra* note 51, at 25, 28.

68. A. Chekhov, *Letter to Alexey S. Suvorin*, Apr. 18, 1892, in The Portable Chekhov 624–25 (A. Yarmolinsky ed. 1947).

69. "In the theater our function is not to fix and assess a penalty, but to feel pity and fear—and to enjoy whatever pleasure may arise from those emotions." G. Else, Aristotle's Poetics: The Argument (1957), quoted in The Modern Theatre 10–11 (D. Seltzer ed. 1967).

70. *See, e.g.,* P. Brook, *supra* note 24, at 136.

71. *See* notes 21–23 *supra* and accompanying text; note 129 *infra* and accompanying text.

72. Davis, *The Requirement of a Trial-Type Hearing*, 70 Harv. L. Rev. 193, 199 (1956).

73. *Id.; see id.* at 195. The allocation of adjudicative fact decisions to trial and of legislative facts to oral argument and briefs is not so rigid as to allow of no exceptions. *See id.* at 216.

74. *Cf.* K. Llewellyn, The Common Law Tradition 121–22 (1960).

75. Davis cites the particular example of Justice Brandeis's dissent in Jay Burns Baking Co. v. Bryan, 264 U.S. 504, 517 (1924). Davis, *supra* note 72, at 193, 215 & n. 82.

76. *See* notes 41–42 *supra* and accompanying text.

77. *See, e.g.,* K. Llewellyn, *supra* note 74, at 240 ("In oral argument lies the opportunity to catch attention and rouse interest").

Notes to Chapter Four

78. *See, e.g.,* Black, *The National Courts of Appeals: An Unwise Proposal,* 83 YALE L. J. 883, 888–90 (1974).
79. Lewis, *Lawyers and Civilization,* 120 U. PA. L. REV. 851, 862 (1972). *See generally* United States v. Dellinger, 472 F.2d 340 (7th Cir. 1972); *In re* Dellinger, 461 F.2d 389 (7th Cir. 1972); United States v. Seale, 461 F.2d 345 (7th Cir. 1972); *In re* Dellinger, 370 F. Supp. 1304 (N.D. Ill., Feb. 14, 1970), *reprinted in In re* Dellinger, 461 F.2d 389, 404 (7th Cir. 1972); Clark, *Foreword,* & Kalven, *Introduction* to CONTEMPT: TRANSCRIPT OF THE CONTEMPT CITATIONS, SENTENCES, AND RESPONSES OF THE CHICAGO CONSPIRACY 10 (1970); Comment, *Invoking Summary Contempt Procedures—Use or Abuse? United States v. Dellinger—The "Chicago Seven" Contempts,* 69 MICH. L. REV. 1549 (1971).
80. Hazard, Book Review, 80 YALE L. J. 433, 446 (1970).
81. *Cf.* Illinois v. Allen, 397 U.S. 337 (1970). Berman has suggested that new rituals are necessary for trials in which defendants seek to proclaim political views, and he cites the trial of the Catonsville Nine as a case in which defendants were allowed to express their views. H. BERMAN, *supra* note 8, at 42. It has been suggested that "rituals will bend" to allow greater participation by criminal defendants, Tigar, *supra* note 12, at 27.
82. Hazard, *supra* note 80, at 446. Hazard concludes,

    The established order . . . by its own terms cannot win the struggle by the threatening mechanisms of legal prescription and penal sanction. It can win only through steadfast and unpretentious fulfillment of official roles, especially that of the judge . . . . [I]t is well to recognize that the struggles represented in political trials will not disappear until fundamental political dissension also disappears. That day may be less welcome than many might think.

    Id. at 450. A Special Committee on Courtroom Conduct of the Association of the Bar of the City of New York discovered that "[i]n many cases [of disruption], the judges reported that they were able to handle the disruptions simply by impressing on the defendants that they would receive a fair trial and acting to protect the defendants' rights." N. DORSEN & L. FRIEDMAN, *supra* note 12, at 6.
83. *Cf., e.g.,* Illinois v. Allen, 397 U.S. 337, 352–56 (1970) (Douglas, J., concurring).
84. Arnold, *The Criminal Trial as a Symbol of Public Morality,* in Y. KAMISAR, F. INBAU, & T. ARNOLD, CRIMINAL JUSTICE IN OUR TIME 137, 143–44 (1965) ("Trials are like the miracle or morality of plays of ancient times. They dramatically present the conflicting moral values of a community in a way that could not be done by logical formalization. Civil trials perform this function as well as do criminal trials"); J. MORTON, THE FUNCTION OF CRIMINAL LAW IN 1962 at 30 (1962) ("It is my contention that the criminal trial is not merely suitable stuff for a play but *is itself a play,* a drama deliberately staged in furtherance of the great general end of the criminal process, that citizens should so conduct themselves as to avoid the types of behavior which society has legally condemned. That the criminal trial is

a contemporary morality play gives new meaning to the whole criminal process").

85. *See* Anon., *The Summoning of Everyman* in THE DEVELOPMENT OF ENGLISH DRAMA 35 (E. Bentley ed. 1950).

86. *Id.*

87. *See* ch. 5, notes 43–46, 82–85 *infra* and accompanying text.

88. 381 U.S. 532 (1965).

89. *Id.* at 575, 576. The Chief Justice's comment appears to grant that the U-2 trial was a good faith attempt to determine guilt as well as an educational lesson. Other Soviet trials may have been only a lesson whose point was not justice or the good faith determination of guilt. *See* A. SOLZHENIT-SYN, THE GULAG ARCHIPELAGO 299–431 (1973). According to Solzhenit-syn, the only purpose of trials was didactic, and they served as glosses on a Stalinistic sermon. They required careful management and had to be given up when they failed to keep to prearranged form. *See id.* at 419–31.

The potentially educative effect of trials is not to be denied. My point in the text is that this effect comes properly from the nature of the trial process as such and not from some superimposed or spurious object lesson. *Cf.* Griffiths, *supra* note 3, at 359–60. Ideally, the process should be instructive of the worth of people, which would be communicated by the respect and concern shown people in the process. *Cf.* Griffiths, *supra*, at 384–85.

90. *See* J. FRAZER, THE GOLDEN BOUGH 675–79 (abr. ed. 1951).

91. *See* E. BENTLEY, THEATRE OF WAR 353 (1972).

92. *See* N. DORSEN & L. FRIEDMAN, *supra* note 12, at 13–15; *cf.* Moore v. Dempsey, 261 U.S. 86 (1923); Frank v. Mangum, 237 U.S. 309 (1915).

93. J. HUIZINGA, *supra* note 12, at 13.

94. *See* J. HUIZINGA, *supra* note 12, at 73, 76–88, 30–31, 48–53, 1–13. Huizinga's study is richly suggestive, and brief references to it must be supplemented by the acknowledgment that this essay has been much aided by it. *See also* notes 69–71 *supra* and accompanying text.

95. J. HUIZINGA, *supra* note 12, at 84.

96. *See* D. BERRIGAN, *supra* note 6.

97. *See* R. HOCHHUTH, THE DEPUTY (R. & C. Winston trans. 1964). The subject of Hochhuth's controversial drama was the relationship of Pope Pius XII to the Third Reich. Specifically, the play raised questions about Pius's failure to take a public stance against the extermination of the Jews.

98. The plays of Pirandello, Ibsen, and Genet are examples of other types that may be likened to judicial theater. *Cf., eg.,* Chiaromonte, *supra* note 53, at 30; McCarthy, *supra* note 51, at 25, 29.

99. *See* notes 69–70 *supra* and accompanying text; notes 127–29 *infra* and accompanying text.

100. *See* Frank, *supra* note 10, at 21.

101. *See* Note, *Video-Tape Trials: A Practical Evaluation and a Legal Analysis,* 26 STAN. L. REV. 619, 623–24 & nn. 29–30 (1974).

Notes to Chapter Four

102. *Cf. id.*, with Note, *Videotape Trials: Legal and Practical Implications*, 9 COL. J. L. & SOC. PROB. 363, 374 n. 67, 381, 389–90 (1973). *See also* Brakel, *Videotape in Trial Proceedings: A Technological Obsession?*, 61 A.B.A.J. 956 (1975); Doret, *Trial by Videotape—Can Justice Be Seen To Be Done?*, 47 TEMP. L. Q. 228, 241–61 (1974). For judicial comment, see Hendricks v. Swenson, 156 F.2d 503, 506, 507–09 (8th Cir. 1972).

103. E. BENTLEY, *supra* note 9, at 207. *Cf.* F. FERGUSSON, *supra* note 47, at 250–55 (on the "histrionic sensibility").

104. In an intriguing analysis of the United Nations as drama, Conor Cruise O'Brien proposed that "for the preservation of peace among actual un-improved men the agonistic element remains of the greatest importance, for letting off steam, for saving face, for sanctifying retreat, for purification, and in other ways." C. O'BRIEN & F. TOPOLSKI, THE UNITED NATIONS: SACRED DRAMA 282 (1968). *See also* J. HUIZINGA, *supra* note 12, at 46–75 ("Play and Contest as Civilizing Functions").

105. Lorenz maintained that "it is particularly the drives that have arisen by ritualization which are so often called upon . . . to oppose aggression, to divert it into harmless channels, and to inhibit those of its actions that are injurious to the survival of the species." K. LORENZ, ON AGGRESSION 67 (1966). *See* C. O'BRIEN & F. TOPOLSKI, *supra* note 104, at 275–85.

106. Chambers v. Baltimore & O.R.R., 207 U.S. 142, 148 (1907). The Court went on to say that the right to sue and defend is "conservative of all other rights, and lies at the foundation of orderly government." *Id. See* Missouri v. Illinois 200 U.S. 496, 520–21 (1906). *See also* J. FRANK *supra* note 10, at 5–9, 26–27.

107. *See* J. HUIZINGA, *supra* note 12, at 49 ("'There is something at stake'—the essence of play is contained in that phrase").

108. J. WIGMORE, A KALEIDOSCOPE OF JUSTICE 487 (1941), *quoted in* Estes v. Texas, 381 U.S. 532, 570 (1965) (Warren, C.J., concurring). Huizinga reports from an English newspaper the story that "a judge received a visit from a man who had lost his case on the previous day, but now said contentedly: 'I had a very bad lawyer, you know, all the same I'm glad to have had a good run for my money!'" J. HUIZINGA, *supra* note 12, at 84.

109. *See* notes 93–95 *supra* and accompanying text. Stanley Kauffman has observed that while the seriousness of judicial theater is sufficient in itself to sustain audience interest, ordinary theater requires something more to achieve the same objective.

> For the spectator, what holds it all together between the high points of interest is the constant realization that a live man—right there before you—will or will not have years sheared off his free life because of these proceedings . . . . In the actual courtroom, a civilized man wants primarily to see justice done: At the courtroom play [*i.e.*, a stage drama about a trial or in a trial setting], that same civilized man wants to see blood—either the defendant's or, if he is innocent, the true culprit's. A courtroom play that merely proved the defendant's innocence and found nobody guilty would fizzle.

Kauffman, *supra* note 107, at col. 5.

110. As Huizinga concluded about play and its rules in general,
     real civilization cannot exist in the absence of a certain play-element,
     for civilization presupposes limitation and mastery of the self, the
     ability not to confuse its own tendencies with the ultimate and high-
     est goal, but to understand that it is enclosed within certain bounds
     freely accepted . . . . To be a sound culture-creating force this play-
     element must be pure. It must not consist in the darkening or debas-
     ing of standards set up by reason, faith or humanity. It must not be a
     false seeming, a masking of political purposes behind the illusion of
     genuine play-forms. True play knows no propaganda.
     J. Huizinga, *supra* note 12, at 211.

111. S. Coleridge, *Biographia Literaria* in Selected Poetry and Prose 264
     (D. Stauffer ed. 1951).

112. *Id.* at 349. *See also* S. Coleridge, *Lectures and Notes on Poetry, Drama, Shake-
     speare, and Other Critical Notes, id.* at 403–04.

113. *See* notes 82–83 *supra* and accompanying text. To the degree that the
     theatrics of court contribute to just judgment, they also contribute to the
     acceptance of court rules and forms as just.

114. *See* note 41 *supra* and accompanying text.

115. The complexities of acting, especially with respect to involvement and
     detachment, are helpfully discussed by P. Brook, *supra* note 24, at
     116–19. For an actress's view (Liv Ullman) see Simon, *A Luminous Film
     Star Moves into Ibsen's "A Doll's House,"* N.Y. Times, Feb. 23, 1975, § 2, at 1,
     col. 1; at 7, cols. 1–6.

116. *See* McCarthy, *supra* note 51, at 25, 28–29.

117. Brook, *Introduction to The Persecution and Assassination of Jean Paul Marat
     as Performed by the Inmates of the Asylum of Charenton Under the Direction of
     the Marquis de Sade,* in The Modern Theatre 285, 286 (D. Seltzer ed.
     1967).

118. In a discussion of the way in which the alienation effect is achieved in
     Chinese theater, Brecht said that the performers expressed awareness of
     being watched, unlike performers in the European tradition who act as
     though there were a fourth wall in addition to the three of the stage,
     thus giving the audience the feeling of being unseen spectators. The
     Chinese actor observes himself and "will occasionally look at the au-
     dience as if to say: isn't it just like that?" Brecht, *Alienation Effects in Chi-
     nese Acting,* in The Modern Theatre 276, 277 (D. Seltzer, ed. 1967).

119. *Id.* at 278.

120. It is tempting, but probably false, to draw an analogy between the jury
     and the Greek chorus. Nietzsche noted of the chorus that it was "the
     primary dramatic phenomenon: Projecting oneself outside oneself and
     then acting as though one had really entered another body, another
     character. This constitutes the first step in the evolution of drama." F.
     Nietzsche, *The Birth of Tragedy* in The Birth of Tragedy and The Gene-
     alogy of Morals 55 (1956).

121. After his own service on a jury, drama critic Stanley Kauffmann wrote
     that "legal folk insist on being concerned with matters other than sus-

taining the interest of the spectators, including the jury. There are innu-
merable delays, recesses, readings of documents into the record—most
irritating of all—whispered conferences at the bench between judge and
both counsel, out of earshot." Kauffmann, *Just Like Life, Only Different*,
N.Y. Times, Feb. 27, 1966, § 2 at col. 4. Kauffmann thought this side action to be "poor dramaturgy." It may well have been. But it may also
have been a form of alienation effect in judicial theater, an irritant which
provided distance between the jury and the witnesses and which served
as a reminder that a judgment had to be formed in response to what was
being presented.

122. N. Chiaromonte, The Worm of Consciousness and Other Essays 131
(1976).

123. *Id.* at 131–32.

124. *Id.* at 126. *See also* H. Arendt, *Reflections: Truth and Politics*, The New
Yorker, Feb. 25, 1967, at 49, 86, 88. Homer had been prompted to give
poetic place to Trojans as well as Achaeans, to Hector as well as Achilles.
Later, as I have already noted, Herodotus undertook the celebration of
barbarian as well as of Greek deeds. The Hebraic story also was one of
disinterest. God, as the God of history, was present as much to Assyria,
Egypt, and Babylon as to Israel. And this story directed anticipation toward historical fulfillment of the original covenantal promise that by
Abraham would all the families of the earth bless themselves.

125. Live presentation may encourage what Judge Hutcheson referred to as
"hunching." *See* note 113 *supra* and accompanying text. "Hunching" is
what Judge Frank would call experiencing a gestalt. Frank, *supra* note
10, at 170–71. The word "hunch" has not been used in the present context both because it might be misleading and because it is inadequate to
convey the creative nature of the phenomenon.

126. Craven, *Paean to Pragmatism*, 50 N.C. L. Rev. 977, 978 (1972). Cardozo
estimated 9 out of 10. B. Cardozo, The Growth of the Law 60 (1924).
Both estimates are based on the exercise of rule discretion. In Judge
Frank's view, the exercise of fact discretion is overlooked in such ac-
counts. He maintained that discretion in finding facts is almost bound-
less for trial judges. *See* J. Frank, *supra* note 10, 56–57. If Judge Frank
is right, then it may be said that live presentation is directed to and en-
courages the exercise of fact discretion. The exercise of discretion and
creativity may be more freely exercised by trial courts than by appellate
courts in the finding and statement of fact. But the discretion exists for
both, if to a lesser degree at the appellate level. It may be that there is
creative interpretation of facts by appellate courts in the way the rules
(rather than the facts) are "found." *See generally id.* at 165–70, 316–25. In
any event, the possible inducement to creativity offered by live presentation is equally applicable to trial courts, appellate courts, and trial juries.

127. Live presentation may also make disposition easier. For example, it may
become evident•at trial that a key witness lacks credibility.
 The judge's alternatives may not be as numerous as those of the jury
since the latter need give no reasons for its judgments and may simply

"nullify" the rule. *See* United States v. Maybury, 274 F.2d 899 (2d Cir. 1960).

128. Cases really worth litigating will generally involve competing rules (with competing fact constructions in their support).

129. I. KANT, THE CRITIQUE OF JUDGMENT 171–72 (J. Meredith trans. 1957).

130. *See, e.g.*, White, *The Evolution of Reasoned Elaboration: Jurisprudential Criticism and Social Change*, 59 VA. L. REV. 279, 299–301 (1973). Dewey spoke of a "logic of exposition [which] is different from that of search and inquiry." DEWEY, *supra* note 43, at 24. The statement of reasons for a judgment should not be confused with the act of judgment. What is decided and how the judge explains that decision have a complex interrelationship but are distinguishable. Nor is the judicial opinion to be taken as a report of the process followed by a judge in reaching a decision, just as a play is not to be taken as a direct revelation of the workings of its author's mind. Rather, it is a response to and the concluding part of the courtroom event. It is the public, reasoned apologia for the correctness of what has been done. Insofar as it is a persuasive device and a substitution for (not diary of) the actual decision-making process, it is, like the attorney's case, a metaphor and is suggestive of texts for future productions. Its rule cannot be set down as a precept, for, to return again to Kant and the analogy of art, "the rule [must] be gathered from the performance, i.e. from the product which others may use to put their own talent to the test, so as to let it serve as a model, not for imitation, but for following." I. KANT, *supra* note 129, at 171.

131. Frost, *The Constant Symbol, quoted in* J. WHITE, THE LEGAL IMAGINATION 766, 773, 956 (1973).

132. Marbury v. Madison, 5 U.S. (1 Cranch) 137, 177 (1803).

Chapter 5. The Image of Court as Theater of Beginning

1. W. SHAKESPEARE, HAMLET, act III, scene 2.

2. E. BENTLEY, THE THEATRE OF COMMITMENT 81 (1967).

3. A. COX, THE ROLE OF THE SUPREME COURT IN AMERICAN GOVERNMENT 117 (1976).

4. BENTLEY, *supra* note 2, at 81.

5. R. DWORKIN, TAKING RIGHTS SERIOUSLY (1977); *id. Seven Critics*, 11 GA. L. REV. 1201 (1977).

6. K. BARTH, 2 CHURCH DOGMATICS pt. 2, at 572 (1957). Paul Lehmann has explained: "The quintessence of the Decalogue is the *indicative* reality whose direction and boundaries are defined in covenantal, that is, personal terms through the commandment form. The reality is God's presence in the midst of his people as help and salvation." P. LEHMANN, THE TRANSFIGURATION OF POLITICS 258 (1975) (emphasis added). The Commandments are imperative "only insofar as such an imperative signals the foundation and purposed fitness of things." *Id.*

Lehmann goes on to explain that "this rightness or fitness of things is

Notes to Chapter Five

the human side of the righteousness of God [and] is expressed in the creation of the world and in the destiny of human people." *Id.* Therefore, for Lehmann, the fitness of things has a distinctly political, personal cast. Quite a different conclusion was reached by Jesse Root, who maintained that his ancestors' "common law was derived from the law of nature and of revelation—those rules and maxims of immutable truth and justice, which arise from the eternal fitness of things, which need only to be understood, to be submitted to." Root, *The Origin of Government and Laws in Connecticut*, 1798, in THE LEGAL MIND IN AMERICA 32, 33 (P. Miller ed. 1962).

7. Hutcheson, *The Judgment Intuitive: The Function of the "Hunch" in Judicial Decision*, 14 CORNELL L. Q. 274, 282–83 (1929). *See* J. FRANK, *supra* note 18, at 170–85.

8. I. KANT, THE CRITIQUE OF JUDGEMENT 150–53 (J. Meredith trans. 1957).

9. *Id.* at 153.

10. *Id.* at 151.

11. AUGUSTINE, CONFESSIONS, bk. III, pt. 2, p. 71 (T. Matthew trans. 1957).

12. C. COCHRANE, CHRISTIANITY AND CLASSICAL CULTURE 392 (1957).

13. Act of Apr. 30, 1790, 1 Story's Laws 83, 1 Stat. 115. The statute designates "certain crimes against the United States." Section 12 provides that upon conviction for manslaughter on the high seas, a seaman shall be imprisoned not more than three years and fined not more than one thousand dollars. The problem of jurisdiction was not raised at trial and seems to have been generally assumed.

14. Holmes had been in prison eight to nine months awaiting trial. The six-month sentence was additional.

15. United States v. Holmes, 26 F.Cas. 360, 367 (No. 15, 383) (L.L.E.D. Pa. 1842).

16. *Id.*

17. *Id.* at 366.

18. *Id.* at 368.

19. 14 Q.B.D. 273; 1881–85 All E.R. Rep. 61 (1884).

20. *Id.* at 67–68.

21. H. ARENDT, EICHMANN IN JERUSALEM (1965).

22. *Id.* at 297.

23. 322 U.S. 143, 154 (1944).

24. The courtroom action draws attention away from the rules of decision to the environment of decision.

   The distinction between the rules and the environment of decision was drawn by Paul Lehmann in a discussion of ethical decision making:

   > Obviously the kind of ethical literalism which aims at a one-to-one correlation between a specific word of Jesus and a specific action misses the point of Jesus' teaching. Decision making as the Christian understands it goes on in quite another way. For the Christian, the *environment* of decision, not the *rules* of decision, gives to behavior its ethical significance.

. . . Consequently, Christian ethics in the tradition of the Reformation seeks to provide an analysis of the environment of decision in which the principal foundations and preceptual directives of behavior are displaced by *contextual foundations* and *parabolic directives*. In a word, *the environment of decision is the context for the ethical reality of conscience*.

P. LEHMANN, ETHICS IN A CHRISTIAN CONTEXT 346–47 (1963). Lehmann describes the context of decision making in terms of God's political activity in the world "doing what it takes to make and to keep human life human in the world." *Id.* at 347; *see id.* at 74–86 *passim*. Dean Wellington displays a certain attention to the context for decision making, but for him the context is one of "conventional morality." He claimed,

[W]hen dealing with legal principles a court must take a moral point of view. Yet I doubt that one would want to say that a court is entitled or required to assert *its* moral point of view. Unlike the moral philosopher, the court is required to assert ours. This requirement imposes constraints: Judicial reasoning in concrete cases must proceed from society's set of moral principles and ideals, in much the same way that the judicial interpretation of documents (contracts, statutes, constitutions—especially constitutions) must proceed from the document. And that is why we must be concerned with conventional morality, for it is there that society's set of moral principles and ideals are located.

Wellington, *Common Law Rules and Constitutional Double Standards: Some Notes on Adjudication*, 83 YALE L.J. 221, 244 (1973). Yet, conventional morality, like rules and principles, is not determinative of concrete cases. And live presentation would seem to have little reference to it. The point about live presentation is that it calls into play, or may call into play, sources for judgment a good deal livelier and more dynamic than any abstraction, such as a rule, a principle, or conventional morality.

25. *See* Duncan v. Louisiana, 391 U.S. 145 (1968).
26. *See* Apodaca v. Oregon, 406 U.S. 404 (1972); Williams v. Florida, 399 U.S. 78 (1970); Glasser v. United States, 315 U.S. 60 (1942); Smith v. Texas, 311 U.S. 128 (1940).

Exclusion of a group from the makeup of the jury can be raised by a party even though the party is not a member of the excluded group. *See* Peters v. Kiff, 407 U.S. 493 (1972) (white defendant challenged conviction on grounds that Negroes were excluded). Procedures of selection which are exclusionary "cast doubt on the integrity of the whole judicial process. They create the appearance of bias in the decision of individual cases, and they increase the risk of actual bias as well." *Id.* at 502 (Marshall, J., concurring).

27. Apodaca v. Oregon, 406 U.S. 404 (1972). Burch v. Louisiana, 441 U.S. 130 (1979) (held that conviction by a nonunanimous six-person jury was impermissible.

28. *Id.* at 414, 397–98 (Stewart, J., dissenting).
29. *Id.* at 396 (Brennan, J., dissenting); 402 (Marshall, J., dissenting).

Notes to Chapter Five

30. *Id.* at 402–04 (Marshall, J., dissenting).
31. *Id.* at 407 n.2 (White, J., writing for the Court).
32. Frankel, *Trials and Procedure—From Private Fights Toward Public Justice*, 51 N.Y.U. L. REV. 516 (1976). *See also* Frankel, *The Search for Truth: An Umpireal View*, 123 U. PA. L. REV. 1031 (1975); *id.*, *The Adversary Judge*, 54 TEX. L. REV. 465 (1976).
33. Frankel, *The Search for Truth: An Umpireal View, supra* note 32, at 1037.
34. *Id.*
35. *Id.* at 1036, quoting D. PECK, THE COMPLEMENT OF COURT AND COUNSEL 9 (1954) (13th Annual Benjamin N. Cardozo Lecture).
36. *John* 3:21.
37. *See, e.g.*, Dolan, *Lawyers and the Class Struggle*, JURIS DOCTOR 32–34 (Apr. 1971).
38. D. NEWMAN, CONVICTION: THE DETERMINATION OF GUILT OR INNOCENCE WITHOUT TRIAL 3 (1966). *See generally* THE CHALLENGE OF CRIME IN A FREE SOCIETY, *A Report by the President's Commission on Law Enforcement and Administration of Justice* 333–38 (1968); D. OAKS & W. LEHMAN, A CRIMINAL JUSTICE SYSTEM AND THE INDIGENT (1968); A. Alshuler, *The Prosecutor's Role in Plea Bargaining*, 36 U. CHI. L. REV. 50 (1968); *id.*, *The Defense Attorney's Role in Plea Bargaining*, 84 YALE L. J. 1175 (1975); A. Rossett, *The Negotiated Guilty Plea*, 374 ANNALS OF THE AM. ACAD. OF POL. & SOC. SC. 70 (1967).
39. Frankel, *The Search for Truth: An Umpireal View, supra* note 32, at 1040 n. 18.
40. Frankel, *Trials and Procedure—From Private Fights Toward Public Justice, supra* note 32, at 158.
41. *See* AMERICAN FRIENDS SERVICE COMMITTEE, STRUGGLE FOR JUSTICE 136–37 (1971).
42. Alshuler, *Plea Bargaining and Its History*, 79 COL. L. REV. 1, 41 (1979).
43. Rossett, *The Negotiated Guilty Plea, supra* note 38, at 72.
44. Blackledge v. Allison 431 U.S. 63, 77–78 (1977); Santobello v. New York, 404 U.S. 257 (1971).
45. United States v. Jackson, 390 F.2d 130, 138 (7th Cir. 1968) (Kiley, J., dissenting).
46. Blackledge v. Allison, 431 U.S. 63, 79 n. 17 (1977).
47. *See, e.g.*, Blackledge v. Allison, 431 U.S. 63 (1977); Weinberg & Babcock, Book Review, 76 YALE L. J. 612 (1967); 1974 Amendments to FED. R. CRIM. PROC. 11; ABA STANDARDS RELATING TO PLEAS OF GUILTY 1–3 (Approved Draft 1968); ALI MODEL CODE OF PRE-ARRAIGNMENT PROCEDURE § 350.3, Commentary (1975); Ala. Code, tit. § 1, § 264 (1958); Gallagher, *Judicial Participation in Plea Bargaining: A Search for New Standards*, 9 HARV. CIV. RTS.–CIV. LIB. L. REV. 29 (1974); Note, *Restructuring the Plea Bargain*, 82 YALE L. J. 286 (1972); Note, *Plea Bargaining: The Case for Reform*, 6 U. RICH. L. REV. 325 (1972); Note, *Plea Bargaining and the Transformation of the Criminal Process*, 90 HARV. L. REV. 564 (1977).
48. Alshuler, *Plea Bargaining and Its History, supra* note 42, at 42.
49. 372 U.S. 335 (1963). *See* A. LEWIS, GIDEON'S TRUMPET (1964).
50. 372 U.S. at 344.

51. L. Fried, An Anatomy of Values: Problems of Personal and Social Choice 131 (1970).
52. United States v. Wade, 388 U.S. 218 (1967). On the "critical stages" analysis, see also Powell v. Alabama, 287 U.S. 45 (1932); Escobedo v. Illinois, 378 U.S. 478, 492 (1964); Miranda v. Arizona, 384 U.S. 436 (1966); Coleman v. Alabama, 399 U.S. 1 (1970); Brewer v. Williams, 430 U.S. 385 (1977). *Cf.* Kirby v. Illinois, 406 U.S. 682 (1972); United States v. Ash, 413 U.S. 300 (1973).
53. United States v. Wade, 388 U.S. at 235–36.
54. *See* Coleman v. Alabama, 399 U.S. 1, 24–25 (1970) (Burger, C.J., dissenting); *In re* Groban, 352 U.S. 330 (1957); Steele, *Right to Counsel at the Grand Jury Stage of Criminal Proceedings*, 36 Mo. L. Rev. 193 (1971); 1967 Duke L. J. 97 (1967).
55. *See generally* United States v. Calandra, 414 U.S. 338 (1974); Note, *The Grand Jury: Powers, Procedures, and Problems*, 9 Col. J. L. & Soc. Prob. 681 (1973). I have relied in particular upon the latter.

The Fifth Amendment provides that "no person shall be held to answer for a capital or otherwise infamous crime, unless on presentment or indictment of a grand jury." While this requirement is not applicable to the states, Hurtado v. California, 110 U.S. 516 (1884), it has been embodied in state constitutions. *See* Note, *The Grand Jury: Powers, Procedures, and Problems, supra,* at 683 n. 11. Where it is not required, the trend has been away from its use. *See, e.g., Contemporary Studies Project: Perspectives on the Administration of Criminal Justice in Iowa*, 57 Iowa L. Rev. 598, 629–30 (1972).

Typically described as "a sword and a shield," *In re* Grand Jury, Jan. 1969, 315 F. Supp. 662, 671 (D. Md. 1970), the grand jury both indicts to initiate prosecution and may refuse to indict and thus bar prosecution and so protect. Regardless of its ancient origins, see United States v. Calandra, 414 U.S. 338, 342–43 & n. 3, in this country,

this body has been regarded as a primary security to the innocent against hasty, malicious and oppressive persecution; it serves the invaluable function in our society of standing between the accuser and the accused, whether the latter be an individual, minority group, or other, to determine whether a charge is founded upon reason or was dictated by an intimidating power or by malice and personal ill will.

Wood v. Georgia, 370 U.S. 375, 390 (1962).

To this end, extraordinary powers and procedures are given to grand juries. "No judge presides to monitor its proceedings. It deliberates in secret and may determine alone the course of its inquiry. The grand jury may compel the production of evidence or the testimony of witnesses it considers appropriate, and its operation generally is unrestrained by the technical procedural and evidentiary rules governing the conduct of criminal trials." United States v. Calandra 414 U.S. at 343.

Grand juries are an arm of the court. Their jurisdiction is coextensive with that of the court, and they use court powers of subpoena. Departures from the trial model allowed in grand jury proceedings include the absence of confrontation of witnesses, *see* People v. Vlcek, Ill. App. 2d 178, 215 N.E. 2d 673 (1966); secrecy, *see* Pittsburgh Plate Glass Co. v. United States, 360 U.S. 395 (1959); and the allowance of hearsay evidence, *see* Costello v. United States, 350 U.S. 359 (1956).

These departures may serve to protect. Thus, *e.g.*, secrecy "grew from the need to protect both jurors and private citizens from royal oppression." Note, *The Grand Jury: Powers, Procedures and Problems, supra*, at 682.

The peculiar power and exceptions allowed the grand jury, Justice Marshall has correctly pointed out, have been granted "in heavy reliance on certain essential assumptions" beginning with the function of the grand jury

> to stand between the Government and the citizen . . . . Properly functioning, the grand jury is to be the servant of neither the Government nor the courts, but of the people . . . . The anticipated neutrality of the grand jury . . . may perhaps be relied upon to prevent unwarranted interference with the lives of private citizens and to ensure that the grand jury's subpoena power over the person are exercised in only a reasonable fashion.

United States v. Dionisio, 93 S.Ct. 764, 788 (1973) (Marshall, J., dissenting). If the grand jury has become mainly a prosecutor's tool, then there would be less reason for it to enjoy the special exceptions. On the subject of prosecutor dominance *see* Note, *The Grand Jury: Powers, Procedures and Problems, supra*, at 701 & nn. 114–15.

More troublesome than prosecutorial domination is prosecutorial abuse. *See, e.g.*, Harris, *Annals of Law: Taking the Fifth*, Pt. 1, THE NEW YORKER, Apr. 5, 1976, at 44; *id.*, Pt. 2, Apr. 12, 1976, at 43; *id.*, Pt. 3, Apr. 19, 1976, at 42; Antell, *The Modern Grand Jury: Benighted Supergovernment*, 51 A.B.A.J. 153 (1965).

Thus, in the late 1960s and early 1970s,

> the FBI desperately resorted to a relatively new law-enforcement technique—the use of compliant federal grand juries to help the Bureau do the job that it couldn't do on its own . . . . [N]owadays grand juries are frequently, and improperly, used to amass evidence against people who have already been indicted, to obtain leads on fugitives, and even to find missing persons like Jimmy Hoffa. The FBI merely persuades a co-operative United States Attorney to instruct the federal grand jury he in effect runs to subpoena relatives, friends, and acquaintances of the person being sought, and then the prosecutor forces these witnesses, under threat of imprisonment for contempt of court, to divulge whatever they may know about the fugitive—or, for that matter, about anything under the sun that the prosecutor (or the FBI) feels like asking.

Harris, *Annals of the Law: Taking the Fifth*, pt. 1, *supra*, at 45.

56. *See* McCORMICK, EVIDENCE § 143 (2d ed. 1968); Kastigar v. United States, 406 U.S. 441 (1972).

57. *See* Harris v. United States, 382 U.S. 162 (1965).

58. *See* United States v. Stone, 429 F.2d 138 (2d Cir. 1970).

59. *See* Chase, *The Burger Court, the Individual, and the Criminal Process: Directions and Misdirections*, 52 N.Y.U. L. REV. 518, 594 (1977). I have relied upon Chase's analysis of criminal procedure in the hands of the Burger Court, both as his thoughts are presented in this article and as he has sought to enlighten me privately.

60. Johnson v. Louisiana, 406 U.S. 356, 392 (1972) (Douglas, J., dissenting).

61. On counsel in posttrial situations, see Wolff v. McDonnell, 418 U.S. 539 (1974) (no counsel required in inmate disciplinary proceeding); Morrissey v. Brewer, 408 U.S. 471 (1972) (parole revocation; judgment reserved on counsel requirement); Gagnon v. Scarpelli, 411 U.S. 778 (1973) (probation hearing; counsel required only in special circumstances).

62. The Sixth Amendment specifies: "In all criminal prosecutions the accused shall enjoy the right . . . to have Assistance of counsel for his defense." The phrase "criminal prosecution" may then be read to embrace certain pretrial stages critical to the effectiveness of counsel at trial and so within the mandate of the Sixth Amendment. Or, if the encounter in question does not fall within the start of a criminal prosecution or one of its critical stages, then counsel may nevertheless be appropriate, not because the counsel clause requires it but because the due-process clause requires it. In the latter event, the content of due process is understood as informed by the judicial process, which includes the right to counsel. The result in either case might well be the requirement of counsel but the result would be reached by different analytical paths beginning from different constitutional premises. Either way, the fundamental guide is the paradigmatic character of counsel in judicial theater.

63. 411 U.S. 778 (1973).

64. Griffiths, *Ideology in Criminal Procedure or A Third "Model" of the Criminal Process*, 79 YALE L. J. 359, 386 (1970).

65. *See* Chase, *supra* note 59, at 596 n. 420.

66. *See generally* Chase, *supra* note 59, at 520–50.

67. A distinction between "legal" and "factual" guilt was drawn by Herbert Packer. H. PACKER, THE LIMITS OF THE CRIMINAL SANCTION 179–246 (1968). A "factually" guilty person is one who committed the act to which criminal liability attaches. A "legally" guilty person is one who, in addition to having been found to have committed the act, has been adjudged guilty in a proceeding in which all of the legal limitations and requirements have been satisfied.

68. 417 U.S. 433 (1974).

69. *Id.* at 446–50, 450 n. 25.

70. *Id.* at 450 n. 25. *See also*, Kaplan, *The Limits of the Exclusionary Rule*, 26 STAN. L. REV. 1027, 1036 n. 53 (1974).

71. United States v. Calandra, 414 U.S. 338, 347 (1974) (Powell, J.).

72. On the absence of deterrent effect or absence of proof, see *id.* at 348 n. 5.

73. Brewer v. Williams, 430 U.S. 387, 416–29 (1977) (Burger, C.J., dissenting). *See also* Bivens v. Six Unknown Named Agents, 403 U.S. 388, 415 (1971) (Burger, C.J., dissenting).

74. Tehan v. United States *ex rel.* Shott, 382 U.S. 406, 416 (1966).

Notes to Chapter Five

75. United States v. Calandra, 414 U.S. 338, 357 (1974) (Brennan, J., dissenting). The majority held that the exclusionary rule does not apply to grand jury proceedings. Grand jury proceedings would have seemed a natural circumstance for effectuation of the courtroom image through the exclusionary rule. The majority did not seize the opportunity, but neither did it explicitly reject the notion of judical proceedings as measures of extra-court actions. It is instructive in this regard to compare Justice Powell's opinion for the majority in *Calandra* with his dissent in Goss v. Lopez, 419 U.S. 565, 594–95, 597 n. 13 (1975) (Powell, J., dissenting).

76. Chase, *supra* note 59, at 537. *See generally* Boker & Corrigan, *Making the Constable Culpable: A Proposal to Improve the Exclusionary Rule*, 27 HASTINGS L. J. 1291 (1976); Monroe, *The Imperative of Judicial Integrity and the Exclusionary Rule*, 4 W. ST. U. L. REV. 1 (1976); Schrock & Welsh, *Up from Calandra: The Exclusionary Rule as a Constitutional Requirement*, 59 MINN. L. REV. 251 (1974).

77. Some distance between the courts and the ordinary is necessary. But this distancing does not require removal from human realities. When human realities are lost, overhaul is necessary.

78. *See* H. BERMAN, THE INTERACTION OF LAW AND RELIGION 36–37 (1974); P. LEHMANN, THE TRANSFIGURATION OF POLITICS 75–76 (1975). Lehmann found that too much and the wrong things had been made of courtroom decorum by Chief Justice Burger's address on *The Necessity for Civility*, 52 F.R.D. 211 (1971). The Chief Justice, Lehmann wrote, "chose to take moral flight above the pain and passion of mounting courtroom disorders . . . and to lecture his professional colleagues upon courtroom manners." P. LEHMANN, *supra*, at 75.

Lehmann believes that, properly understood, "[i]n a genuinely civil order, civility means the pursuit of justice under law through the practice of law under justice." *Id*. *See also* Weaver, *Nixon Court Gives a Conservative Ruling on the Laws of Fashion and Decorum*, N.Y. TIMES, Mar. 11, 1974, at 19, col. 3 (new requirement of conservative dress for attorneys appearing before Supreme Court "reportedly a reaction to dismay expressed by Chief Justice Burger when a lawyer rose to plead his case wearing a pearl-grey vest under his morning coat instead of the traditional dark one").

79. See Letter from the Panther 21 to Judge John M. Murtagh, Mar. 2, 1970: "We know very well what is meant by your statement, 'This court is responsible for maintaining proper respect for the administration of criminal justice and preventing any reflection on the image of American justice.' Properly translated, it simply means that the farce must go on. The image must remain intact."

80. *See* N.Y. TIMES, May 14, 1971, at 1, col. 8; Kempton, *Free at Last?*, N.Y. REV. OF BOOKS, June 17, 1971, at 30.

81. *See* M. KEMPTON, THE BRIAR PATCH 280 (1973).

82. A. SOLZHENITSYN, THE GULAG ARCHIPELAGO 399 (1973).

83. *Id*. at 419.

84. *Cf. id*. at 419–31.

85. *Id.* at 431.
86. REPORT OF THE NATIONAL ADVISORY COMMISSION ON CIVIL DISORDERS 337 (Bantam ed. 1968).
87. W. SHAKESPEARE, A MIDSUMMER NIGHT'S DREAM, act V, scene 1, line 18.

✿ Chapter 6. *Personae*

1. Barker, *Introduction to O. Gierke*, NATURAL LAW AND THE THEORY OF SO-CIETY lxx–lxxi, lxxv–vi (1960). *See also* J. NOONAN, PERSONS AND MASKS OF THE LAW (1976).
2. Barker, *supra* note 1, lxxi.
3. *Id.* at lxx. The founding fathers referred to the state as a stage or theater. *Cf.* G. Washington, *Address to Congress on Resigning His Commission*, Dec. 23, 1783, in 27 WRITINGS OF WASHINGTON 284, 285 (J. Fitzpatrick ed. 1938); D. MALONE, JEFFERSON AND THE RIGHTS OF MAN 274 (1951) (Jefferson); H. ARENDT, ON REVOLUTION 200 (1963) (Madison). It was the platform upon which citizens acted out public parts of importance and responsibility from local town meetings to the national congress. *Cf.* H. ARENDT, *supra*, at 111–37.
4. J. WHITE, THE LEGAL IMAGINATION 859 (1973).
5. 397 U.S. 254 (1970).
6. 419 U.S. 565 (1975).
7. *See, e.g.*, Davis, *The Goss Principle*, 16 SAN DIEGO L. REV. 284 (1979).
8. 397 U.S. 254, 267–71 (1970); Davis, *supra* note 7, at 290.
9. *Id.* at 292.
10. Davis's belief in the future potential of *Goss* was not shaken by its fate in subsequent Supreme Court cases. *Ingraham v. Wright*, 430 U.S. 651 (1977) involved the paddling (beating) of a junior high school student. No hearing was given, and the Court required none. A footnote appeared to reject the *Goss* notion of an informal hearing. 430 U.S. 682 n. 55. In *Board of Curators of the Univ. of Mo. v. Horowitz*, 435 U.S. 78 (1978), a senior medical student had been excluded from school for academic reasons and was not permitted to graduate and was dismissed from school. She had an excellent academic record but her clinical performance had been evaluated as abysmal. She was given warnings and, after the initial decision denying graduation, special oral exams. The Court concluded that she had not been denied procedural due process. The opportunity to rehabilitate *Goss* after *Ingraham* was not seized.
11. 419 U.S. at 583–84.
12. *Id.* at 597 (Powell, J., dissenting).
13. *Id.* at 594.
14. *Id.* at 594–95 n. 13.
15. *See* Miranda v. Arizona, 384 U.S. 436 (1966).
16. In their famous article introducing the right of privacy, Brandeis and Warren made the observation, now at least commonplace, that from "cor-

poreal property arose the incorporeal rights issuing out of it; then there opened the wide realm of intangible property, in the products and processes of the mind, as works of literature and art, goodwill, trade secrets, and trademarks." S. Warren & L. Brandeis, *The Right to Privacy*, 4 HARV. L. REV. 193, 193–94 (1890). More recently, Charles Reich identified emerging forms of property: government largess as well as "franchises in private business, equities in corporations, the right to receive privately furnished utilities and services, status in private organizations." Reich, *The New Property*, 73 YALE L. J. 733, 786 (1964). He argued for the legal protection of these emerging forms as a "new property" so that the "presumption should be that the professional man will keep his license, and the welfare recipient his pension." *Id.* at 786. And he proposed a kind of "Homestead Act for rootless twentieth century man," *id.* at 787, whereby there would be protected "zones" for the maintenance of "independence, dignity and pluralism in society." *Id.* at 786.

Reich's program bears the defect of dependence upon property as the possession of status. William Van Alstyne has pointed out the dangers of Reich's idea as it relates to individuals holding status in public offices. Van Alstyne, *Cracks in the "New Property: Adjudicative Due Process in the Administrative State*, 62 CORNELL L. REV. 445, 483 (1977). Van Alstyne grants the indispensability of private property to a person's sense of self, but he finds incorrect the attempted application of a new, vindicated property to the problems of arbitrary administrative adjudication. *Id.* at 483–84. For protection against governmental arbitrariness, what is required in his estimation is not a new property but "the more general protection of the old liberty." *Id.* at 487. Van Alstyne certainly perceives the nexus between property and liberty, *see id.* at 483–84 & n. 111, but he frames his understanding of property in terms of possession. *See id.* at 484. When the notion of property is freed from the constricting errors of ownership, then it does serve as a protection against governmental arbitrariness, for it is a mode for effecting the old liberty. Reich's basic notion remains satisfactory if we retain its spatial but strike off and discard its possession and status-related content.

17. Harless v. Florida *ex rel*. Schellenberg, 360 So.2d 83, 90–91 (Fla. App. 1978) (Smith, J.) ("We have long understood that worship and speech are constitutionally protected, not only for their benefits to a democratic state [footnote omitted], but also because liberty in such matters is of the essence of personhood. We know now that the United States Constitution similarly protects privacy, another fundamental aspect of personhood, and that it does so without pretext.")

18. *Cf.* Reich, *Reflections: The Limits of Duty*, THE NEW YORKER, June 19, 1971, at 52.

19. *See, e.g.*, Bell v. Burson, 402 U.S. 535 (1971) (driver's license); Fuentes v. Shevin, 407 U.S. 67 (1972) (prejudgment replevin); Morrissey v. Brewer, 408 U.S. 471 (1972) (parole); Perry v. Sindermann, 408 U.S. 593 (1972) (teacher's job).

20. *See, e.g.,* Javins v. First National Realty Corp., 428 F.2d 1071 (D.C. Cir.), *cert. denied,* 400 U.S. 925 (1970); Marini v. Ireland, 56 N.J. 130, 265 A.2d 526 (1970).
21. United States v. Grunewald, 233 F.2d 556, 581–82, (2d Cir.) (Frank, J., dissenting), *rev'd,* 353 U.S. 391 (1957).
22. *Id.* at 582. Justice Frankfurter also recognized that "[t]he history of liberty has largely been the history of observance of procedural safeguards." McNabb v. United States, 318 U.S. 332, 347 (1943).
23. 233 F.2d at 582. Judge Frank noted that the privilege against self-incrimination, mistakenly viewed as a mere procedural matter, had come to seem "an unjustifiable obstacle to the judicial ascertainment of the truth." *Id.* at 581. By wiping out all private worlds, the enclaves protected in part by the privilege, totalitarians "boast of the resulting greater efficiency in obtaining all the evidence in criminal prosecutions." *Id.* at 582. *Cf.* Edward Chase's study of the Burger Court's operations on criminal procedure, which betray "total empiricist" preoccupation with efficiency, accuracy, and factual guilt. Chase, *The Burger Court, the Individual, and the Criminal Process: Directions and Misdirections,* 52 N.Y.U.L. Rev. 518, 588–92 (1977).
    Laurence Tribe also notes that "those procedural formalities that are implicit in treating persons with respect as members of the community should thus be required by due process for reasons more basic than any utilitarian calculus of accuracy, although accuracy of course matters as well when the procedure is ancillary to a substantive interest of great importance to the individual." L. Tribe, American Constitutional Law 554 (1978).
24. M. Farrand, 4 The Records of the Federal Convention of 1787, at 31 (1966).
25. *Letter from Thomas Jefferson to Reverend James Madison,* Oct. 28, 1787, in The Life and Selected Writings of Thomas Jefferson, 388, 390 (A. Koch & W. Peden eds. 1944).
26. *See* P. Emerson, Public Policy and the Changing Structure of American Agriculture (1978); R. Marshall & A. Thompson, Status and Prospects of Small Farmers in the South (1976); United States General Accounting Office, Changing Character and Structure of American Agriculture: An Overview (1978).
27. In Germany long years after the days of Jefferson and Madison and in a situation far removed from theirs, Dietrich Bonhoeffer foresaw that
    [i]n the revolutionary times ahead the greatest gift will be to know the security of a good home. It will be a bulwark against all dangers from within and without.
    . . . .
    In spite of man's longing for peace and solitude, these will be difficult to find. But with all these changes [brought about by the urbanization of the country], it will be an advantage to have under one's feet a plot of land from which to draw the resources of a new,

> natural, unpretentious, and contented day's work and evening's leisure.
>
> D. Bonhoeffer, *Thoughts on the Baptism of D.W.R.*, LETTERS AND PAPERS FROM PRISON 165, 167–68 (E. Bethge ed. 1967). Earlier, he had been led to ask "whether there have ever before in human history been people with so little ground under their feet, people to whom every available alternative seemed equally intolerable, repugnant, and futile." *Id.*, *After Ten Years*, at 25, 26.

28. *See* H. ARENDT, ON REVOLUTION 102–03, 296 n. 42 (1964).

29. *Id.* Williams v. Rhodes, 393 U.S. 23 (1968). *But see* American Party of Texas v. White, 415 U.S. 767 (1974); Storer v. Brown, 415 U.S. 724 (1974); Jenness v. Fortson, 403 U.S. 431 (1971).

30. *See* Harper v. Virginia Bd. of Elections, 383 U.S. 663 (1966).

31. *See* text at notes 38–40 *infra*.

32. ARISTOTLE, THE POLITICS, bk. I, ch. 2, at 28 (T. Sinclair trans. 1962).

33. Whitney v. California, 274 U.S. 357, 375 (1927) (Brandeis, J., concurring).

34. *See* Columbia Broadcasting System, Inc. v. Democratic National Committee, 412 U.S. 94 (1973); Red Lion Broadcasting Co. v. FCC, 395 U.S. 367 (1969).

35. *See* Grayned v. Rockford, 408 U.S. 104 (1972); Colten v. Kentucky, 407 U.S. 104 (1972); Bachellar v. Maryland, 397 U.S. 564 (1970); Cox v. Louisiana, 379 U.S. 559 (1965); Cox v. Louisiana, 379 U.S. 536 (1965).

36. *See* Prune Yard Shopping Center v. Robins, 100 S.Ct. 2035 (1980). *Compare* Hudgens v. NLRB, 424 U.S. 507 (1976); Lloyd Corp. v. Tanner, 407 U.S. 551 (1972); and Central Hardware Co. v. NLRB, 407 U.S. 539 (1972), *with* Food Employees Union Local 590 v. Logan Valley Plaza, Inc., 391 U.S. 308 (1968).

37. Kalven, *The Concept of the Public Forum*: Cox v. Louisiana, 1965 SUP. CT. REV. 1, 12.

38. ARENDT, *supra* note 3, at 236–42, 252–56.

39. *Id.* at 256–57, 272–73.

40. *Cf.* L. TRIBE, *supra* note 23, at 607 ("It is at least incomplete to say that Americans took [the causes of the 1960s] to the streets because other channels of communication were closed to their protest. Rather, they marched, paraded, and picketed because no other medium could adequately register either the intensity of their protest or the solidarity of their movement").

41. And it is of the essence therefore that citizens have access to court. *See* Boddie v. Connecticut, 401 U.S. 371 (1971); NAACP v. Button, 371 U.S. 415 (1963).

42. Chayes, *The Role of the Judge in Public Law Litigation*, 89 HARV. L. REV. 1281 (1976).

43. *See* Goldberg & Schwartz, *Supreme Court Denial of Citizen Access to Federal Courts to Challenge Unconstitutional or Other Unlawful Actions: The Record of the Burger Court*, A Statement of the Board of Governors of the Society of American Law Teachers, October, 1976.

44. *See, e.g.,* Citizens to Preserve Overton Park, Inc. v. Volpe, 401 U.S. 402

(1971); EDF v. Ruckelshaus, 439 F.2d 584 (D.C. Cir. 1971); Calvert Cliffs' Co-ordinating Committee, Inc. v. AEC, 449 F.2d 1109 (D.C. Cir. 1971); Scenic Hudson Preservation Conference v. FPC, 354 F.2d 608 (2d Cir. 1965), *cert. denied*, 384 U.S. 941 (1966).

45. 435 U.S. 519 (1978).

46. For a recent article suggesting that *Vermont Yankee* will be so confined, see Rodgers, *A Hard Look at* Vermont Yankee: *Environmental Law Under Close Scrutiny*, 67 GEORGETOWN L. J. 699 (1979). For other commentary on the case, see the symposium on the subject presented in the *Harvard Law Review*, 91 HARV. L. REV. 1803 (1978). For comment on the subject of environmental decision making generally, see the worthy symposium published by the *Iowa Law Review*, 62 IOWA L. REV. 637 (1977).

47. That we must inquire into law, government, and politics from a standpoint altogether different from interest representation is a major distinction between the notion pursued here and Richard Stewart's *The Reformation of American Administrative Law*, 88 HARV. L. REV. 1669 (1975). Stewart has made an exhaustive study of the administrative process as, under judicial intervention, it has been increasingly molded to interest representation. He has carefully assessed the problems and limited prospects for administrative law on the interest representation model. (The same category of problems and prospects, as they impinge upon the potential of the judicial system for interest representation, was subsequently addressed by Chayes. *See* Chayes, *supra* note 42.)

What remains to do is to examine the administrative process in a qualitatively different context than that of interests. The kind of alienation implicit in interest representation (analyzed by Arendt) and the inherent impossibility of satisfying all interests (diagnosed by Augustine) indicate how pursuit of interests is bankrupting of politics and of administrative law as a political process. A different context for analysis and point of fresh departure is suggested by the reality which Adams sought to describe as the "passion for distinction." *See infra.*

Such an analysis would diverge at significant points from that of Stewart, which is, for all that it is heroic, restricted by the concept of the antipolitics of interest. Thus, for example, a future exploration might depart from some point other than interest representation, give more thought to procedure (the administrative process itself, like the performance of a play, as the good sought), and have less concern for efficiency, accuracy, outcome, and "input" (as in technocracy).

Also, it would examine the judicial process as a model for the administrative process. This is not to say that agencies ought to be viewed "as courts under another name." *Id.* at 1806. It is to say that the judicial process may be a model for the way citizens (not interests) are to be considered by their government in any process, *i.e.*, for the development and testing of administrative like any law through experimentation by citizens where what counts is the power of argument rather than the power of interest.

In a footnote, Stewart remarks, "How bewildered would be the Found-

Notes to Chapter Six

ers to hear the courtroom touted as the cockpit of democracy!" Stewart, *supra*, at 1761 n. 437. How bewildered would they be to hear the government of the republic touted as managing a cockfight of interests?

48. Augustine, The City of God, bk. II, ch. 21, at 61–63; bk. XIX, ch. 21, at 699–700 (M. Dods trans., 1950).

49. *Id.* bk. XIX, ch. 24, at 706.

50. C. Cochrane, Christianity and Classical Culture 501 (1957).

51. Tribe argues for a constitutionally mandated dialogic process which bears some resemblance to the argument of the present text. *See, e.g.,* Tribe, *Structural Due Process*, 10 Harv. Civ. Rts.–Civ. Lib. L. Rev. 269 (1975). It is no bar to such a process to say that the declaration of a rule by a legislative or administrative body speaks the community's mind, for "[i]n a society whose legislative and administrative processes of value-formation and conflict resolution seem to resemble less the ancient ideal of the polis than the contemporary notion of pluralist compromise, any suggestion that bartered rules are necessarily expressions of true substantive consensus seems difficult to maintain." *Id.* at 315. Moreover, in a situation of moral flux, fixed rules pose

> a question of process values in its communal dimension: should we not regard individual human confrontation as an intrinsically more fitting response than codification to the predicament of moral uncertainty . . .? One might, indeed, regard such confrontations between decisionmaker and disputants as the *only* fitting response to any serious human controversy in a community worthy of the name. Resolution of disputes by reliance on fixed rules that settle in advance the boundaries between persons and the shape of their entitlements might conceivably be thought inconsistent with any but an unacceptable atomistic, anomic, anti-communal conception of social life.

Id. at 311.

52. His point is made in Adams, *Discourses on Davilla*, in 6 The Works of John Adams 221 (C.F. Adams ed. 1851), and is introduced there at *id.* 232.

53. *Id.* at 234. According to Adams's insight, the desire to be observed and praised is one of the most powerful human dispositions. *Id.* at 232. A poor man's lot is made all the worse by the cruelty of invisibility. "He is not disapproved, censured, or reproached; *he is only not seen." Id.* at 239. Avarice can be understood as an attempt to satisfy the need for respect because riches attract attention. *Id.* at 238–39. But, Adams went on to note, the pride of possessions issues only in "meanness of sentiment and a sordid scramble for money." *Id.* at 271. What has to be done is not to temper the passion for distinction but to direct it away from such things as accumulation of wealth and toward virtue, *i.e.,* "activity for the good of others," and then to stimulate it when it is so directed with the rewards of esteem and admiration. *Id.* at 234, 398, 246. Thus, Adams concluded, "[i]t is a principal end of government to regulate this passion, which in turn becomes a principal means of government." *Id.* at 234.

54. Aeschylus, *The Eumenides*, in The Oresteian Trilogy, at p. 173, line 755 (P. Vellacott trans. 1967).

55. *Id.* at p. 176, line 867.
56. *Id.* at p. 177, line 916.
57. *Id.* line 904.

✥ Chapter 7. Judicial Protection of the Powerless

1. D. GREGORY, DICK GREGORY'S POLITICAL PRIMER 203 (1972).
2. 5 WRITINGS OF JAMES MADISON 272 (G. Hunt ed. 1904).
3. *Id.*
4. *Id.*
5. THE FEDERALIST No. 10, at 57 (J. Cooke ed. 1961) (Madison).
6. *Id.* at 58–60.
7. *Id.* at 60–65.
8. THE FEDERALIST No. 51, *supra* note 5, at 349.
9. *Id.*, No. 10, at 60.
10. *Id.* at 61.
11. *Id.* at 60.
12. *Id.* at 63–64; No. 51, at 351–52.
13. *Id.*, No. 51, at 351–52.
14. *Id.* at 352.
15. Madison, *Letter to James Monroe*, Oct. 5, 1786, in THE COMPLETE MADISON 45 (S. Padover ed. 1953).
     Reinhold Niebuhr observed: "Man's capacity for justice makes democracy possible, but man's inclination to injustice makes democracy necessary." R. NIEBUHR, THE CHILDREN OF LIGHT AND THE CHILDREN OF DARKNESS xiii (2d ed. 1944). *Cf.* the formulation of John Rawls: "If men's inclination to self-interest makes their vigilance against one another necessary, their public sense of justice makes their secure association together possible." J. RAWLS, A THEORY OF JUSTICE 5 (1971).
16. Wills notes how Jefferson, instructed by the same Scottish moral sense school as Madison and equally devoted to equality, came to the opposite conclusion, that homogeneity is necessary to society. *See* G. WILLS, INVENTING AMERICA 301–02, 305–06 (1978).
17. *See id.* at 289.
18. *Id.* at 289–92.
19. *Speech in Virginia Convention*, June 14, 1788, in THE COMPLETE MADISON, *supra* note 15, at 47.
20. Winthrop, *A Modell of Christian Charity*, in AN AMERICAN PRIMER 26, 40 (D. Boorstin ed. 1968).
21. *Galatians* 3:28 (RSV).
22. I *Corinthians* 12:24–25 (RSV).
23. P. LEHMANN, ETHICS IN A CHRISTIAN CONTEXT 255 (1963).
24. *Speech in the Virginia Constitutional Convention*, Dec. 2, 1829, in 9 *Writings of James Madison*, *supra* note 2, at 358.
25. *Id.*
26. THE FEDERALIST No. 78, *supra* note 5, at 525–27 (Hamilton).

Notes to Chapter Seven

27. *Id.*
28. *Id.* at 523. *But see* R. McCloskey, The Modern Supreme Court 304 (1972) (The Court is a governing agency which faces some of the same power problems faced by others).
29. Jaffe, *Aristotle*, in History of Political Philosophy 64, 65 (1963).
30. Aristotle, Politics 1200.b.27–29 (bk. II, i, 1) (Loeb Classical Library 1967).
31. *Id.* at 1252.b.31–1253.a.3 (bk. I, i, 8–9). *See also* Aristotle, The Nicomachean Ethics 1094.a.19–1094.b.7 (bk. I, ii, 1–7); 1141.b.23–34 (bk. VI, viii, 1–4); 1180.b.28–1181.b.12 (bk. X, ix, 18–21) (Loeb Classical Library 1932).
32. Hans Kelsen stressed the point that his theory of positive law sought "to answer the question what, and how the law *is*, and not how it ought to be. It is a science of law (jurisprudence), not legal politics." H. Kelsen, Pure Theory of Law 1 (1967). A trenchant analysis of Kelsen's theory concluded with the conviction that the occasion for contemporary thinking about law is exactly what *Pure Theory of Law* omits: "it is time to pass to more important matters that Kelsen would dismiss as 'legal politics.'" Clark, *Hans Kelsen's Pure Theory of Law*, 22 J. Legal Ed. 170 (1970). Indeed it is.
33. Winthrop, *supra* note 20, at 38.
34. The Court "must know us better than we know ourselves," Archibald Cox says, and "sometimes be the voice of the spirit, reminding us of our better selves." A. Cox, The Role of the Supreme Court in American Government 117 (1976).
35. 416 U.S. 312 (1974).
36. 438 U.S. (1978).
37. *The Landmark Bakke Ruling*, Newsweek, July 10, 1978, at 19.
38. 438 U.S. 265, 324 (1978) (Brennan, J., concurring).
39. *Id.* Justice Powell was "in agreement with the view that race may be taken into account as a factor in an admissions program," and so agreed with Justices Brennan, White, Marshall, and Blackmun "that the portion of the [state court] judgment that would proscribe all consideration of race must be reversed." 438 U.S. 296 n. 36 (1980). One commentator has correctly concluded that, based on the tie-breaking opinion of Justice Powell, the *Bakke* ruling is "that race may be *a* factor but not *the* factor in admissions criteria of state universities." Dixon, Bakke: *A Constitutional Analysis*, 67 Calif. L. Rev. 69 (1979).
40. 443 U.S. 193 (1979).
41. 65 L.Ed.2d 902 (1980).
42. Chief Justice Burger announced the judgment of the Court and delivered an opinion in which Justices White and Powell joined. Justice Powell filed a separate, concurring opinion. Justice Marshall, joined by Justices Brennan and Blackmun, also filed a concurring opinion. Justice Stewart filed a dissenting opinion and was joined by Justice Rehnquist. Justice Stevens filed a separate dissenting opinion. The six-vote majority was thus two

plus one plus three, and the minority was two plus one. The major but not only difference in vote from *Bakke* was that of the Chief Justice. The only account which he gave of the change was to say, "This opinion does not adopt, either expressly or implicitly, the formulas of analysis articulated in such cases as [*Bakke*]. However, our analysis demonstrates that the [challenged] provision would survive judicial review under either 'test' articulated in the several *Bakke* opinions." 65 L.Ed.2d 902, 933 (1980).

Among the issues which the Chief Justice focused upon in his opinion and which could account for the difference in vote are: the provision in issue was found in an act of Congress; it could be based upon constitutional regulation of interstate commerce or spending power; and participation in the program was voluntary for local grantees. Furthermore, the set-aside was remedial and could be administratively waived. Also, the challenge was brought against the statute on its face, not as specifically applied; and to the extent a burden was to be borne by nonminority businesses, it was a light one.

43. 65 L.Ed.2d 902, 953.
44. *Id.* at 954 n. 2.
45. If the Justice's statement is true, then how does he explain those cases, *Jones v. Alfred H. Mayer & Co.*, 392 U.S. 409 (1968), notable among them, which recognize Congress's competence to determine that certain private action is racial discrimination forbidden by the Thirteenth Amendment?
46. As regards the Chief Justice's change, see note 42 *supra*.

Justice Powell provides a careful explanation of the difference which he perceived between *Bakke* and *Fullilove* and of the corresponding difference in his vote. His position is that racial classification is prohibited unless there is a compelling interest which the classification is a necessary means for achieving. Redress of past discrimination is a compelling interest when an appropriate authority has found that the detrimental effects have been caused by a constitutional or statutory violation. The Regents in *Bakke*, according to Justice Powell, lacked the necessary authority and made no finding of past discrimination. Congress, on the other hand, passed both these tests in *Fullilove*. Also the set-aside was a reasonable means: alternatives had failed, it was temporary, and it was related to the percentage of minorities.

Justices Marshall, Brennan, and Blackmun remained consistent and articulated what I believe to be the correct position, *i.e.*, that the impermissibility of racial classifications does not apply in the remedial context but that such classifications may be misused and, therefore, are justifiable only when they are shown to justify important governmental ends and are substantially related to these ends.

47. *See* Bell, Bakke, *Minority Admissions, and the Usual Price of Racial Remedies*, 67 CALIF. L. REV. 3, 5–7 (1979); Comment, *The Case for Minority Participation in Reverse Discrimination Litigation*, 67 CALIF. L. REV. 191 (1979).
48. Arendt, *Reflections: Truth and Politics*, THE NEW YORKER, Feb. 25, 1967, at 49, 62. *See* ch. 1, n. 12 *supra*.

Notes to Chapter Seven

> Gary Wills finds the matrix of Jefferson's ideas in the Scottish moral sense school and the notion of "self-evident truth" in particular in Thomas Reid's epistemology. WILLS, *supra* note 16, at 181–92.

49. WILLS, *supra* note 16, at 237.
50. *Id.* at 237–38.
51. *Id.* at 191.

Chapter 8. *Carolene Products*

1. 304 U.S. 144, 152–53 n. 4 (1938).
2. The footnote is described as "famous" in Ely, *The Wages of Crying Wolf: A Comment on Roe v. Wade*, 82 YALE L. J. 920, 933 (1973); G. GUNTHER & N. DOWLING, CASES AND MATERIALS ON CONSTITUTIONAL LAW, 1051 (1970); *The Supreme Court, 1971 Term*, 86 HARV. L. REV. 1, 82 (1972). Justice Brennan called it "prescient." Braunfeld v. Brown, 366 U.S. 599, 613 (1961) (Brennan, J., concurring and dissenting). Mr. Justice Frankfurter said of it, "A footnote hardly seems to be an appropriate way of announcing new constitutional doctrine, and the *Carolene* footnote did not purport to announce any new doctrine; incidentally, it did not have the concurrence of a majority of the Court." Kovacs v. Cooper, 336 U.S. 77, 90–91 (1949) (Frankfurter, J., concurring). *See also* Dennis v. United States, 341 U.S. 494, 526–27 (1951) (Frankfurter, J., concurring).

   Herbert Wechsler observed that this first expression of Justice Stone on civil liberties "comes characteristically in a footnote." Wechsler, *Stone and the Constitution*, 46 COLUM. L. REV. 764, 795 (1946). And Samuel Konefsky said that, "[a]lthough by no means clear and direct, if not actually oblique, these observations did contain the key to the alleged contradiction in outlook. Considering their nature, they were hardly calculated to commit the Court to the undeviating course of decision." S. KONEFSKY, CHIEF JUSTICE STONE AND THE SUPREME COURT 196 (1945). Ely observed:

   > In his famous *Carolene Products* footnote, Justice Stone suggested that the interests to which the Court can responsibly give extraordinary constitutional protection include not only those expressed in the Constitution but also those that are unlikely to receive adequate consideration in the political process, specifically the interests of "discrete and insular minorities" unable to form effective political alliances. There can be little doubt that such considerations have influenced the direction, if only occasionally the rhetoric, of the recent Courts. (Footnotes omitted.)

   Ely, *supra*, at 933 (footnotes omitted).

   Archibald Cox said that "Justice Stone's suggestion is not often cited nowadays." A. COX, THE WARREN COURT 94 (1968). The frequency seems to be increasing, as should be evident from the material already cited and that which is to follow.

   It has been reported that

Louis Lusky, today a professor at Columbia University Law School, is generally credited as the source of a fruitful idea contained in a footnote of an opinion by the late Justice Harlan Fiske Stone. The note, attached to a 1938 decision upholding a federal law that restricted milk marketing, warned that while the court was unwilling to interfere with this economic regulation, it might take a closer look at laws that affected civil liberties or discriminated against minority groups. The footnote helped open the way to expansion of court activity in the civil liberties and civil rights fields.

Mr. Lusky emphasizes, however, that "I never got an idea into a Stone opinion that the Justice didn't want there, and I couldn't have if I had tried."

Falk, *High Court Law Clerks Rarely Sway Decisions, But Job is Prestigious,* THE WALL STREET JOURNAL, July 22, 1971, at 1, col. 1.

3. The footnote in its entirety reads:

There may be narrower scope for operation of the presumption of constitutionality when legislation appears on its face to be within a specific prohibition of the Constitution, such as those of the first ten amendments, which are deemed equally specific when held to be embraced with the Fourteenth. See *Stromberg v. California*, 283 U.S. 359, 369–370; *Lovell v. Griffin*, 303 U.S. 444, 452.

It is unnecessary to consider now whether legislation which restricts those political processes which can ordinarily be expected to bring about repeal of undesirable legislation, is to be subjected to more exacting judicial scrutiny under the general prohibitions of the Fourteenth Amendment than are most other types of legislation. On restrictions upon the right to vote, see *Nixon v. Herndon*, 272 U.S. 536; *Nixon v. Condon*, 286 U.S. 73; on restraints upon the dissemination of information, see *Near v. Minnesota* ex rel. Olson, 283 U.S. 697, 713–14, 718–720, 722; *Grosjean v. American Press Co.*, 297 U.S. 233; *Lovell v. Griffin, supra*; on interferences with political organizations, see *Stromberg v. California, supra*, 369; *Fiske v. Kansas*, 274 U.S. 380; *Whitney v. California*, 274 U.S. 357, 373–378; *Herndon v. Lowry*, 301 U.S. 242; and see Holmes, J., in *Gitlow v. New York*, 268 U.S. 652, 673; as to prohibition of peaceable assembly, see *De Jonge v. Oregon*, 299 U.S. 353, 365.

Nor need we enquire whether similar considerations enter into the review of statutes directed at particular religious, *Pierce v. Society of Sisters*, 268 U.S. 510, or national, *Meyer v. Nebraska*, 262 U.S. 390; *Bartels v. Iowa*, 262 U.S. 404; *Farrington v. Tokushige*, 273 U.S. 484, or racial minorities, *Nixon v. Herndon, supra; Nixon v. Condon, supra*: whether prejudice against discrete and insular minorities may be a special condition, which tends seriously to curtail the operation of those political processes ordinarily to be relied upon to protect minorities, and which may call for a correspondingly more searching judicial inquiry. Compare *McCulloch v. Maryland*, 4 *Wheat.* 316, 428;

188

Notes to Chapter Eight

> *South Carolina v. Barnwell Bros.*, 303 U.S. 177, 184, n.2, and cases cited.
> United States v. Carolene Products Co., 304 U.S. 144, 152–53 n.4 (1938).
> Lusky divulges that the first paragraph was a later addition to the footnote as it was originally circulated. J. LUSKY, BY WHAT RIGHT? 108–11 (1975).

4. John Hart Ely has not worked himself completely free of this error. *See* J. ELY, DEMOCRACY AND DISTRUST 76–77 *passim* (1980).
5. What appear to be examples of this mistake are to be found in Karst, *Invidious Discrimination: Justice Douglas and the Return of the "Natural-Law-Due-Process Formula,"* 16 U.C.L.A. L. REV. 716, 725 (1969), and *The Supreme Court, 1971 Term,* 86 HARV. L. REV. 1 (1972); the latter states:

   > Two important justifications for relatively strict scrutiny of legislative determinations, as expressed in Justice Stone's famous footnote in *United States v. Carolene Products Co.*, are applicable [to the standard of review in *Furman*]: that a specific prohibition of the Bill of Rights is involved, and that the beneficiaries of the protection are unlikely to be able to protect their interests through the political process.

   Id. at 82.
6. *See* notes 33–34 *infra* and accompanying text.
7. 310 U.S. 586, 601 (1940) (Stone, J., dissenting).
8. *Id.* at 591, 600.
9. *Id.*
10. *Id.* at 605–06. The salute requirement and the expulsion from school for not meeting it were the action of a board of education, not a legislature. *Id.* at 541, 586–87. A distinction was drawn neither by Justice Stone nor by Justice Frankfurter, who wrote the opinion of the Court. The quoted phrase is taken from the Frankfurter opinion. *Id.* at 599.
11. *Id.* at 606.
12. *Id.* (emphasis added).
13. *Id.; see id.* at 606–07.
14. Restriction of political processes may be a threat to the majority or to a minority or to both.
15. The term "powerless" is adopted in place of "discrete and insular" as explained.
16. This formulation may fall far short of what Justice Stone might say. His own thoughts on the issue were not given extended, final expression. Wechsler wrote:

    > We can not know where the lines will ultimately be drawn in this emerging area of protection, where, indeed, Justice Stone would have had them drawn had he remained somewhat longer with the task. But we may judge from the evidence of his labors the governing standard he would have set: to preserve the essentials of freedom without impairing the power to govern.

    Wechsler, *supra* note 42, at 800. Another view is presented in Frank, Book Review, 9 STAN. L. REV. 621 (1957):

189

In general summary, the spectacular nature of Stone's lone dissent in the first *Flag Salute* case, holding a position to which he eventually rallied the majority of the Court plus Stone's very important intellectual contribution in the *Carolene Products* case, has tended to overemphasize the orientation of Stone's views in matters of personal liberty. Generally speaking in these areas he was a substantial but not a ground-breaking adherent of the rights of man.

. . . .

In short, Stone's was a mind which was creative within the boundaries of the known. Really path-breaking thought tended to leave him a little hurt, a little bewildered and sometimes even a little angry.

Id. at 624–25.

17. Regents of the University of California v. Bakke, 438 U.S. 265, 298–99 (1978).
18. 403 U.S. 365 (1971).
19. *See id.* at 366–68.
20. *See id.* at 382–83.
21. *Id.* at 372.
22. 413 U.S. 634, 645–46 (1973).
23. 413 U.S. 717, 721 (1973).
24. *Id.* at 656–57 (Rehnquist, J., dissenting).
25. It is not clear that protection of powerless minorities would qualify as "constitutionally justified" to the satisfaction of Justice Rehnquist even though the phrase "discrete and insular minorities" is more than a formula and can be understood as a mandate for the Court.
26. Ely, *supra* note 2, at 935. In *Democracy and Distrust, supra* note 4, Ely has attempted to elaborate a theory of judicial review which is neither interpretivist (judges deciding constitutional questions are confined to application of norms implicit in the written constitution) nor noninterpretivist (judges enforce fundamental values not found in the document). Ely's third option takes its lead from the Warren Court, which he views as not so much seized by the desire to vindicate certain fundamental values as by the desires both to insure the openness of the political process and to correct discrimination against minorities. The book's resulting "participation-oriented, representation-reinforcing" notion gives a fuller reading to the *Carolene Products* theory than had his articles which preceded it. But it is still inaccurate. He continues to believe that politics is a market, that courts intervene only to correct market malfunctions, and that *Carolene Products* is directed primarily at protection of participation in the market rather than at protection of minorities.

By far the most suggestive recent work in this general area is that of Owen Fiss. *See* Fiss, *The Supreme Court, 1978 Term: Foreword: The Forms of Justice*, 93 HARV. L. REV. 1 (1979). Fiss challenges us to see the tasks of judges as "giving meaning to our public values and adjudication as the process through which that meaning is revealed or elaborated." *Id.* at 14.

Notes to Chapter Eight

He has misgivings about that subscription to *Carolene Products* which reads it (mistakenly, in my view) as making judicial review a reflexive action to legislative failure. The resurgence of this attitude, he observes, "does not stem from doubts about the special capacity of courts and their processes to move us closer to a correct understanding of our constitutional values, but from the frail quality of our substantive vision. We have lost our confidence in the existence of the values that underlie the litigation of the 1960's, or, for that matter, in the existence of any public values." *Id.* at 16–17. I am not interested in rehabilitating *Carolene Products*. I am interested in making a statement about underlying, public values and the way courts give reality to them. I believe that stating these values in terms of beginning, as I have, can employ *Carolene Products* fruitfully and that the result is not so far from Fiss's idea of structural reform. In any event, this recent essay, like the numerous works which preceded it, is richly insightful and instructive.

Justice Powell outlines some of the potential difficulties in protecting minorities:

> First, it may not always be clear that a so-called preference is in fact benign. Courts may be asked to validate burdens imposed upon individual members of particular groups in order to advance the group's general interest. See *United Jewish Organizations v. Carey*, 430 U.S. 144, 172–173 (Brennan, J., concurring in part). Nothing in the Constitution supports the notion that individuals may be asked to suffer otherwise impermissible burdens in order to enhance the societal standing of their ethnic groups. Second, preferential programs may only reinforce common stereotypes holding that certain groups are unable to achieve success without special protection based on a factor having no relationship to individual worth. See *DeFunis v. Odegaard*, 416 U.S. 312, 343 (Douglas, J., dissenting). Third, there is a measure of inequity in forcing innocent persons in respondent's position to bear the burdens of redressing grievances not of their making.

Regents of the University of California v. Bakke, 438 U.S. 265, 298 (1978).

27. It is true, of course, that when viewed in the abstract, women do not constitute a small and powerless minority. Nevertheless, in part because of past discrimination, women are vastly underrepresented in this nation's decisionmaking councils. There has never been a female President, nor a female member of this Court. Not a single woman presently sits in the United States Senate, and only 14 women hold seats in the House of Representatives. And, as appellants point out, this underrepresentation is present throughout all levels of our State and Federal Government.

See Joint Reply Brief of Appellants and American Civil Liberties Union (*Amicus Curiae*) 9. Frontiero v. Richardson, 411 U.S. 677, 686 n. 17 (1973) (Brennan, J.).

The District of Columbia's blacks are more numerous than its whites,

but, even so, they constituted a powerless minority in the context of de-
segregation of the District's schools.

> While in the District it is whites who are the minority, Negroes are
> unable to translate their superior numbers into political power, for
> the obvious reason that citizens in the District are disenfranchised
> with respect to local government. Ultimate responsibility for the Dis-
> trict's schools is lodged in the Congress and its District Committees;
> immediate responsibility in a Board of Education on which until last
> week Negroes had only a minority vote, and only a one-third vote
> when the basic decisions on desegregation were reached in 1954.

> And since they are neither elected nor re-elected, but appointed by
> the judges of the District Court, Negro Board members are neither
> responsive nor responsible to the public will of the local, largely poor
> Negro community.

Hobson v. Hansen, 269 F. Supp. 401, 508 n. 198 (D. D.C. 1967), *aff'd sub
nom.* Smuck v. Hobson, 408 F.2d 175 (D.C. Cir. 1969).

28. Ely suggests that

> in every legislative balance one of the competing interests loses to
> some extent; indeed usually, as here, they both do. On some occa-
> sions the Constitution throws its weight on the side of one of them,
> indicating the balance must be restruck. And on others—and this is
> Justice Stone's suggestion—it is at least arguable that, constitutional
> directive or not, the Court should throw *its* weight on the side of a
> minority demanding in court more than it was able to achieve politi-
> cally. But even assuming this suggestion can be given principled
> content, it was clearly intended and should be reserved for those
> interests which, *as compared with the interests to which they have been
> subordinated,* constitute minorities unusually incapable of protecting
> themselves.

Ely, *supra* note 2, at 934 (footnotes omitted).

> Justice Powell noted about the *Carolene Products* type of rationale "that
> judicial scrutiny of classifications touching on racial and ethnic back-
> ground [would] vary with the ebb and flow of political forces." Regents
> of the University of California v. Bakke, 438 U.S. 265, 298 (1978). He
> thought this to be a disqualifying drawback, whereas I believe it a
> strength of the approach.

29. United States v. Carolene Products Co., 304 U.S. 144, 152–53 n.4 (1938).
30. 17 U.S. (4 Wheat.) 316, 428 (1819).
31. 303 U.S. 177, 184 n. 2 (1938).
32. It is true that, by their absence, the truckers were not able to make their
voice heard through the political processes. But neither could they defend themselves in other ways. The critical factor was their discreteness
and insularity, not the unavailability of intrastate political processes to
them.

> The citation of *Barnwell* indicates that economic groups were not to be
> excluded from Justice Stone's discrete and insular minorities.

Notes to Chapter Eight

33. *See* Wright, *The Role of the Supreme Court in a Democratic Society—Judicial Activism or Restraint?*, 54 CORNELL L. REV. 1 (1968), wherein the author stated:

> The Court must continue carefully to distinguish those groups whose rights are consistently trammelled and whose interests are consistently neglected in the political arena, from those groups whose interests are occasionally submerged in legislative compromise. This the Court has done. It has applied and extended the principles and ideals of our society to those "insular" minorities, which, either because they are unpopular or because the vindication of their rights is expensive, are persecuted or neglected by the legislatures. In so doing, it has tried to secure the integrity of the legislative processes themselves. These are tasks for which the courts, the "deviant" institutions in our democratic society, are required (footnotes omitted).

Id. at 26.

34. Minersville School Dist. v. Gobitis, 310 U.S. 586, 606 (1940) (Stone, J., dissenting).

35. For a discussion of poverty, a more inclusive term than indigency, *see* text accompanying notes 69–76, *infra*.

36. 406 U.S. 205 (1972).

37. 408 U.S. 238 (1972).

38. 406 U.S. at 207, 209.

39. *Id.* at 217.

40. *Id.* at 226.

41. 408 U.S. at 239–40.

42. *Id.* at 249–52.

43. The quotation for *The Supreme Court, 1971 Term*, 86 HARV. L. REV. 1, 82 (1972) took account of the applicability of the Stone rationale to *Furman*.

44. 408 U.S. at 249–52, 255–57 (1971) (Douglas, J., concurring); *id.* at 309–10 (Stewart, J., concurring); *id.* at 364–66 (Marshall, J., concurring).

45. The textual statement is worded in terms of a de jure classification. A statute may also produce a de facto classification. The latter may be as suspect as the former and will be so treated.

> This need for investigating justification is strengthened when the practice, though not explicitly singling out for special treatment any of the groups for which the Constitution has a special solicitude, operates in such a way that one such group is harshly and disproportionately disadvantaged . . . .
>
> The explanation for this additional scrutiny of practices which, although not directly discriminatory, nevertheless fall harshly on such groups relates to the judicial attitude toward legislative and administrative judgments. Judicial deference to these judgments is predicated in the confidence courts have that they are just resolutions of conflicting interests. This confidence is often misplaced when the vital interests of the poor and of racial minorities are involved.

For these groups are not always assured of a full and fair hearing through the ordinary political processes, not so much because of the chance of outright bias, but because of the abiding danger that the power structure—a term which need carry no disparaging or abusive overtones—may incline to pay little heed to even the deserving interests of a politically voiceless and invisible minority.

Hobson v. Hansen, 269 F. Supp. 401, 507–08 (D. D.C. 1967) (footnote omitted), *aff'd sub nom.* Smuck v. Hobson, 408 F.2d 175 (D.C. Cir. 1969).

46. Loving v. Virginia, 388 U.S. 1, 11 (1967); McLaughlin v. Florida, 379 U.S. 184, 192 (1964); Bolling v. Sharpe, 347 U.S. 497, 499 (1954).

47. Oyama v. California, 332 U.S. 633, 646 (1948); Korematsu v. United States, 323 U.S. 214, 216 (1944).

48. *Compare* Weber v. Aetna Cas. & Sur. Co., 406 U.S. 164, 172–76 (1972), *and* Levy v. Louisiana, 391 U.S. 68, 70–71 (1968), *with* San Antonio Indep. School Dist. v. Rodriguez, 411 U.S. 1, 108–09 (1973) (Marshall, J., dissenting).

49. Frontiero v. Richardson, 411 U.S. 677, 682–84 (1973); *cf.* Reed v. Reed, 404 U.S. 71, 75–76 (1971).

50. 403 U.S. 365, 372 (1971).

51. South Carolina Highway Dep't v. Barnwell Bros., 303 U.S. 177 (1938).

52. 303 U.S. at 189. There was at least enough of a surmise that absence makes the legislative heart grow fonder of imposing burdens to justify scrutiny.

53. *See* notes 68–75 *infra* and accompanying text.

54. Concurring in San Antonio Indep. School Dist. v. Rodriguez, 411 U.S. 1 (1973), Justice Stewart said that "the basic concern of the Equal Protection Clause is with state legislation whose purpose or effect is to create discrete and objectively identifiable classes." *Id.* at 60. Legislation only "creates" discrete and insular minorities in the special sense described in the text following. And equal protection would seem to extend to more than just these specialized cases.

55. A large number of permutations, both plain and subtle, are imaginable.

56. Possible reasons in support of the discrimination could, perhaps, be dutifully trotted out by a state: the measure is reformatory and positive in nature; the mechanics of the ballot might become so cumbersome that it would become mechanically impossible for any to vote; the fisc is too limited to supply the logistics necessary for taking and counting the vote; etc.

57. *See generally* Tussman & tenBroek, *The Equal Protection of the Laws*, 37 CALIF. L. REV. 341, 347–53 (1949).

58. The same case may require analysis of both the classification and the interest. Issues belonging to each, however, are best kept separate but equal.

59. This separating of issues is not to gainsay the danger of creating instant minorities instantly deprived of power. Correcting a wrong of this type is better managed under the rubric of redressing denial of a fundamental

interest, since instant powerlessness would likely entail deprivation of a fundamental right.

Care must also be exercised against closing the class of powerless minorities against newcomers. New minorities are to be brought into existence and encouraged. It is likely, however, that they will have as a birthright traditionally recognizable traits like religion. Protection of new minorities should not require creation of new judicially cognizable categories.

60. "Personal poverty may entail much the same social stigma as historically attached to certain racial or ethnic groups." San Antonio Indep. School Dist. v. Rodriguez, 411 U.S. 1, 121 (1973) (Marshall, J., dissenting).

61. *See generally* Michelman, *The Supreme Court, 1968 Term, Foreword: On Protecting the Poor Through the Fourteenth Amendment,* 83 HARV. L. REV. 1 (1964) [hereinafter cited as Michelman].

62. *See, e.g.,* Bullock v. Carter, 405 U.S. 134, 142–44 (1972); McDonald v. Board of Election Comm'rs, 394 U.S. 802, 806–07 (1969); Harper v. Virginia Bd. of Elections, 383 U.S. 663, 667–68 (1966); Griffin v. Illinois, 351 U.S. 12, 16–20 (1956). In the *McDonald* case, the court stated, "[A] careful examination on our part is especially warranted where lines are drawn on the basis of wealth or race, . . . two factors which would independently render a classification highly suspect and thereby demand a more exacting judicial scrutiny." 394 U.S. at 807.

63. 411 U.S. 1 (1973).

64. *Id.* at 25.

65. *Id.* at 22–23.

66. *Id.* at 23.

67. 405 U.S. 134 (1972).

68. *Bullock* struck down Texas's candidate filing fee as violative of equal protection. 405 U.S. at 149. The disparity resulting from the required payment of fees was found not the less offensive because it could not "be described by reference to discrete and precisely defined segments of the community as is typical of inequities challenged under the Equal Protection Clause." *Id.* at 144. This language was cited in *Rodriguez* by dissenting Justices White, 411 U.S. 1, 70 and Marshall, *id.* at 94.

69. Michelman offers a corollary, expanded explanation. Uniform suspicion is justifiably raised about de jure wealth classifications, he argues, but de facto pecuniary discriminations present a different case. De facto wealth classifications can be justified because, in the usual form of charging a price, they only make markets, exposure to the decisions of which are not deemed objectionable by our society. Certain "commodities," like the vote, are exceptional, however, and the invidiousness of a given de facto wealth classification should accordingly turn on whether it deprives a class of poor of a "good" with exceptional qualities. *See* Michelman *supra* note 61, at 27–33. Thus, inquiry should be focused "on the crucial variable—the nature and quality of the deprivation—and thereby [avoid] the distractions, false stirring of hopes, and tunneling of

vision which results from a rhetorical emphasis on acts of 'discrimination' that consist of nothing more than charging a price." *Id.* at 32.

70. 411 U.S. at 121–22 (Marshall, J., dissenting) (footnotes omitted).

71. Michelman, *supra* note 61, at 33.

72. A marketplace is scarcely what the fathers meant by "a more perfect Union." Nor is it the very model for modern justice. *Cf.* J. RAWLS, A THEORY OF JUSTICE 359–61 (1971).

73. Devotion to "free enterprise" cannot be allowed to override the commitment of enlightened self-interest to nourish minorities, whether poor or racial or otherwise. The Court should not forbear to remind of this commitment.

74. Black, Book Review, N.Y. TIMES, Feb. 29, 1976, at 23, 24.

75. *Id.*

76. In Psalm 72, a song upon the accession of a new king, the prayer is that the king may judge "thy poor with justice! . . . May he defend the cause of the poor of the people, give deliverance to the needy, and crush the oppressor!" *Psalm* 72:1ff. Likewise, in the messianic vision of Isaiah, the coming one "shall not judge by what his ears hear; but with righteousness he shall judge the poor, and decide with equity for the meek of the earth." *Isaiah* 11:3–4.

77. Dunn v. Blumstein, 405 U.S. 330, 336 (1972); Harper v. Virginia Bd. of Elections, 383 U.S. 663, 667 (1966); Reynolds v. Simms, 377 U.S. 533, 562 (1964).

78. *See* Douglas v. California, 372 U.S. 353, 357–58 (1963); Griffin v. Illinois, 351 U.S. 12, 18 (1956).

79. Shapiro v. Thompson, 394 U.S. 618, 633 (1969).

80. Roe v. Wade, 410 U.S. 113, 152–53 (1973); Griswold v. Connecticut, 381 U.S. 479, 485 (1965).

81. *See* Skinner v. Oklahoma, 316 U.S. 535, 541 (1942).

82. *See* Loving v. Virginia, 388 U.S. 1, 12 (1967); Skinner v. Oklahoma, 316 U.S. 535, 541 (1942).

83. Attention should be called to possibilities for expanding protection under the Thirteenth Amendment. *See* Sullivan v. Little Hunting Park, Inc., 396 U.S. 229, 235–36 (1969); Jones v. Alfred H. Mayer Co., 392 U.S. 409, 439 (1968); Contract Buyers' League v. F & F Investment, 300 F. Supp. 210, 215 (N.D. Ill. 1969), *aff'd on other grounds on interlocutory appeal sub. nom.* Baker v. F & F Investment, 420 F.2d 1191 (7th Cir. 1970); Note, *Discriminatory Housing Markets, Racial Unconscionability, and Section 1988: The Contract Buyers League Case*, 80 YALE L. J. 516., 558–66 (1971); Note, *The "New" Thirteenth Amendment: A Preliminary Analysis*, 82 HARV. L. REV. 1294 (969).

84. *See* authorities cited notes 50–61 *supra.*

85. *See, e.g.,* San Antonio Indep. School Dist. v. Rodriguez, 411 U.S. 1, 40–44 (1973); Lindsey v. Normet, 405 U.S. 56, 69–74 (1972); Dandridge v. Williams, 397 U.S. 471, 486–87 (1970).

86. This is a recurrence of the bosom compunction as diagnosed by Judge

Learned Hand, who noted that phrases like "equal protection" and "due process" are "moral adjurations, the more imperious because inscrutable, but with only that content which each generation must pour into them anew in the light of its own experience. If an independent judiciary seeks to fill them from its own bosom, in the end it will cease to be independent." L. HAND, THE SPIRIT OF LIBERTY 163 (Dillard ed. 1952). *See* Furman v. Georgia, 408 U.S. 238, 467 (1972); Williams v. Illinois, 399 U.S. 235, 259–60 (1970) (Harlan, J., concurring); Shapiro v. Thompson, 394 U.S. 618, 660–62 (1969) (Harlan, J., dissenting); *cf.* Lochner v. New York, 198 U.S. 45, 74–76 (1905) (Holmes, J., dissenting). In *Furman*, Justice Rehnquist stated, "The most expansive reading of the leading constitutional cases does not remotely suggest that this Court has been granted a roving commission, either by the Founding Fathers or by the framers of the Fourteenth Amendment, to strike down laws that are based upon notions of policy or morality suddenly found unacceptable by a majority of this Court." 408 U.S. at 467.

87. *Cf.* Michelman *supra* note 61, at 18–19, 58.

88. Since the minimum is a function of the maximum, the movement will be toward equality. *See id.* Predisposition to equality is reinforced by awareness that it is in the interest of all to allow only inequalities which enhance the position of the least advantaged. *See* notes 35–41 *supra* and accompanying text. Equal protection will at least tend to assure that the least advantaged are not abused. As Justice Jackson said in his concurrence in Railway Express Agency v. New York, 336 U.S. 106 (1949),

> The framers of the Constitution knew and we should not forget today, that there is no more effective practical guaranty against arbitrary and unreasonable government than to require that the principles of law which officials would impose upon a minority must be imposed generally. Conversely, nothing opens the door to arbitrary action so effectively as to allow those officials to pick and choose only a few to whom they will apply legislation and thus to escape the political retribution that might be visited upon them if larger numbers were affected. Courts can take no better measure to assure that laws will be just than to require that laws be equal in operation. *Id.* at 112–13 (Jackson, J., concurring).

That measure of equality also has the advantage of freeing the Court from questionable decisions about adequate minima.

89. 411 U.S. at 35.

90. *Id.* at 36. Appellees did not seek equal protection of more effective speech or of more informed utilization of the vote. What they sought was equality of education. They argued that education is a fundamental right because of its relation to speech and the franchise. And they asked the Court to guarantee equal access to it. They did not ask the Court to guarantee more effective speech or more intelligent voting. Appellees did not ask for what the Court said, in turning down their request, it could not give.

91. *Id.* at 25 n. 60, 37.
92. 397 U.S. 471 (1970).
93. 405 U.S. 56 (1972).
94. 411 U.S. at 37.
95. Whatever merit appellees' argument might have if a State's financing system occasioned an absolute denial of educational opportunities to any of its children, that argument provides no basis for finding an interference with fundamental rights where only relative differences in spending levels are involved and where—as is true in the present case—no charge fairly could be made that the system fails to provide each child with an opportunity to acquire the basic minimal skills necessary for the enjoyment of the rights of speech and of full participation in the political process.
   Id.
96. In his dissent in *Rodriguez*, Justice White expressed disagreement about the amount of variance in the Texas system and raised the possibility that the variance might itself be taken as an indication of fundamentality:
   Perhaps the majority believes that the major disparity in revenues provided and permitted by the Texas system is inconsequential. I cannot agree, however, that the difference of the magnitude appearing in this case can sensibly be ignored, particularly since the State itself considers it so important to provide opportunities to exceed the minimum state educational expenditures.
   Id. at 69.
97. *Id.* at 33–34 (citation omitted).
98. *Id.* at 62–63.
99. *Id.* at 102–03.
100. *Id.* at n. 74.
101. The need to distinguish *Dandridge* and *Lindsey* may have caused incremental degrees in proximity or distance to appear where none in fact exist. The alternative to distinguishing food and housing from education is acknowledgment that *Dandridge* and *Lindsey* were wrongly decided.
102. 411 U.S. at 109 (Marshall, J., dissenting).
103. It could be argued, however, that a minority has a right to survival equal to that of a majority and that the uniqueness of a minority's discrete need should not be allowed to bar realization of this equal right.
104. Positive governmental satisfaction of a minority's singular need is to be distinguished from remedial legislation, which gives some advantage to a minority by way of compensating for previous denial of satisfaction of a want shared by all. In the former case, the interest is critical to the minority because only the minority has the particular need. In the latter case, the interest is critical to the minority because only the minority has previously been denied fulfillment of the general need.
105. Roe v. Wade, 410 U.S. 113 (1973); Doe v. Bolton, 410 U.S. 179 (1973).
106. 410 U.S. at 153.
107. It may be that poor women were the real minority whose interests were

vindicated by the Court. *But see* Maher v. Roe, 432 U.S. 464 (1977); Harris v. McRae, 100 S.Ct.2671 (1980). (See especially the dissenting opinion of Justice Marshall, 100 S.Ct.2706 (1980). For a discussion of the discriminatory effect of anti-abortion legislation upon poor women, *see* Clark, *Religion, Morality and Abortion: A Constitutional Appraisal*, 2 LOYOLA U.L.A. L. REV. 1, 6–7 (1969); THE CASE FOR LEGALIZED ABORTION 11, 58, 64 (Guttmacher ed. 1967); U.S. DEP'T OF HEALTH, EDUCATION, AND WELFARE, THE EFFECT OF CHANGES IN THE STATE ABORTION LAWS 9–10 (1971); Note, *The Right of Equal Access to Abortions*, 56 IOWA L. REV. 1015 (1971).

108. "Note that the claim . . . has to do with the capacity of the earlier decisions to be *rationalized* in terms of some value highlighted by the Constitution, not with the skill with which they were in fact rendered." Ely, *supra* note 2, at 936 n. 97.

109. *Id.* at 935–36. Ely understands the *Carolene Products* footnote to suggest that "the interests to which the Court can responsibly give extraordinary constitutional protection include not only those expressed in the Constitution but also those that are unlikely to receive adequate consideration in the political process, specifically the interests of 'discrete and insular minorities' unable to form effective political alliances." *Id.* at 933. The construction of the footnote proposed here would eliminate Ely's last qualifying phrase ("unable to form political alliances") and would read the footnote as implying three rather than two categories of interests qualifying for strict scrutiny.

110. Ely, *supra* note 2, at 934–35.

111. Just who is a powerless minority is determined in relation to the power of the group with which the minority has come into conflict. Generally, this will mean that two powerless minorities will not be adversaries; in a given context one group will be powerful and the other powerless. However, it is a classic tactic of oppression to set minorities against one another, and conflicts between powerless minorities are conceivable. For example, a legislature might provide that the franchise is to be extended to either minority X or minority Y but not to both. The remedy in this kind of case is to put minorities X and Y on a parity with each other *and* with the majority. In the *Abortion Cases* and *Yoder*, two minorities are not pitted against one another in this hypothetical way. These cases present situations in which there is potential conflict between a minority and a subminority, a subgroup with the primary group.

112. In *Yoder*, the Amish children are a subclassification within the class of Amish. In the *Abortion Cases* the fetuses are not a subclassification of the class of women but are "within" the minority. In both instances, interests of the subminority are dependent upon, but may conflict with, those of the minority of which they are a part.

113. Obviously, if a right to life attaches to the unborn at the time of conception, then the rights of fetus and mother will be in direct conflict for the entire term of pregnancy. There would be no way to grant the right to an abortion and then go on to fashion some protection for the fetus.

See generally Louisell, *Abortion, the Practice of Medicine and the Due Process of Law*, 16 U.C.L.A. L. Rev. 233 (1969).

Wade did not find a direct conflict between the rights of mother and fetus. The ensuing compromise worked out by the Court might have given wider play to the rights of the fetus. The Court held that the potential life of the fetus ripens at the point of viability, 410 U.S. at 163, and from then until delivery justifies state proscription of abortion except when necessary for preserving "the life or health of the mother." *Id.* at 165. That would appear to leave the option for an abortion considerably more viable than the life of the fetus. In *Bolton*, and in the light of *United States v. Vuitch*, 402 U.S. 62 (1971), the Court said that the medical judgment concerning the need for abortion to preserve a woman's "health" is to be "exercised in the light of all factors—physical, emotional, psychological, familial, and the woman's age—relevant to the well-being of the patient. All these factors may relate to health. This allows the attending physician the room he needs to make his best medical judgment." 410 U.S. at 192. If a doctor decides that it is in the woman's best medical interest, broadly construed, then even during the last phase of pregnancy the abortion may be performed. Maximum discretion is reposed in the physician. The practical effect, one may assume, will be to give physicians some pause but no legal stop before performing abortions after viability.

Viability, said the Court, occurs when the fetus is "potentially able to live outside the mother's womb, albeit with artificial aid." 410 U.S. at 160. *See also* Byrn, *Abortion-on-Demand: Whose Morality?*, 46 N.D. Lawyer 5, 12–14 (1970); Oteri, Benjoia, & Souweine, *Abortion and the Religious Liberty Clauses*, 7 Harv. Civ. Rights–Civ. Lib. L. Rev. 559, 597–98 (1972). If the fetus is capable of life, but there is a liberal practice of abortion after viability, then what happens to the fetus separated from its mother's womb? If it is capable of life without artificial aid, is it, in the current euphemism, "not encouraged to live?" If it could live with artificial aid, on what grounds is the artificial aid withheld? Potential mothers may find liberal opportunity for abortion after viability. The fetuses thus separated from their mothers' wombs should be protected (as *e.g.*, by making them wards of the state). *See* Colautti v. Franklin, 439 U.S. 379 (1979).

114. Wisconsin v. Yoder, 406 U.S. 205, 244–46 (1972) (footnotes omitted). The unborn in *Wade* and *Bolton* could not be heard, but their decision in favor of continued existence was to be assumed and presumed.

115. "Strict review" or "strict scrutiny," as Frank Michelman explained, entails "requirement that the challenged classification be strictly relevant to whatever purpose is claimed by the state to justify its use, and also that it be the fairest and least restrictive alternative evidently available for the pursuit of that purpose ('necessity'); and (b) a requirement that the infringement of fundamental interests resulting from the classification's use be outweighed by the claimed state purpose ('compellingness')." Michelman, *supra* n. 61, at 20 n. 34 (citation omitted).

Notes to Chapter Eight

116. Gunther, *The Supreme Court, 1971 Term—Foreword: In Search of Evolving Doctrine on a Changing Court: A Model for a Newer Equal Protection*, 86 HARV. L. REV. 1, 8 (1972).

117. *See* San Antonio Indep. School Dist. v. Rodriguez, 411 U.S. 1, 98–110 (1973) (Marshall, J., dissenting); Harris v. McRae, 100 S.Ct. 2671, 2708–09 & nn. 3, 6 (1980) (Marshall, J., dissenting).

118. *See* Gunther, *supra*, note 116. *See also* Boraas v. Village of Belle Terre, 476 F.2d 806 (2d Cir. 1973):

> [Courts] are no longer limited to the either-or choice between the compelling state interest test and the minimal scrutiny . . . formula. . . . [T]he Supreme Court appears to have moved from this rigid dichotomy, sometimes described as a "two-tiered" formula, toward a more flexible and equitable approach, which permits consideration to be given to evidence of the nature of the unequal classification under attack, the nature of the rights adversely affected, and the governmental interest urged in support of it. Under this approach the test for application of the Equal Protection Clause is whether the legislative classification is *in fact* substantially related to the object of the statute.
>
>   .   .   .   .
>
> In thus being required to focus on the actual rationality of the legislative means under attack, we are asked to do what courts are historically suited to do—apply the law to factual contexts rather than accept one hypothetical legislative justification to the exclusion of others that represent the true rationale of the classification. This more realistic judicial scrutiny in cases in which the compelling state interest test is not invoked serves to render the Equal Protection Clause effective rather [than] permit all but egregious inequalities to go unchecked, as was sometimes the case under the minimal scrutiny test. This approach is particularly appropriate in cases of the present type, where individual human rights of groups as opposed to business regulations are involved.
>
> *Id.* at 814–15 (footnotes omitted).

❧ Chapter 9. Law, Language, Death, and Life

1. Burger, *The Future of Legal Education*, STUDENT LAW, Jan. 1970, at 18, 20.
2. *Id.* at 21.
3. *Report and Recommendations of the Task Force on Lawyer Competency: The Role of the Law Schools of the ABA Section of Legal Education and Admissions to the Bar.*
4. *Id.* at 2.
5. *Id.*
6. Burger, *supra* note 1, at 19. *See also* Brewer v. Williams, 430 U.S. 387, 416–29 (1977) (Burger, C.J., dissenting).
7. Burger, *supra* note 1, at 19.

8. McDougal, *Law as a Process of Decision: A Policy-Oriented Approach to Legal Study*, NATURAL L. FOR. 53. 54–55 (1956). *See also* Lasswell & McDougal, *Legal Education and Public Policy: Professional Training in the Public Interest*, 52 YALE L. J. 203, 208–09 (1943).

9. Burger, *supra* note 1, at 19.

10. *See* J. Dickey, *Metaphor as Pure Adventure, A Lecture Delivered at the Library of Congress*, Dec. 4, 1967.

11. J. WHITE, THE LEGAL IMAGINATION (1973) [hereinafter cited as WHITE].

12. WHITE xxxi.

13. Another unusual book with wide-reaching selections is W. BISHIN & C. STONE, LAW, LANGUAGE, AND ETHICS (1972). I hold that it is not as radically innovative as White's on the ground, among others, that it is a collection of readings in jurisprudence and not a casebook. *The Legal Imagination*, I will argue, is a casebook.

14. *Quoted in* Arnold, *Criminal Attempts—The Rise and Fall of an Abstraction*, 40 YALE L. J. 53, 58 (1930).

15. 52. A.B.A.J. (1966) (ad follows p. 788) (emphasis added).

16. WHITE 49.

17. *See, e.g.*, E. HANKS, A. TARLOCK & J. HANKS, ENVIRONMENTAL LAW AND POLICY (1974) (economics is to be found throughout the book; theology at 82–88).

18. One of the last selections in *The Legal Imagination* is an interview with Morris Abram, then president of Brandeis University, who is questioned about a proposal for a new law school. Experimental though his ideas are, Abram nevertheless speaks of the curriculum as including "the basic 'building block' courses." WHITE 938, 940.

19. *Id.* at 927.

20. MacLeish, *Apologia*, 85 HARV. L. REV. 1505, 1510 (1972).

21. WHITE 10.

22. *Id.* at xxi.

23. *Id.* at 757.

24. *Id.*

25. K. EBLE, A PERFECT EDUCATION 10–11 (1966). The statement is made in the context of a discussion about public schools.

26. WHITE 360.

27. K. MANNHEIM, IDEOLOGY AND UTOPIA 253 (L. Wirth & E. Shils trans. 1936).

28. *Id.* at 262.

29. Utopian education requires teachers who are not angling for appointment to the bench or some seat of influence upon public affairs. As Chiaromonte notes: "The essential conclusion is that the proponent of a Utopia, be he philosopher, intellectual, or mere conscious protester, does not want to rule or to be a councilor of the prince, but simply to convince those who share his condition and his dissatisfaction with the present state of affairs." N. Chiaromonte, *Modern Tyranny*, in THE WORM OF CONSCIOUSNESS AND OTHER ESSAYS 231 (1976).

30. REPORT, *supra* note 3, at 22–23.

Notes to Chapter Nine

31. WHITE 631.
32. I infer his knowledge from the context of the question about a course on justice. It is asked in conjunction with discussion of excerpts from Plato.
33. P. RICOEUR, THE SYMBOLISM OF EVIL 348 (1967).
34. *See* Jee v. Audley, 29 Eng. Rep. 1186 (Ch. 1787).
35. *See* Loring v. Balke, 98 Mass. 253, 259 (1867).
36. *See* Sherwood v. Walker, 66 Mich. 568, 33 N.W. 919 (1887).
37. WHITE xxxii.
38. *See id.* at 317–63.
39. *Id.* at 319–24.
40. *Id.* at 329–33.
41. *Id.* at 334.
42. 164 Colo. 130, 433 P.2d 108 (1967). The case is reproduced in digested form in WHITE 335.
43. WHITE 336.
44. *Id.*
45. *Id.* at 335.
46. *Id.* at 325–27.
47. *Id.* at 327.
48. MacLeish, *supra* note 25, at 1508 (emphasis added).
49. *See also* WHITE 64, 761, 956. White describes the judicial opinion as metaphor. The judge speaks of life in terms of law in his opinions and expresses his own thoughts in traditional judicial language. Furthermore, the judicial ritual, he proposes, may be regarded as a kind of social metaphor. *Id.* at 773–74.

    Lon Fuller addressed the subject of the use of metaphor in law. L. FULLER, LEGAL FICTIONS 24–27 (1967). White's central notion is that law not only employs metaphor but also that it is itself a metaphor.

    Fuller's book was first published as a series of articles in the *Illinois Law Review*, which was then edited as a joint venture by students from the University of Chicago, the University of Illinois, and Northwestern University, 25 U. ILL. L. REV. 363, 513, 877 (1930–31). Then Edward Levi of the school drew attention to the manner in which law proceeds by analogy (legal reasoning as reasoning by example). E. LEVI, AN INTRODUCTION TO LEGAL REASONING (1949) (first published at 15 U. CHI. L. REV. 501 [1948]). It is parabolic that White's advance from metaphor and analogy in law to law as metaphor should continue at the same school.
50. WHITE xxxiii. *See also id.* at 807.
51. The supposed lifelessness of legal education has a substantial history. The young James Madison, for example, once wrote a letter of commiseration to a friend: "I was afraid you would not easily have loosened your Affections for the Belles Lettres. A Delicate Taste and warm imagination like yours must find it hard to give up such refined & exquisite enjoyments for the coarse and dry study of the Law: It is like leaving a pleasant flourishing field for a barren desert." J. Madison, Letter to William Bradford of Jan. 24, 1774, in 1 THE PAPERS OF JAMES MADISON 104, 105 (W. Hutchinson & M. Rachal eds. 1962).

52. W. Stringfellow, An Ethic for Christians and Other Aliens in a Strange Land 84–86 (1973). He adds, "Every sanction or weapon or policy or procedure—including law where law survives distinct from authority—which the State commands against both human beings and against the other principalities carries the connotation of death, implicitly threatens death, derives from and symbolizes death." *Id.* at 110.

53. White 760.

54. *Id.*

55. *Id.*

56. The original use of legal words and legal forms of thought is the function, in White's phrase, of a "controlling intelligence or imagination." *See* text at note 11 *supra*.

Index

Abortion Cases, 122–24
Adam and Eve, 86, 87
Adams, John, 93, 140 (n. 10), 181 (n. 47), 182 (n. 53)
Administrative process, 90–91
Adversary technique, 73–74
Aeschylus, 1, 19, 43, 60, 93
Affection, 15, 97–98
Aggression, 58
Akropolis, 49
Alienation effect, 60, 167 (n. 118)
American Bar Association Task Force, 127, 132
American beginning. *See* Beginning
American Revolution: and French Revolution, 38
American story, 42
Arendt, Hannah, xi, 2, 8, 9, 11, 13, 71, 89, 143 (nn. 10, 14), 150 (n. 72), 181 (n. 47)
Aristotle, 88, 100
Arnold, Matthew, 140 (n. 12)
Ashcraft v. Tennessee, 72
Auden, W. H., 21
Audience, 46–47
Augustine, 11, 12, 13, 37, 39, 68, 92, 181 (n. 41)
Augustinian, 15
Authority, 5, 7–15, 18, 29, 63, 91, 126

Bakke, Regents of the University of California v., 101–3, 110, 184–85 (n. 42), 185 (n. 46), 191 (n. 28)
Barth, Karl, xi, 3, 29, 65
Beaird, Ralph, xi
Beginning, 2, 3, 5, 13, 16, 20, 22, 28, 29, 63, 64, 65, 66, 68, 85, 94; biblical, 4, 11, 15, 16, 17, 18, 19, 25, 42, 64, 72, 98, 105, 107, 125; new, 4, 11, 92, 132, 138; American, 4, 13, 17, 18, 19, 21, 25, 27, 42, 64, 68, 72, 98, 126; and principle, 10; story of, 18, 20, 22, 25, 27, 29, 42, 43, 53, 62, 105; theater of, 43, 64, 81; and *personae*, 85; and the powerless, 94, 96, 97; and truth, 105; and the

poor, 118; and minorities, 125; and the classroom, 126; and justice, 133
Bentham, Jeremy, 35, 157 (n. 23)
Bentley, Eric, 64, 156–57 (n. 9)
Berman, Harold, 163 (n. 66)
Berrigan, Daniel, 43, 57
Bible, 17, 18, 22; Old Testament, 16, 17, 24; New Testament, 17, 24
Biblical story, 28
Biblical tradition, 2
Black, Charles, 148 (n. 48)
Black, Hugo, 26
Blackmun, Harry, 110
Blacks, 4, 102, 109, 136–37, 144 (n. 26); black labor and misery, 15
Blackstone, William, 35, 36
Board of Curators of the University of Missouri v. Horowitz, 177 (n. 10)
Bonhoeffer, Dietrich, xi, 3, 33, 179 (n. 27)
Bradford, William, 30
Brecht, Bertolt, 60
Brennan, William, 79, 120
Broadway, 43
Bullock v. Carter, 116
Burger, Warren, 31, 38, 114, 127, 128, 176 (n. 78)
Burger Court, 78, 90, 125

Calvin, John, 13, 139 (n. 2)
Cardozo, Benjamin, 26
Carolene Products. See *United States v. Carolene Products*
Carter, Jimmy, 154–55 (n. 57)
Centers, 155 (n. 64)
Chase, Edward, xi, 175 (nn. 59, 65, 66), 176 (n. 76), 179 (n. 23)
Chayes, Abram, 90, 181 (n. 47)
Chekov, Anton, 52; *The Cherry Orchard*, 49
Chiaromonte, Nicola, 6, 50, 60, 143 (n. 10), 201 (n. 29)
Christ, 13
Christian people, 13
Cicero, 31, 71, 92, 153 (nn. 52, 53)
Clark, Roger, xi, 184 (n. 32)

Index

Classroom: and beginning, 126
Clothes, 153 (n. 39)
Cochrane, Charles, 145 (n. 29), 153
   (n. 53), 155 (n. 70)
Common law, 24, 129, 147 (n. 47)
Communal, 15, 19, 105, 182 (n. 51)
Community, 6, 12, 15, 62, 98; New
   Testament, 4; of faith, 63, 68; of
   interests, 92
Concordia, 73
Consent, 8, 14
Constitution, 7, 8, 9, 15, 25, 29, 30, 79,
   99, 118, 120; and constituting act, 15
Constitutional assembly, 63
Context, 1, 13; and judgment, 118, 171
   (n. 24)
Cornford, F. M., 30
Counsel, 76–78, 88; right to, 160 (n. 42),
   175 (n. 67)
Court House, 40–41
Courtrooms, 9, 16, 17, 40, 44, 45, 49
Courts: as theater, 9, 16, 29, 44, 46, 95
Covenant, 13, 14, 20, 62, 86, 98; people,
   65; partners, 70
Covenantal tradition, 10, 13, 14
Cox, Archibald, 184 (n. 34), 186 (n. 2)

Dandridge v. Williams, 119
Darrow, Clarence, 1
Davis, Kenneth Culp, 53, 83, 177 (n. 10)
Declaration of Independence, 8, 9, 10,
   14, 15, 73, 105, 141 (n. 12)
De Funis v. Odegaard, 101–3
The Deputy, 57
Deuteronomy, 16, 19, 28, 29, 65, 103
Dewey, John, 48–49, 169 (n. 130)
Dickey, James, 148 (n. 53)
Dickinson, Emily, 134
Douglas, William O., 77, 123
Dramatis personae. See *Persona*
Due process, 7, 72, 84, 147–48 (n. 48)
Dworkin, Ronald, 64, 145 (n. 28), 147
   (nn. 42, 45)

Eastlake v. Forest City Enterprises, 38
Eble, Kenneth, 201 (n. 25)
Edwards, Jonathan, 139 (n. 2), 149
   (nn. 67, 68)
Eichmann, Adolf, 71

Eighth Amendment, 114
Ely, John Hart, 111, 122, 148 (n. 52), 186
   (n. 2), 188 (n. 4), 189 (n. 26), 191
   (n. 28), 198 (nn. 108, 109)
Enlarged mind, 67
Equality, 98, 101–5
Equal protection, 7, 101–5, 110–24
Estes v. Texas, 45, 56
Eudaemonia, 145 (n. 29)
The Eumenides, 93
Exclusionary rule, 78
Exodus, 17, 18, 19

Faces: masks, 84–85
Fairbanks, Russell, xi
Federalism, 31, 151 (nn. 17, 21)
Fergusson, Francis, 49
Ferrin v. People, 134
First Amendment, 99, 109, 119
Fiss, Owen, 189 (n. 26)
Format, trial, 47–48
Founding fathers, 14, 23, 146 (n. 32). *See
   also* Adams, John; Jefferson, Thomas;
   Madison, James
Fourteenth Amendment, 107
Frank, Judge, 179 (n. 23)
Frankel, Marvin, 73, 74
Frankfurter, Felix, 2, 179 (n. 22)
Freedom, 9, 20, 36, 53
French Revolution, 38
Friedell, Steven, 50 (n. 3)
Fuller, Lon, 51, 202 (n. 49)
Fullilove v. Klutznick, 101–3
Furman v. Georgia, 114
Fussell, Paul, 145–46 (n. 30), 149 (n. 70)

Gagnon v. Scarpelli, 77
Gettysburg Address, 9
Gideon v. Wainwright, 76
God, 3, 4, 8, 12, 13, 14, 16, 19, 29, 33, 53,
   62, 65, 70, 86, 96, 135
Goldberg v. Kelly, 83–84
Goss v. Lopez, 83–84
Graham v. Richardson, 110, 115
Grand jury, 77, 173 (n. 55)
Gregory, Dick, 95
Griffiths, John, 156 (n. 5)
Grotowski, Jerzy, 47, 49
Gunther, Gerald, 152 (n. 21), 200 (n. 118)

Index

Harless v. Florida ex rel. *Schellenberg*, 178 (n. 17)
Harris, Richard, 174 (n. 55)
Hazard, Geoffrey, 55, 164 (n. 82)
Herodotus, 18, 19, 23, 142 (n. 2), 145 (n. 29), 150 (n. 72), 168 (n. 124)
Hobbes, Thomas, 141 (n. 36)
Hochhuth, Rolf, 57
Holmes, Oliver Wendell, 34, 52
Holmes, Seaman, 69, 83, 91, 104
Homer, 168 (n. 124)
Huizinga, Johann, 165 (n. 94), 166–67 (n. 109)
Hunch, 66, 168 (n. 125)
Hutcheson, Joseph C., 66, 168 (n. 125)
Huxtable, Ada Louise, 155 (n. 64)

Illinois v. Allen, 26
Impartiality, 59
Ingraham v. Wright, 177 (n. 10)
Insanity defense, 133–36

Jefferson, Thomas, 4, 14, 15, 39, 40, 104, 105, 140 (n. 8), 141 (n. 12), 150 (n. 12), 151 (n. 14); and wards, 40
Jesus, 4, 17
Johnson, Lyndon, 18
Jones v. Alfred H. Mayer & Co., 185 (n. 45)
Judge, 47, 59
Judgment, 1, 23, 43, 61, 64, 100, 105; and live presentation, 43; and process, 64; and judicial theater, 66–72; contextual, 118, 171 (n. 24)
Judicial integrity: and exclusionary rule, 78–79
Judicial process, 5, 17, 40, 72–81; as theater, 5; and American beginning, 72
Judicial review, 2, 124–25
Judicial theater. *See* Theater
Jury, 47, 59, 70, 72, 171 (n. 26)
Justice, 52, 59, 95, 133, 158 (n. 30), 176 (n. 79); theater of, 76; assembly line, 81; and beginning, 133; and truth, 162 (n. 65)

Kant, Immanuel, 61, 68, 169 (n. 130)
Kauffman, Stanley, 166 (n. 109), 167 (n. 121)
Kelsen, Hans, 184 (n. 32)

Kennedy, John F., 21
King Lear, 42

Law school, 29, 126–38
Legal education, 126–38
The Legal Imagination, 128–38
Lehmann, Paul L., xi, 139 (n. 2), 145 (n. 2), 163 (n. 65), 169–70 (n. 6), 170 (n. 24), 176 (n. 78), 202 (n. 49)
Levi, Edward, 202 (n. 49)
Lilburn, John, 25
Lincoln, Abraham, 9, 18, 98, 141 (n. 12)
Lindsey v. Normet, 119
Lippmann, Walter, 36
Locke, John, 15, 142 (n. 37), 153 (n. 52)
Logos, 27
Love, 12, 15, 27, 92, 98
Lusky, Louis, 187 (n. 2), 188 (n. 3)
Luther, Martin, 13, 63

McCarthy, Mary, 50, 161 (n. 55), 162 (n. 62)
McCulloch v. Maryland, 112
McDougal, Myres, 127
MacLeish, Archibald, 131, 136
M'Naghten rule, 135
Macpherson v. Buick Motor Co., 26
Madison, James, 20, 30, 31, 32, 39, 96–97, 99, 139 (n. 3), 147 (n. 47), 152 (n. 27), 154 (n. 54), 183 (n. 16), 202 (n. 51)
Marbury v. Madison, 51 (n. 16)
Marlowe, Christopher, 135
Marshall, John, 62, 139 (n. 3)
Marshall, Thurgood, 116, 120, 121, 125
Mask. *See Persona*
The Mayflower, 9, 10, 141 (n. 15)
Mayflower Compact, 9, 15, 30, 141 (n. 15)
Metaphor, 5, 48–53, 98, 136–38, 169 (n. 130)
Michelman, Frank, 117, 194 (n. 69), 199 (n. 115)
Michigan v. Tucker, 78
Miller, Charles, 143 (n. 7)
Minersville School District v. Gobitis, 108–9
Minorities, 2, 96–97, 108–9; judicial protection of, 5, 95–125 passim; powerless, 2, 5, 22, 112; identified, 111–14

208

Index

Miranda v. Arizona, 25
Montesquieu, 32
Morality play, 55
Moses v. Macferlan, 149 (n. 60)
Mueller, Gerhard, 46

Narrative. *See* Story
Natural law, 3, 8, 23, 140 (n. 8), 142 (n. 37)
New Testament. *See* Bible
Niebuhr, Reinhold, 154–55 (n. 57), 183 (n. 15)
Nonverbal information, 58

Old Testament. *See* Bible
Oral argument, 42

Packer, Herbert, 156 (n. 5), 175 (n. 67)
Palsgraf v. Long Island R.R., 149 (n. 63)
Panther, 21, 80, 176 (n. 79)
Participation, 20, 21, 22
People, the, 8, 14, 65; Christian, 13
Performance, 62–63
The Persians, 60
Persona, 5, 82–94; *dramatis*, 55, 82–94 passim; *juris*, 82–94 passim, 93, 95, 126; and beginning, 85; and private sphere, 86–87; and public sphere, 89
Persons, right-and-duty-bearing, 85
Place, 29–41; private, 32, 33; public, 32, 89; and story, 41
Plato, 2, 10
Platonists, 11
Play, 58–59
Plea-bargaining, 74–76
Polis, 106
Politeia, 9, 140 (nn. 10, 11)
Political theater, 41
Politics, 7, 13, 15, 63, 89, 92, 97, 100, 113; and property, 33–40 passim
Poor, the, 115–18 passim, 137; and beginning, 118; poor women, 197 (n. 107). *See also* Poverty
Possession, 35–39 passim
Poverty, 115, 116–18, 194 (n. 60)
Powell, Lewis, 84, 85, 110, 116, 119
Powell, Thomas Reed, 128
Power, 34, 35, 100
Powerless: and beginning, 94, 96, 97

Priesthood of believers, 13, 63, 137
Principium, 10, 11, 12, 25, 92; and principle, 10, 11, 12; and beginning, 10, 11, 12; and Christ, 12
Principle, 4, 8, 10, 64, 65
Privacy, right of, 87
Private sphere. *See* Place
Promise, 10, 19, 63; exchange of, 9; and common deliberation, 10
Property, 5, 6, 14, 26, 34, 53, 85–89, 95, 153 (nn. 52, 54), 178 (n. 16); and politics, 34, 36; and *persona*, 85–89; and vote, 153 (n. 54); *res privata* and *res publica*, 155 (n. 70)
Proposition, 9
Public sphere. *See* Place

Queen v. Dudley, 71

Rawls, John, 141 (n. 14), 183 (n. 15)
Regents of the University of California v. Bakke, 101–3, 110, 184–85 (n. 42), 185 (n. 46), 191 (n. 28)
Rehnquist, William, 111, 151 (n. 21)
Reich, Charles, 178 (n. 16)
Representation, 160 (n. 42)
Res privata / res publica. *See* Property
Reverse discrimination, 101
Revolution, American, 7
Robe, 157 (n. 10)
Roberts v. State, 44
Rodgers, William, 181 (n. 46)
Rodriguez, San Antonio Independent School District v., 116, 119, 120
Rousseau, 91
Rules, 17, 65
Rusk, Dean, xi

San Antonio Independent School District v. Rodriguez, 116, 119, 120
Saturnalia, 56
Schleiermacher, Friedrich, 139 (n. 2)
Sennett, Richard, 34, 154 (n. 55)
Shakespeare, William, 43; *King Lear*, 42; *Hamlet*, 169 (n. 1); *A Midsummer Night's Dream*, 177 (n. 87)
Sixth Amendment, 159 (n. 38), 175 (n. 67); right to counsel, 160 (n. 42)
Social contract, 14

Solzhenitsyn, Aleksandr I., 80, 81
South Carolina v. Barnwell Brothers, Inc.,
   112, 115
Space, 5; of freedom, 57. See also Place
Spirit, 13
Stare decisis, 7
Stewart, Potter, 73, 79
Stewart, Richard, 181 (n. 47)
Stone, Harlan Fiske, 106, 108, 109, 112,
   113
Story, 5, 16, 17, 18, 19, 41, 143 (n. 4), 146
   (n. 34); exodus, 17, 19; of beginning,
   18, 20, 22, 25, 27, 29, 42, 57, 62, 105;
   biblical, 28; and place, 41; American, 42
Stringfellow, William, 136, 204 (n. 52)
Structuralism, 161 (n. 56)
Suburbs, 38
Supreme Court, 17, 26, 31, 54, 73, 76,
   77, 99

Taylor, Hunter, xi, 139 (n. 2)
Teaching, 130–38 passim
Television, 45
Ten Commandments, 65
Theater, 5, 42, 63; and judicial process, 5,
   29, 63, 66; and beginning, 5, 43, 63, 64,
   66, 81, 95; and courts, 16, 29, 44, 45,
   54, 95; of justice, 46, 76; of absurd, 55;
   of fact, 57; judgment and, 66–72
Theology, 2, 3, 7, 17, 143 (n. 7), 145
   (n. 29)
Thompson v. Stahl, 44
Thoreau, Henry David, 33
Thucydides, 1
Tribe, Laurence, 151 (n. 17), 152 (n. 21),
   179 (n. 23), 180 (n. 40), 182 (n. 51)

Truth, 52, 74, 95; and justice, 52, 162
   (n. 65); and biblical beginning, 105;
   communal, 105; self-evident, 105,
   140 (n. 8)
Twain, Mark, 131
Typology, 23–27, 68

United States v. Calandra, 176 (n. 75)
United States v. Carolene Products, 96,
   106–25
United States v. Holmes, 69–71
United States v. Nixon, 151 (n. 15)
United Steelworkers of America
   AFL–CIO–CLC v. Weber, 101–3
Utopia, 132, 201 (n. 29)

Van Alstyne, William, 178 (n. 16)
Videotape, 43
Virgil, 2, 11
Von Rad, Gerhard, 16

Wards, 40. See also Jefferson, Thomas
Warren, Earl, 25, 56
Warren Court, 78, 95
Weber, United Steelworkers of America
   AFL–CIO–CLC v., 101–3
Wellington, Harry, 171 (n. 24)
White, James, 128–38 passim, 146 (n. 34)
Willing suspension of disbelief, 59
Wills, Gary, 14, 150 (n. 12), 183 (n. 16)
Winthrop, John, 99
Wisconsin v. Yoder, 114, 119, 123–24
Wright, Skelly, 192 (n. 33)
Wythe, George, 26

Yoder, Wisconsin v., 114, 119, 123–24